SACREDSPACE

the prayer book 2011

Inspired by one of the most successful spirituality websites around (and for good reason), *Sacred Space* offers readers short but profound meditations on the daily scriptures. Friendly, concise, and consistently thought-provoking, these books are perfect for anyone who would like to pray more and be more connected to God, but may feel too busy to do so. In other words, everyone!

James Martin, S.J.
Author of *My Life with the Saints*

The website Sacred Space has been helping millions to pray for some years. Now Ave Maria Press makes these very helpful and easily usable prayer-helps available in handsome and accessible form, including pocket-sized booklets for the Advent-Christmas and Lenten seasons. What a great service to God's people! I hope millions more will buy the books. God is being well served.

William A. Barry, S.J.
Author of *Paying Attention to God: Discernment in Prayer*

I don't know any other guides to prayer that are so direct, profound, and effective. It's no wonder that right around the world they have proved extraordinarily helpful in leading busy people to stay in touch with the presence of God.

Gerald O'Collins, S.J.
Author of *Jesus: A Portrait*

Sacred Space has provided countless people with a clear and concise resource to pray alone—any time and anywhere—and yet consciously united with numerous others worldwide. This timely, unassuming aid to daily prayer is a gem.

Peter van Breemen, S.J.
Author of *The God Who Won't Let Go*

SACREDSPACE

the prayer book 2011

from the website www.sacredspace.ie

The Irish Jesuits

ave maria press AmP notre dame, indiana

acknowledgement

The publisher would like to thank Piaras Jackson, S.J., and Alan McGuckian, S.J., for their kind assistance in making this book possible. Piaras Jackson, S.J., can be contacted on feedback@jesuit.ie where comments or suggestions related to the book or to www.sacredspace.ie will always be welcome.

First published in Australia 2010 by Michelle Anderson Publishing Pty., Ltd.

Founded in 1865, Ave Maria Press is a ministry of the Indiana Province of Holy Cross.

www.avemariapress.com

ISBN-10: 1-59471-250-6   ISBN-13: 978-1-59471-250-0

Cover design by Andy Wagoner.

Text design by K. Hornyak.

Printed and bound in the United States of America.

prayer for the journey

As the rain hides the stars,
as the autumn mist hides the hills,
as the clouds veil the blue of the sky,
so the dark happenings of my lot
hide the shining of your face from me.
Yet, if I may hold your hand in the darkness,
it is enough, since I know that,
though I may stumble in my going,
you do not fall.

Celtic prayer

contents

how to use this book

We invite you to make a sacred space in your day and spend ten minutes praying here and now, wherever you are, with the help of a prayer guide and scripture chosen specially for each day. Every place is a sacred space so you may wish to have this book in your desk at work or available to be picked up and read at any time of the day, whilst traveling or on your bedside table, a park bench. . . . Remember that God is everywhere, all around us, constantly reaching out to us, even in the most unlikely situations. When we know this, and with a bit of practice, we can pray anywhere.

The following pages will guide you through a session of prayer stages.

Something to think and pray about each day this week
The Presence of God
Freedom
Consciousness
The Word (leads you to the daily scripture and provides help with the text)
Conversation
Conclusion

It is most important to come back to these pages each day of the week as they are an integral part of each day's prayer and lead to the scripture and inspiration points.

Although written in the first person the prayers are for "doing" rather than for reading out. Each stage is a kind of exercise or meditation aimed at helping you to get in touch with God and God's presence in your life.

We hope that you will join the many people around the world praying with us in our sacred space.

november 28–december 4

Something to think and pray about each day this week:

Cloaked with Christ

Ignatius Loyola failed with at least two sets of companions before he settled on the small group who, with him, founded the Jesuits. His experience with his first followers was sobering. They were strong on enthusiasm and made the right spiritual noises, but they fell away when Ignatius was arraigned by the Inquisition, imprisoned, and humiliated. While Ignatius could see his experience as donning the livery of Christ, the young men who admired him were dismayed, and felt something had gone wrong. So when Peter Faber, Francis Xavier, and others gathered round Ignatius in Paris, he held them off from any commitment until he had put them through the Spiritual Exercises, especially the meditation on "Two Standards," in which a person is invited to consider their personal choice to serve "under the standard," or banner, of Christ. They needed to taste the failure and hopelessness of the suffering Jesus, and maintain their faith and hope through it.

The Presence of God
Lord, help me to be fully alive to your holy presence.
Enfold me in your love.
Let my heart become one with yours.

Freedom
Many countries are at this moment suffering
the agonies of war.
I bow my head in thanksgiving for my freedom.
I pray for all prisoners and captives.

Consciousness
At this moment, Lord, I turn my thoughts to You.
I will leave aside my chores and preoccupations.
I will take rest and refreshment in your presence, Lord.

The Word
The Word of God comes down to us through the scriptures. May the Holy Spirit enlighten my mind and my heart to respond to the gospel teachings. (Please turn to your scripture on the following pages. Inspiration points are there should you need them. When you are ready, return here to continue.)

Conversation
Sometimes I wonder what I might say
if I were to meet you in person, Lord.
I might say "Thank you, Lord" for always being there for me.
I know with certainty there were times when you carried me.
When through your strength I got through the dark times in my life.

Conclusion
Glory be to the Father, and to the Son, and to the Holy Spirit,
As it was in the beginning, is now, and ever shall be,
World without end. Amen

Sunday 28th November,
First Sunday of Advent **Matthew 24:37–44**

For as the days of Noah were, so will be the coming of the Son of Man. For as in those days before the flood they were eating and drinking, marrying and giving in marriage, until the day Noah entered the ark, and they knew nothing until the flood came and swept them all away, so too will be the coming of the Son of Man. Then two will be in the field; one will be taken and one will be left. Two women will be grinding meal together; one will be taken and one will be left. Keep awake therefore, for you do not know on what day your Lord is coming. But understand this: if the owner of the house had known in what part of the night the thief was coming, he would have stayed awake and would not have let his house be broken into. Therefore you also must be ready, for the Son of Man is coming at an unexpected hour.

- Jesus is not asking us to stay awake all night, but to live in the present, so that I can recognize the Lord when he appears in my life. He shows himself in the unrehearsed moments, the interruptions and accidents that can throw me off balance.
- Teach me, Lord, to recognize you wherever I encounter you.

Monday 29th November **Matthew 8:5–11**

When Jesus entered Capernaum, a centurion came to him, appealing to him and saying, "Lord, my servant is lying at home paralyzed, in terrible distress." And he said to him, "I will come and cure him." The centurion answered, "Lord, I am not worthy to have you come under my roof; but only speak the word, and my servant will be healed. For I also am a man under authority, with soldiers under me; and I say to one, 'Go,' and he goes, and to another, 'Come,' and he comes, and to my slave,

'Do this,' and the slave does it." When Jesus heard him, he was amazed and said to those who followed him, "Truly I tell you, in no one in Israel have I found such faith. I tell you, many will come from east and west and will eat with Abraham and Isaac and Jacob in the kingdom of heaven."

- Now, at the beginning of a new church year, we hear Jesus' mission statement or policy. The faith of a Roman soldier—a hated person for the local people—was the picture and sign of the coming of all nations into God's kingdom.
- Prayer humbles us to let us know that we are of these nations, getting into God's kingdom and love by his gracious gift and legacy, not by our own self-esteem or self-importance. Advent is the month of the humble God, the child who is God.

Tuesday 30th November,
St. Andrew, Apostle **Matthew 4:18–22**

As he walked by the Sea of Galilee, he saw two brothers, Simon, who is called Peter, and Andrew his brother, casting a net into the lake—for they were fishermen. And he said to them, "Follow me, and I will make you fish for people." Immediately they left their nets and followed him. As he went from there, he saw two other brothers, James son of Zebedee and his brother John, in the boat with their father Zebedee, mending their nets, and he called them. Immediately they left the boat and their father, and followed him.

- Peter, Andrew, James, and John gave up lucrative businesses to be Jesus' faithful followers.
- What have I had to give up in order to follow Jesus more faithfully? What are the attachments in my life that I am reluctant to give up?

Wednesday 1st December **Matthew 15:29–37**

Jesus went on from there and reached the shores of the Sea of Galilee, and he went up into the hills. He sat there, and large crowds came to him bringing the lame, the crippled, the blind, the dumb, and many others. The crowds were astonished to see the dumb speaking, the cripples whole again, the lame walking and the blind with their sight, and they praised the God of Israel. But Jesus called his disciples to him and said, "I feel sorry for all these people; they have been with me for three days now and have nothing to eat. I do not want to send them off hungry, they might collapse on the way." The disciples said to him: "Where could we get enough bread in this deserted place to feed such a crowd?" Jesus said to them: "How many loaves have you?" "Seven," they said, "and a few small fish." Then he instructed the crowd to sit down on the ground, and he took the seven loaves and the fish, and he gave thanks and broke them and handed them to the disciples who gave them to the crowds. They all ate as much as they wanted, and they collected what was left of the scraps, seven baskets full.

- There are times when I need to be healed from over-anxiousness, shame, anger, or a broken relationship. Am I willing to place my need for healing before the risen Jesus and ask for his help?
- Jesus gives thanks before breaking the seven loaves and the fish. What do I wish to thank God for today?

Thursday 2nd December **Matthew 7:21, 24–27**

Jesus said to the people, "Not everyone who says to me, 'Lord, Lord,' will enter the kingdom of heaven, but only one who does the will of my Father in heaven. Everyone then who hears these words of mine and acts on them will be like a wise man who built his house on rock. The rain fell, the floods came, and the winds blew and beat on that house, but it did not fall, because it had been founded on rock. And everyone who hears these words of mine and does not act on them will be like a foolish man who built his house on sand. The rain fell, and the floods came, and the winds blew and beat against that house, and it fell—and great was its fall!"

- There are many ways to "hear" words. They can be just sound with practical content, like giving information or directions. The Word of God is more like the word of a friend, spoken to the mind and to the heart.
- The Word of God gives meaning to life and is spoken always in love.

Friday 3rd December,
St. Francis Xavier **Matthew 28:16–20**

Now the eleven disciples went to Galilee, to the mountain to which Jesus had directed them. When they saw him, they worshipped him; but some doubted. And Jesus came and said to them, "All authority in heaven and on earth has been given to me. Go therefore and make disciples of all nations, baptizing them in the name of the Father and of the Son and of the Holy Spirit, and teaching them to obey everything that I have commanded you. And remember, I am with you always, to the end of the age."

- Saint Francis Xavier built his life and missionary efforts in what we now call Asia on the firm rock of faith. A man in the Gospels once prayed "Lord I believe, help my unbelief."
- Can I make that my prayer today?

Saturday 4th December **Matthew 9:35–10:1, 6–8**

Jesus went about all the cities and villages, teaching in their synagogues, and proclaiming the good news of the kingdom, and curing every disease and every sickness. When he saw the crowds, he had compassion for them, because they were harassed and helpless, like sheep without a shepherd. Then he said to his disciples, "The harvest is plentiful, but the laborers are few; therefore ask the Lord of the harvest to send out laborers into his harvest." Then Jesus summoned his twelve disciples and gave them authority over unclean spirits, to cast them out, and to cure every disease and every sickness. These twelve Jesus sent out with the following instructions: "Go rather to the lost sheep of the house of Israel. As you go, proclaim the good news, 'The kingdom of heaven has come near.' Cure the sick, raise the dead, cleanse the lepers, cast out demons. You received without payment; give without payment."

- In Jesus' time, people believed that those who had serious psychiatric illnesses were "possessed" by demons. Even today we talk of alcoholics as being possessed by the "demon" drink. Maybe I need to examine my "demons."
- Jesus' good news was the love and forgiveness of God poured out on all of us, whatever our "demons." When we love and forgive others, especially the poor and those on the margins, we spread the good news of God's kingdom, God's reign of love.

december 5–11

Something to think and pray about each day this week:

Making Sense of Life

Scripture makes sense when it meets the non-scriptural world inside us. God works on us and touches us through experience and through scripture—the Word of God. So in prayer, when we feel moved either by consolation or by disturbance, it is good to stop, to linger on the movement we feel. It is a theophany, a self-showing of God. We are on holy ground, as Moses sensed before the burning bush on Sinai. God is spirit, invisible, untouchable. But when we are alert we can sense God's effect on us.

This can happen when we feel in utter desolation and reach outside ourselves: "There must be something beyond this." It can happen in communion and joy, like that of Peter at the Transfiguration: "This should go on forever; let the party never stop." It can happen in our places of prayer, during religious celebrations, in a park, or wherever we pray. In all cases it is a gift, a grace, a promise, a lifting of the veil. For many devout people, the veil was seldom lifted. The great mystic John of the Cross wrote, "Love is the fruit of faith, that is to say, of darkness."

The Presence of God

God is with me, but more, God is within me, giving me existence.
Let me dwell for a moment on God's life-giving presence
in my body, my mind, my heart
and in the whole of my life.

Freedom

God is not foreign to my freedom.
Instead the Spirit breathes life into my most intimate desires,
gently nudging me towards all that is good.
I ask for the grace to let myself be enfolded by the Spirit.

Consciousness

Help me, Lord, to be more conscious of your presence.
Teach me to recognize your presence in others.
Fill my heart with gratitude for the times your love
has been shown to me through the care of others.

The Word

I read the Word of God slowly, a few times over, and I listen to what God is saying to me. (Please turn to your scripture on the following pages. Inspiration points are there should you need them. When you are ready, return here to continue.)

Conversation

How has God's Word moved me? Has it left me cold?
Has it consoled me or moved me to act in a new way?
I imagine Jesus standing or sitting beside me,
I turn and share my feelings with him.

Conclusion

Glory be to the Father, and to the Son, and to the Holy Spirit,
As it was in the beginning, is now, and ever shall be,
World without end. Amen

Sunday 5th December,
Second Sunday of Advent **Matthew 3:1–6**

In those days John the Baptist appeared in the wilderness of Judea, proclaiming, "Repent, for the kingdom of heaven has come near." This is the one of whom the prophet Isaiah spoke when he said, "The voice of one crying out in the wilderness: 'Prepare the way of the Lord, make his paths straight.'" Now John wore clothing of camel's hair with a leather belt around his waist, and his food was locusts and wild honey. Then the people of Jerusalem and all Judea were going out to him, and all the region along the Jordan, and they were baptized by him in the river Jordan, confessing their sins.

- Isn't it extraordinary how a mortified man draws people. We admire one whose needs are minimal, who is the master of his own appetites, who has a deep interior freedom. John the Baptist, with minimal clothes and minimal food, was a magnet. People trusted him because clearly he could not be bought.
- Where are the chains on me, the appetites that I have not mastered, and that pull me in ways I do not want? Help me towards a freer heart and body, Lord.

Monday 6th December **Luke 5:17–26**

One day, while he was teaching, Pharisees and teachers of the law were sitting near by (they had come from every village of Galilee and Judea and from Jerusalem); and the power of the Lord was with him to heal. Just then some men came, carrying a paralyzed man on a bed. They were trying to bring him in and lay him before Jesus; but finding no way to bring him in because of the crowd, they went up on the roof and let him down with his bed through the tiles into the middle of the crowd in front of Jesus. When he saw their faith, he said, "Friend, your sins are forgiven you." Then the scribes and the Pharisees began to question, "Who is this who is speaking blasphemies? Who can forgive sins but God alone?" When Jesus perceived their questionings, he answered them, "Why do you raise such questions in your hearts? Which is easier, to say, 'Your sins are forgiven you,' or to say, 'Stand up and walk'? But so that you may know that the Son of Man has authority on earth to forgive sins"—he said to the one who was paralyzed—"I say to you, stand up and take your bed and go to your home." Immediately he stood up before them, took what he had been lying on, and went to his home, glorifying God. Amazement seized all of them, and they glorified God and were filled with awe, saying, "We have seen strange things today."

- Only God can forgive sin. That is why the scribes and Pharisees thought that Jesus was blaspheming. They did not miss the implication: Jesus was implying that God's power to heal and forgive sin was made manifest in his own words and deeds.
- Not only did Jesus forgive sin, he gave his apostles the power to do the same. Where can I find that power this day?

Tuesday 7th December **Matthew 18:12–14**

Jesus said to his disciples: "What do you think? If a shepherd has a hundred sheep, and one of them has gone astray, does he not leave the ninety-nine on the mountains and go in search of the one that went astray? And if he finds it, truly I tell you, he rejoices over it more than over the ninety-nine that never went astray. So it is not the will of your Father in heaven that one of these little ones should be lost."

- We are the little ones; all we are and have is from God who wants us to be at our best, our most alive. God wants nothing good in us to perish. Nothing good we have done or have tried to do is wasted. All is valued in the mind and heart of God, and we are saved, honoured, and loved by the one who creates us each day.
- Advent reminds us of what it is like to be a little one, dependent on others and on God for so much in life.

Wednesday 8th December, The Immaculate Conception of the Blessed Virgin Mary **Luke 1:26–38**

In the sixth month the angel Gabriel was sent by God to a town in Galilee called Nazareth, to a virgin engaged to a man whose name was Joseph, of the house of David. The virgin's name was Mary. And he came to her and said, "Greetings, favored one! The Lord is with you." But she was much perplexed by his words and pondered what sort of greeting this might be. The angel said to her, "Do not be afraid, Mary, for you have found favor with God. And now, you will conceive in your womb and bear a son, and you will name him Jesus. He will be great, and will be called the Son of the Most High, and the Lord God will give to him the throne of his ancestor David. He will reign over the house of Jacob forever, and of his kingdom there will be no end." Mary said to the angel, "How can this be, since I am a virgin?" The angel said to her, "The Holy Spirit will come upon you, and the power of the Most High will overshadow you; therefore the child to be born will be holy; he will be called Son of God. And now, your relative Elizabeth in her old age has also conceived a son; and this is the sixth month for her who was said to be barren. For nothing will be impossible with God." Then Mary said, "Here am I, the servant of the Lord; let it be with me according to your word." Then the angel departed from her.

- Mary held no special office. She was powerless: young in a world that valued age, female in a world ruled by men, poor in a stratified economy. So her being "favoured" by God to be the mother of the long-awaited Messiah would have seemed to people in Jesus' time as a complete reversal of expectations.
- By responding positively to God's messenger, Mary becomes the model believer, servant and disciple, responding wholeheartedly to God's plan of salvation. Do I ever model myself on Mary in my response to God's call?

Thursday 9th December **Matthew 11:11–15**

Truly I tell you, among those born of women no one has arisen greater than John the Baptist; yet the least in the kingdom of heaven is greater than he. From the days of John the Baptist until now the kingdom of heaven has suffered violence, and the violent take it by force. For all the prophets and the law prophesied until John came; and if you are willing to accept it, he is Elijah who is to come. Let anyone with ears listen!

- Some modern thinkers insist that faith is a private matter, not to be discussed in the public arena, and religious belief something to be treated with scorn.
- In the midst of such opposition and scorn, how content am I to profess my Christian faith openly?

Friday 10th December **Matthew 11:16–19**

Jesus spoke to the crowds, "But to what will I compare this generation? It is like children sitting in the marketplaces and calling to one another, 'We played the flute for you, and you did not dance; we wailed, and you did not mourn.' For John came neither eating nor drinking, and they say, 'He has a demon'; the Son of Man came eating and drinking, and they say, 'Look, a glutton and a drunkard, a friend of tax collectors and sinners!' Yet wisdom is vindicated by her deeds."

- Jesus compares his generation to children playing "make believe" games. Some refuse to play the wedding game ("we piped for you") while others refuse to play the funeral game ("you did not mourn").
- Do I play games with God so that I can remain undisturbed and maintain my lifestyle no matter what it does to others, especially the poor and the excluded?

Saturday 11th December **Matthew 17:10–13**

The disciples asked Jesus, "Why do the scribes say that Elijah must come first?" He replied, "Elijah is indeed coming and will restore all things; but I tell you that Elijah has already come, and they did not recognize him, but they did to him whatever they pleased. So also the Son of Man is about to suffer at their hands." Then the disciples understood that he was speaking to them about John the Baptist.

- Elijah was one of the great prophets in Israel. Jesus is saying that John the Baptist is the new Elijah because he has acted as Jesus' prophetic forerunner. But just as people did not believe John, and he was put to death, so they do not believe Jesus who will also be put to death.
- Jesus suffered primarily because he claimed to be God's son. Am I prepared to suffer for my Christian faith when people mock my beliefs, or do I simply accommodate myself to the values of those around me?

december 12–18

Something to think and pray about each day this week:

Seeking God

Jesus shows how to find goodness where others see only bad. The prime example is the father of the prodigal son. Once the boy has turned towards home, the father falls on his neck and throws a party. The party is neither for the son nor for the rest of the family. It is the father expressing his own joy; it is his party: "there is more joy among the angels in heaven over one sinner . . ." Jesus urges us to be perfect in this way, going the extra mile, generous to a fault. It is a counsel of perfection, rare in this world, but when it happens, God is shown.

The Presence of God

What is present to me is what has a hold on my becoming.
I reflect on the presence of God always there in love,
amidst the many things that have a hold on me.
I pause and pray that I may let God
affect my becoming in this precise moment.

Freedom

There are very few people
who realize what God would make of them
if they abandoned themselves into his hands,
and let themselves be formed by his grace. (St. Ignatius)
I ask for the grace to trust myself totally to God's love.

Consciousness

In the presence of my loving Creator,
I look honestly at my feelings over the last day,
the highs, the lows, and the level ground.
Can I see where the Lord has been present?

The Word

God speaks to each one of us individually. I need to listen to hear what he is saying to me. Read the text a few times, then listen. (Please turn to your scripture on the following pages. Inspiration points are there should you need them. When you are ready, return here to continue.)

Conversation

What is stirring in me as I pray?
Am I consoled, troubled, left cold?
I imagine Jesus himself standing or sitting at my side,
and share my feelings with him.

Conclusion

Glory be to the Father, and to the Son, and to the Holy Spirit,
As it was in the beginning, is now, and ever shall be,
World without end. Amen

Sunday 12th December,
Third Sunday of Advent **Matthew 11:2–11**

When John heard in prison what the Messiah was doing, he sent word by his disciples and said to him, "Are you the one who is to come, or are we to wait for another?" Jesus answered them, "Go and tell John what you hear and see: the blind receive their sight, the lame walk, the lepers are cleansed, the deaf hear, the dead are raised, and the poor have good news brought to them. And blessed is anyone who takes no offense at me." As they went away, Jesus began to speak to the crowds about John: "What did you go out into the wilderness to look at? A reed shaken by the wind? What then did you go out to see? Someone dressed in soft robes? Look, those who wear soft robes are in royal palaces. What then did you go out to see? A prophet? Yes, I tell you, and more than a prophet. This is the one about whom it is written, 'See, I am sending my messenger ahead of you, who will prepare your way before you.' Truly I tell you, among those born of women no one has arisen greater than John the Baptist; yet the least in the kingdom of heaven is greater than he."

- There is real comfort in this story. John the Baptist had his moments of darkness. Imprisoned in Herod's dungeon, he wondered, "Am I a fool? Was I wrong about Jesus?" He does not just brood on the question but sends messengers to Jesus. And Jesus does not send back reassurances; he just asks the messengers to open their eyes and see the evidence of Jesus' life.
- Lord, in my moments of doubt and darkness, may I fill my eyes with you.

Monday 13th December **Matthew 21:23–27**

When Jesus entered the temple, the chief priests and the elders of the people came to him as he was teaching, and said, "By what authority are you doing these things, and who gave you this authority?" Jesus said to them, "I will also ask you one question; if you tell me the answer, then I will also tell you by what authority I do these things. Did the baptism of John come from heaven, or was it of human origin?" And they argued with one another, "If we say, 'From heaven,' he will say to us, 'Why then did you not believe him?' But if we say, 'Of human origin,' we are afraid of the crowd; for all regard John as a prophet." So they answered Jesus, "We do not know." And he said to them, "Neither will I tell you by what authority I am doing these things."

- The chief priests and elders will be the main opponents of Jesus during his passion. They hope to force Jesus into a public admission that his power comes directly from God, thus opening him up to a charge of blasphemy.
- How would I answer my opponents today if I were asked about my faith in Jesus? Would I know Jesus well enough to give a good account of my Christian belief?

Tuesday 14th December **Matthew 21:28–32**

Jesus said, "What do you think? A man had two sons; he went to the first and said, 'Son, go and work in the vineyard today.' He answered, 'I will not'; but later he changed his mind and went. The father went to the second and said the same; and he answered, 'I go, sir'; but he did not go. Which of the two did the will of his father?" They said, "The first." Jesus said to them, "Truly I tell you, the tax collectors and the prostitutes are going into the kingdom of God ahead of you. For John came to you in the way of righteousness and you did not believe him, but the tax collectors and the prostitutes believed him; and even after you saw it, you did not change your minds and believe him."

- Tax collectors worked closely with the occupying Roman forces, collecting taxes on their behalf. They were regarded as traitors by nationalist Jews. Prostitutes often sold their services to Roman soldiers.
- Jesus welcomed repentant tax collectors and prostitutes among his followers. Would I do that?

Wednesday 15th December **Luke 7:18–23**

The disciples of John reported all these things to him. So John summoned two of his disciples and sent them to the Lord to ask, "Are you the one who is to come, or are we to wait for another?" When the men had come to him, they said, "John the Baptist has sent us to you to ask, 'Are you the one who is to come, or are we to wait for another?'" Jesus had just then cured many people of diseases, plagues, and evil spirits, and had given sight to many who were blind. And he answered them, "Go and tell John what you have seen and heard: the blind receive their sight, the lame walk, the lepers are cleansed, the deaf hear, the dead are raised, the poor have good news brought to them. And blessed is anyone who takes no offence at me."

- John and his disciples wonder whether Jesus is the expected Messiah. Jesus answers them by telling them of all the miracles he has worked. Jesus' works of healing, preaching, and raising the dead are signs that he is the Messiah, the one in and through whom God "visits" his people.
- Do I ever take offence at Jesus' teaching? Do I truly believe? Do I love? Am I a disciple?

Thursday 16th December **Isaiah 54:7–10**

For a brief moment I abandoned you, but with great compassion I will gather you. In overflowing wrath for a moment I hid my face from you, but with everlasting love I will have compassion on you, says the Lord, your Redeemer. This is like the days of Noah to me: Just as I swore that the waters of Noah would never again go over the earth, so I have sworn that I will not be angry with you and will not rebuke you. For the mountains may depart and the hills be removed, but my steadfast love shall not depart from you, and my covenant of peace shall not be removed, says the Lord, who has compassion on you.

- The prophet's message is one of good news, of God's compassion, of hope and new beginnings, all proclaimed with exaltation.
- Lord, in this Advent season, you offer me the possibility to undo, to please, to apologize, to change, to surrender, and to grow. Give me grace and courage.

Friday 17th December **Matthew 1:1–11**

An account of the genealogy of Jesus the Messiah, the son of David, the son of Abraham. Abraham was the father of Isaac, and Isaac the father of Jacob, and Jacob the father of Judah and his brothers, and Judah the father of Perez and Zerah by Tamar, and Perez the father of Hezron, and Hezron the father of Aram, and Aram the father of Aminadab, and Aminadab the father of Nahshon, and Nahshon the father of Salmon, and Salmon the father of Boaz by Rahab, and Boaz the father of Obed by Ruth, and Obed the father of Jesse, and Jesse the father of King David. And David was the father of Solomon by the wife of Uriah, and Solomon the father of Rehoboam, and Rehoboam the father of Abijah, and Abijah the father of Asaph, and Asaph the father of Jehoshaphat, and Jehoshaphat the father of Joram, and Joram the father of Uzziah, and Uzziah the father of Jotham, and Jotham the father of Ahaz, and Ahaz the father of Hezekiah, and Hezekiah the father of Manasseh, and Manasseh the father of Amos, and Amos the father of Josiah, and Josiah the father of Jechoniah and his brothers, at the time of the deportation to Babylon.

- Matthew's Gospel opens with a genealogy to place Jesus' birth within the context of Jewish history from the time of Abraham. Alongside the patriarchs, kings, and unknowns are four women, all outsiders: Tamar, Rahab, Ruth, and Bathsheba, each with a marital history that contained elements of human scandal. In this way Matthew prepares his readers for the extraordinary way in which Jesus was conceived, and Mary's place in this history.
- God writes not in copperplate but with crooked lines. Lord, help me recognize my role in spreading the good news.

Saturday 18th December **Matthew 1:18–25**

Now the birth of Jesus the Messiah took place in this way. When his mother Mary had been engaged to Joseph, but before they lived together, she was found to be with child from the Holy Spirit. Her husband Joseph, being a righteous man and unwilling to expose her to public disgrace, planned to dismiss her quietly. But just when he had resolved to do this, an angel of the Lord appeared to him in a dream and said, "Joseph, son of David, do not be afraid to take Mary as your wife, for the child conceived in her is from the Holy Spirit. She will bear a son, and you are to name him Jesus, for he will save his people from their sins." All this took place to fulfill what had been spoken by the Lord through the prophet: "Look, the virgin shall conceive and bear a son, and they shall name him Emmanuel," which means, "God is with us." When Joseph awoke from sleep, he did as the angel of the Lord commanded him; he took her as his wife, but had no marital relations with her until she had borne a son; and he named him Jesus.

- Just as God created all that exists in the heavens and the earth, now, through the power of God's Spirit, Jesus is conceived in Mary's womb by a specific and special case of God's creativity.
- The birth of any child brings with it a sense of awe and wonderment. Can I share a sense of awe and wonderment at the incredible fact that God becomes human in a baby boy?

december 19–25

Something to think and pray about each day this week:

The Joy of Waiting

This last week of Advent is a time of waiting—and that has its own pleasures: for children, perhaps the sound of Dad's car on the drive, the key turning in the front door. Anticipation is a joy, and at Christmas the Eve is often better than the indulgence of the Day. Our preparation is for a guest. Life and human history is not just one thing after another. God broke in on human history two thousand years ago and nothing is the same since. The world is young though it may feel old. Christmas is a birthday. We survive on the bright spots, when things are special: light at the end of the tunnel. Advent is the tunnel, and it used to have its share of fasting and repentance, sharpening the contrast between anticipation and Event.

In what sense does God arrive at Christmas? In Innsbruck they re-enact the arrival, putting a live baby and mother on a sleigh drawn through the lighted town. That is lovely, but imaginary. The real arrival is partly in our hearts, partly in our Mass. True, that happens more than once a year. But on this feast, as on a birthday, we celebrate that Bethlehem event which showed (as birthday presents show), that we are the children God wanted, that we matter to him.

The Presence of God
God is with me, but more, God is within me.
Let me dwell for a moment on God's life-giving presence
in my body, in my mind, in my heart,
as I sit here, right now.

Freedom
A thick and shapeless tree-trunk would never believe
that it could become a statue, admired as a miracle of sculpture,
and would never submit itself to the chisel of the sculptor,
who sees by her genius what she can make of it. (St. Ignatius)
I ask for the grace to let myself be shaped by my loving Creator.

Consciousness
Knowing that God loves me unconditionally,
I can afford to be honest about how I am.
How has the last day been, and how do I feel now?
I share my feelings openly with the Lord.

The Word
I read the Word of God slowly, a few times over, and I listen to what God is saying to me. (Please turn to your scripture on the following pages. Inspiration points are there should you need them. When you are ready, return here to continue.)

Conversation
Do I notice myself reacting as I pray with the Word of God?
Do I feel challenged, comforted, angry?
Imagining Jesus sitting or standing by me,
I speak out my feelings, as one trusted friend to another.

Conclusion
Glory be to the Father, and to the Son, and to the Holy Spirit,
As it was in the beginning, is now, and ever shall be,
World without end. Amen

Sunday 19th December,
Fourth Sunday of Advent **Romans 1:1–7**

Paul, a servant of Jesus Christ, called to be an apostle, set apart for the gospel of God, which he promised beforehand through his prophets in the holy scriptures, the gospel concerning his Son, who was descended from David according to the flesh and was declared to be Son of God with power according to the spirit of holiness by resurrection from the dead, Jesus Christ our Lord, through whom we have received grace and apostleship to bring about the obedience of faith among all the Gentiles for the sake of his name, including yourselves who are called to belong to Jesus Christ, to all God's beloved in Rome, who are called to be saints: Grace to you and peace from God our Father and the Lord Jesus Christ.

- As Paul presents himself to the believers in Rome, he echoes the nativity stories we read in both Luke and Matthew: the child Jesus is "son of David," sprung from the Jewish tradition, and Jesus is also "son of God," through the power of his resurrection. This Jesus brings salvation to the Jews and to Gentiles alike.
- What is my Christian ministry? How would I describe myself? What are the key points in my Christian journey?

Monday 20th December **Isaiah 7:10–14**

Again the Lord spoke to Ahaz, saying, "Ask a sign of the Lord your God; let it be deep as Sheol or high as heaven." But Ahaz said, "I will not ask, and I will not put the Lord to the test." Then Isaiah said: "Hear then, O house of David! Is it too little for you to weary mortals, that you weary my God also? Therefore the Lord himself will give you a sign. Look, the young woman is with child and shall bear a son, and shall name him Immanuel."

- "Emmanuel"—a mantra for Advent and Christmas prayer. If we speak it from the heart we are in touch with the mystery of the God who is near, close to the God who is present in our hearts. God is as near as the air we breathe.
- With each breath in prayer, just say "Emmanuel." This is our Christmas welcome to the child who is our God.

Tuesday 21st December **Luke 1:39–45**

In those days Mary set out and went with haste to a Judean town in the hill country, where she entered the house of Zechariah and greeted Elizabeth. When Elizabeth heard Mary's greeting, the child leapt in her womb. And Elizabeth was filled with the Holy Spirit and exclaimed with a loud cry, "Blessed are you among women, and blessed is the fruit of your womb. And why has this happened to me, that the mother of my Lord comes to me? For as soon as I heard the sound of your greeting, the child in my womb leapt for joy. And blessed is she who believed that there would be a fulfillment of what was spoken to her by the Lord."

- Two strong women meet, both of them blessed in a special way by God, and both willing to carry out God's unexpected plans.
- How do I react when my life takes unexpected turns?

Wednesday 22nd December **Luke 1:46–56**

And Mary said, "My soul magnifies the Lord, and my spirit rejoices in God my Savior, for he has looked with favor on the lowliness of his servant. Surely, from now on all generations will call me blessed; for the Mighty One has done great things for me, and holy is his name. His mercy is for those who fear him from generation to generation. He has shown strength with his arm; he has scattered the proud in the thoughts of their hearts. He has brought down the powerful from their thrones, and lifted up the lowly; he has filled the hungry with good things, and sent the rich away empty. He has helped his servant Israel, in remembrance of his mercy, according to the promise he made to our ancestors, to Abraham and to his descendants forever." And Mary remained with Elizabeth about three months and then returned to her home.

- Having heard that her son is to be son of David and Son of God, Mary translates this into good news for the lowly and hungry people of the world, and a warning for the rich and powerful. Her *Magnificat* demonstrates what God will do: he will scatter the arrogant, pull down the mighty, send the rich away empty, exalt the lowly, fill the hungry, and lead his people by the hand. This is the reversal that Jesus announces in the Beatitudes.
- Do I find myself on the side of the lowly or, without openly admitting it, on the side of the arrogant?

Thursday 23rd December **Luke 1:57–66**

Now the time came for Elizabeth to give birth, and she bore a son. Her neighbors and relatives heard that the Lord had shown his great mercy to her, and they rejoiced with her. On the eighth day they came to circumcise the child, and they were going to name him Zechariah after his father. But his mother said, "No; he is to be called John." They said to her, "None of your relatives has this name." Then they began motioning to his father to find out what name he wanted to give him. He asked for a writing tablet and wrote, "His name is John." And all of them were amazed. Immediately his mouth was opened and his tongue freed, and he began to speak, praising God. Fear came over all their neighbors, and all these things were talked about throughout the entire hill country of Judea. All who heard them pondered them and said, "What then will this child become?" For, indeed, the hand of the Lord was with him.

- When the people turn to the dumb Zechariah, they watch him writing on a tablet, confirming what his wife has said. At that very moment, his power of speech returns and he starts to praise God. They are in awe, and the whole affair becomes a talking point throughout the hill country of Judea as people wonder what the future holds for baby John.
- With any birth, we may wonder what the future holds for the little baby. As I look back on my own life, what have I become?

Friday 24th December **Luke 1:67–79**

Then his father Zechariah was filled with the Holy Spirit and spoke this prophecy: "Blessed be the Lord God of Israel, for he has looked favorably on his people and redeemed them. He has raised up a mighty savior for us in the house of his servant David, as he spoke through the mouth of his holy prophets from of old, that we would be saved from our enemies and from the hand of all who hate us. Thus he has shown the mercy promised to our ancestors, and has remembered his holy covenant, the oath that he swore to our ancestor Abraham, to grant us that we, being rescued from the hands of our enemies, might serve him without fear, in holiness and righteousness before him all our days. And you, child, will be called the prophet of the Most High; for you will go before the Lord to prepare his ways, to give knowledge of salvation to his people by the forgiveness of their sins. By the tender mercy of our God, the dawn from on high will break upon us, to give light to those who sit in darkness and in the shadow of death, to guide our feet into the way of peace."

- Zechariah recalls God's interventions in Israelite history. Now God has intervened again for, as Zechariah says, God has visited his people in the person of Jesus.
- On this Christmas Eve, how do I prepare for Christ's coming? Will he find a "dwelling" in the inn of my heart, or will I be so preoccupied with presents and the food on my table that I miss the significance of this momentous event?

Saturday 25th December,
Feast of the Nativity of the Lord **Luke 2:1–14**

In those days a decree went out from Emperor Augustus that all the world should be registered. This was the first registration and was taken while Quirinius was governor of Syria. All went to their own towns to be registered. Joseph also went from the town of Nazareth in Galilee to Judea, to the city of David called Bethlehem, because he was descended from the house and family of David. He went to be registered with Mary, to whom he was engaged and who was expecting a child. While they were there, the time came for her to deliver her child. And she gave birth to her firstborn son and wrapped him in bands of cloth, and laid him in a manger, because there was no place for them in the inn. In that region there were shepherds living in the fields, keeping watch over their flock by night. Then an angel of the Lord stood before them, and the glory of the Lord shone around them, and they were terrified. But the angel said to them, "Do not be afraid; for see—I am bringing you good news of great joy for all the people: to you is born this day in the city of David a Savior, who is the Messiah, the Lord. This will be a sign for you: you will find a child wrapped in bands of cloth and lying in a manger." And suddenly there was with the angel a multitude of the heavenly host, praising God and saying, "Glory to God in the highest heaven, and on earth peace among those whom he favors!"

- Luke tells us about some shepherds who live in the fields and watch their flocks by night. The scribes and Pharisees would have regarded these men as ritually unclean, as "outsiders." Luke mentions them to give encouragement to all those who lacked status in society, and for whom Jesus had a special regard.
- In Luke's story Mary and Joseph are portrayed as transients, somewhat like "the homeless" of our contemporary city streets. Are such people in my thoughts and concerns this Christmas?

december 26–january 1

Something to think and pray about each day this week:

Into the New Year

Lord, this has been another difficult year across the globe. As it slips away in these last few days, I pray about what has happened to me, and to my world, since last January. How was I touched by the great events of the year? Have I become more compassionate, or more selfish and defensive? It seems that year after year there are momentous events, in nature, business, and government. We could easily droop with depression, crying in the old Gaelic lament, "Ochón agus ochón agus ochón!"

Success is what we do with our failures. Somewhere in all this misery, Lord, you have a lesson for us. We do not learn it if we simply circle the wagons and defend the way we have always been. We have seen the consequences of unbridled greed. As we wish one another a happy new year, we might think twice before adding "and prosperous." The blinkered pursuit of prosperity has not spread happiness wider. Teach me, Lord.

The Presence of God

As I sit here, the beating of my heart,
the ebb and flow of my breathing, the movements of my mind
are all signs of God's ongoing creation of me.
I pause for a moment, and become aware
of this presence of God within me.

Freedom

I ask for the grace
to let go of my own concerns
and be open to what God is asking of me,
to let myself be guided and formed by my loving Creator.

Consciousness

In the presence of my loving Creator,
I look honestly at my feelings over the last day,
the highs, the lows, and the level ground.
Can I see where the Lord has been present?

The Word

I take my time to read the Word of God, slowly, a few times, allowing myself to dwell on anything that strikes me. (Please turn to your scripture on the following pages. Inspiration points are there should you need them. When you are ready, return here to continue.)

Conversation

Remembering that I am still in God's presence,
I imagine Jesus himself standing or sitting beside me,
and say whatever is on my mind, whatever is in my heart,
speaking as one friend to another.

Conclusion

Glory be to the Father, and to the Son, and to the Holy Spirit,
As it was in the beginning, is now, and ever shall be,
World without end. Amen

Sunday 26th December,
The Holy Family **Matthew 2:13–15, 19–23**

Now after they had left, an angel of the Lord appeared to Joseph in a dream and said, "Get up, take the child and his mother, and flee to Egypt, and remain there until I tell you; for Herod is about to search for the child, to destroy him." Then Joseph got up, took the child and his mother by night, and went to Egypt, and remained there until the death of Herod. This was to fulfill what had been spoken by the Lord through the prophet, "Out of Egypt I have called my son." When Herod died, an angel of the Lord suddenly appeared in a dream to Joseph in Egypt and said, "Get up, take the child and his mother, and go to the land of Israel, for those who were seeking the child's life are dead." Then Joseph got up, took the child and his mother, and went to the land of Israel. But when he heard that Archelaus was ruling over Judea in place of his father Herod, he was afraid to go there. And after being warned in a dream, he went away to the district of Galilee. There he made his home in a town called Nazareth, so that what had been spoken through the prophets might be fulfilled, "He will be called a Nazorean."

- Like all of us, Joseph and Mary had their family difficulties—their child could have been killed by King Herod, and they couldn't go home for fear of him; Joseph died leaving Mary a widow, and Jesus was murdered in front of his mother.
- The Holy Family know what family life is about, in its good and loving times, and its bad times, and our faith is a support to family life. I pray today for my family, living and dead.

Monday 27th December,
St. John, Evangelist **John 20:2–8**

So Mary Magdalene ran and went to Simon Peter and the other disciple, the one whom Jesus loved, and said to them, "They have taken the Lord out of the tomb, and we do not know where they have laid him." Then Peter and the other disciple set out and went toward the tomb. The two were running together, but the other disciple outran Peter and reached the tomb first. He bent down to look in and saw the linen wrappings lying there, but he did not go in. Then Simon Peter came, following him, and went into the tomb. He saw the linen wrappings lying there, and the cloth that had been on Jesus' head, not lying with the linen wrappings but rolled up in a place by itself. Then the other disciple, who reached the tomb first, also went in, and he saw and believed.

- John links the end of Jesus' passion and death with the new life of the resurrection: Christmas with Easter. All of our prayer is from this side of Easter. We are the ones who know by faith that the Christ child is the risen Lord. Christmas is the feast of glory, the glory of God hidden in the child who would rise from death.
- The glory of God is hidden in each of God's people. With faith in the mystery of the risen Emmanuel we reach out to embrace all, so that we see the incarnate and risen God in each person.

Tuesday 28th December,
The Holy Innocents **Matthew 2:13–18**

Now after they had left, an angel of the Lord appeared to Joseph in a dream and said, "Get up, take the child and his mother, and flee to Egypt, and remain there until I tell you; for Herod is about to search for the child, to destroy him." Then Joseph got up, took the child and his mother by night, and went to Egypt, and remained there until the death of Herod. This was to fulfill what had been spoken by the Lord through the prophet, "Out of Egypt I have called my son." When Herod saw that he had been tricked by the wise men, he was infuriated, and he sent and killed all the children in and around Bethlehem who were two years old or under, according to the time that he had learned from the wise men. Then was fulfilled what had been spoken through the prophet Jeremiah: "A voice was heard in Ramah, wailing and loud lamentation, Rachel weeping for her children; she refused to be consoled, because they are no more."

- My heart goes out this Christmas time to all those who have lost children. Theirs is a heart-break beyond telling. I remember them in my prayers today.

Wednesday 29th December **Luke 2:25–32**

Now there was a man in Jerusalem whose name was Simeon; this man was righteous and devout, looking forward to the consolation of Israel, and the Holy Spirit rested on him. It had been revealed to him by the Holy Spirit that he would not see death before he had seen the Lord's Messiah. Guided by the Spirit, Simeon came into the temple; and when the parents brought in the child Jesus, to do for him what was customary under the law, Simeon took him in his arms and praised God, saying, "Master, now you are dismissing your servant in peace, according to your word; for my eyes have seen your salvation, which you have prepared in the presence of all peoples, light for revelation to the Gentiles and for glory to your people Israel."

- Simeon's prayer, the night prayer of the Church, invites us to let go of conflict, disappointment and loss; of all that keeps us from God and from living life to the full. We live in the light of God's promise to grace us with the light of peace, joy, and security.

- Even in times of unhappiness, confusion, and lack of faith, the love and peace of God are near. Our heart "sees" the salvation and the loving presence of God in prayer, in service, and in love.

Thursday 30th December **Luke 2:36–40**

There was also a prophet, Anna the daughter of Phanuel, of the tribe of Asher. She was of a great age, having lived with her husband for seven years after her marriage, then as a widow to the age of eighty-four. She never left the temple but worshipped there with fasting and prayer night and day. At that moment she came, and began to praise God and to speak about the child to all who were looking for the redemption of Jerusalem. When they had finished everything required by the law of the Lord, they returned to Galilee, to their own town of Nazareth. The child grew and became strong, filled with wisdom; and the favor of God was upon him.

- Mary, Joseph, and their baby return to their hometown of Nazareth, and Luke tells us, "the child grew and became strong, filled with wisdom." In order to be the model for his disciples, Jesus had to be fully human. Jesus learned step-by-step, as every human must: how to lace his sandals, how to react to skinned knees, and what it meant to be Jesus of Nazareth and Son of God.
- What does all this tell me about my image of Jesus?

Friday 31st December **John 1:1–5**

In the beginning was the Word, and the Word was with God, and the Word was God. He was in the beginning with God. All things came into being through him, and without him not one thing came into being. What has come into being in him was life, and the life was the light of all people. The light shines in the darkness, and the darkness did not overcome it.

- John's Gospel opens with a Prologue, a hymn that sums up his view of who Jesus was. John asserts, in opposition to the synagogue leaders, that Jesus was a divine being. In trying to explain what he meant, he drew on ideas from the Old Testament that spoke of God's Word. From John's point of view, Jesus was God's Word spoken to the people of Israel.
- At his birth, Jesus was truly God, but he no longer knew it. In the same way, each of us is born male or female, but it takes us a long time to grasp even a hazy understanding of what that means. So it was with Jesus. Just as with each one of us, his lifetime was a series of new insights into who he was.

Saturday 1st January,
Solemnity of Mary, Mother of God **Luke 2:16–21**

So they went with haste and found Mary and Joseph, and the child lying in the manger. When they saw this, they made known what had been told them about this child; and all who heard it were amazed at what the shepherds told them. But Mary treasured all these words and pondered them in her heart. The shepherds returned, glorifying and praising God for all they had heard and seen, as it had been told them. After eight days had passed, it was time to circumcise the child; and he was called Jesus, the name given by the angel before he was conceived in the womb.

- We are named and loved by God before birth. From the moment of conception we are named in the mind and love of God just as Jesus was. We carry that love through life.
- In prayer you might repeat your baptismal—or "Christian"—name like a mantra, and allow God's choice of you to fill that name with thanks, love, and commitment.
- Happy new year!

january 2–8

Something to think and pray about each day this week:

Seeking the Father

We are forever sorting out our sense of God. Jesus took a big gamble when he called God our Father. God is beyond gender, beyond our imagination, and if we have bad associations or memories of either father or mother, we risk contaminating our idea of God with them. Those who have known a father as a tyrant or drunk, will have strange overtones to "Our Father in heaven." It takes many years of reflection to see what mother and father did to us, for better or worse.

Yet if we look for the "star" to navigate towards the true heart of Jesus, the point to which he returned with joy and longing, we find it in one recurring word: "my father," meaning God. Philosophers and theologians speak abstract words about God, the First Mover, Creator, Transcendent and Everlasting. Jesus' picture is different: it is the father in the story of the Prodigal Son. His clearest picture of the Father shows God coming out to meet us as soon as we turn God-wards.

The Presence of God

I pause for a moment
and reflect on God's life-giving presence
in every part of my body, in everything around me,
in the whole of my life.

Freedom

Many countries are at this moment suffering
the agonies of war.
I bow my head in thanksgiving for my freedom.
I pray for all prisoners and captives.

Consciousness

Knowing that God loves me unconditionally,
I look honestly over the last day, its events and my feelings.
Do I have something to be grateful for? Then I give thanks.
Is there something I am sorry for? Then I ask forgiveness.

The Word

God speaks to each one of us individually. I need to listen to hear what he is saying to me. Read the text a few times, then listen. (Please turn to your scripture on the following pages. Inspiration points are there should you need them. When you are ready, return here to continue.)

Conversation

How has God's Word moved me? Has it left me cold?
Has it consoled me or moved me to act in a new way?
I imagine Jesus standing or sitting beside me,
I turn and share my feelings with him.

Conclusion

Glory be to the Father, and to the Son, and to the Holy Spirit,
As it was in the beginning, is now, and ever shall be,
World without end. Amen

Sunday 2nd January,
The Epiphany of the Lord **Matthew 2:1–2, 7–12**

In the time of King Herod, after Jesus was born in Bethlehem of Judea, wise men from the East came to Jerusalem, asking, "Where is the child who has been born king of the Jews? For we observed his star at its rising, and have come to pay him homage." Herod secretly called for the wise men and learned from them the exact time when the star had appeared. Then he sent them to Bethlehem, saying, "Go and search diligently for the child; and when you have found him, bring me word so that I may also go and pay him homage." When they had heard the king, they set out; and there, ahead of them, went the star that they had seen at its rising, until it stopped over the place where the child was. When they saw that the star had stopped, they were overwhelmed with joy. On entering the house, they saw the child with Mary his mother; and they knelt down and paid him homage. Then, opening their treasure chests, they offered him gifts of gold, frankincense, and myrrh. And having been warned in a dream not to return to Herod, they left for their own country by another road.

- Can you remember some time in life when you were overcome with joy?
- Joy is a gift from God and a share in the nature of God, for God is joy. Allow this joy be part of your life and part of your prayer this day. Allow the tough times to find their place there too.

Monday 3rd January **Matthew 4:23–25**

Jesus went throughout Galilee, teaching in their synagogues and proclaiming the good news of the kingdom and curing every disease and every sickness among the people. So his fame spread throughout all Syria, and they brought to him all the sick, those who were afflicted with various diseases and pains, demoniacs, epileptics, and paralytics, and he cured them. And great crowds followed him from Galilee, the Decapolis, Jerusalem, Judea, and from beyond the Jordan.

- These were people who wanted a cure for their neighbours, family, and friends. Something about Jesus drew the helping side of people to the sick, and to him.
- Let me reflect on what it was that drew them to Jesus. Who might emerge in my prayer today who needs care and help?

Tuesday 4th January **Mark 6:34–44**

As he went ashore, he saw a great crowd; and he had compassion for them, because they were like sheep without a shepherd; and he began to teach them many things. When it grew late, his disciples came to him and said, "This is a deserted place, and the hour is now very late; send them away so that they may go into the surrounding country and villages and buy something for themselves to eat." But he answered them, "You give them something to eat." They said to him, "Are we to go and buy two hundred denarii worth of bread, and give it to them to eat?" And he said to them, "How many loaves have you? Go and see." When they had found out, they said, "Five, and two fish." Then he ordered them to get all the people to sit down in groups on the green grass. So they sat down in groups of hundreds and of fifties. Taking the five loaves and the two fish, he looked up to heaven, and blessed and broke the loaves, and gave them to his disciples to set before the people; and he divided the two fish among them all. And all ate and were filled; and they took up twelve baskets full of broken pieces and of the fish. Those who had eaten the loaves numbered five thousand men.

- "Come and see" is an invitation we have heard in prayer. The invitation and command now is to "go and see." Jesus knows there are basic needs in the big crowd that gathers around him. The apostles are to go and see what is needed and what is to be done.
- Let me watch and listen today for the needs of the people around me, and see how I can express the compassion of God.

Wednesday 5th January **Mark 6:45–52**

Immediately he made his disciples get into the boat and go on ahead to the other side, to Bethsaida, while he dismissed the crowd. After saying farewell to them, he went up on the mountain to pray. When evening came, the boat was out on the sea, and he was alone on the land. When he saw that they were straining at the oars against an adverse wind, he came towards them early in the morning, walking on the sea. He intended to pass them by. But when they saw him walking on the sea, they thought it was a ghost and cried out; for they all saw him and were terrified. But immediately he spoke to them and said, "Take heart, it is I; do not be afraid." Then he got into the boat with them and the wind ceased. And they were utterly astounded, for they did not understand about the loaves, but their hearts were hardened.

- He went to pray—something Jesus did very often. We know little of how he prayed, what he said, how he sat or stood. It doesn't seem to matter.
- Similarly with ourselves—*how* we pray is not as important as *that* we pray: "Pray as you can, not as you can't."

Thursday 6th January **Luke 4:14–21**

Then Jesus, filled with the power of the Spirit, returned to Galilee, and a report about him spread through all the surrounding country. He began to teach in their synagogues and was praised by everyone. When he came to Nazareth, where he had been brought up, he went to the synagogue on the sabbath day, as was his custom. He stood up to read, and the scroll of the prophet Isaiah was given to him. He unrolled the scroll and found the place where it was written: "The Spirit of the Lord is upon me, because he has anointed me to bring good news to the poor. He has sent me to proclaim release to the captives and recovery of sight to the blind, to let the oppressed go free, to proclaim the year of the Lord's favor." And he rolled up the scroll, gave it back to the attendant, and sat down. The eyes of all in the synagogue were fixed on him. Then he began to say to them, "Today this scripture has been fulfilled in your hearing."

- Jesus was praised by everyone. Something about him caught their attention, their attraction, and their love. Maybe it was his words and the way he spoke them. The people knew Jesus' life as well as hearing his words. Only later would they reject him.
- For now, in your prayer, how would you praise Jesus? What do you like about him? Praise and prayer go together.

Friday 7th January **Psalm 147:12–15, 19–20**

Praise the Lord, O Jerusalem! Praise your God, O Zion! For he strengthens the bars of your gates; he blesses your children within you. He grants peace within your borders; he fills you with the finest of wheat. He sends out his command to the earth; his word runs swiftly. He declares his word to Jacob, his statutes and ordinances to Israel. He has not dealt thus with any other nation; they do not know his ordinances.

- In the five psalms of praise that close the Book of Psalms, the psalmist prays with hope and confidence that God's mighty deeds of the past can be trusted and relied on in the future.
- Do I express my hope and trust in God by giving praise, or am I nervous and tentative? Can I speak with the Lord about this?

Saturday 8th January **Psalm 149:1–6, 9**

Praise the Lord! Sing to the Lord a new song, his praise in the assembly of the faithful. Let Israel be glad in its Maker; let the children of Zion rejoice in their King. Let them praise his name with dancing, making melody to him with tambourine and lyre. For the Lord takes pleasure in his people; he adorns the humble with victory. Let the faithful exult in glory; let them sing for joy on their couches. Let the high praises of God be in their throats; this is glory for all his faithful ones.

- Prayer is joyful! Praise for God flows from the hope we have in the God who creates, who protects, and who is compassionate and merciful when we fail.
- Do I sing to the Lord? Play songs of praise? What holds me back?

january 9–15

Something to think and pray about each day this week:

Open to Weakness

For many of us in early life, and for most of us as we grow old, the experience of weakness hits hard. But it links us with Jesus, as the Letter to the Hebrews (2:18; 4:15; 5:2) describes: "Because Jesus himself has suffered and been emptied, he is able to help those who are tempted . . . for we have not a high priest who is unable to sympathize with our weaknesses, but one who in every respect has been tempted as we are, yet without sinning. He can deal gently with the ignorant and wayward since he himself is beset with weakness."

What does weakness mean here? Not the experience of sin, but almost its opposite. Weakness is the experience of a peculiar liability to suffering, a profound sense of inability both to do and to protect: an inability, even after a great effort, to perform as we should want, or achieve what we had determined, or succeed with the completeness that we might have hoped. It means openness to suffering. It means that we are unable to secure our own future, or to protect ourselves from any adversity, or to live with easy clarity and assurance, or to ward off shame, pain, or even interior anguish.

The Presence of God

The world is charged with the grandeur of God. (Gerard Manley Hopkins)
I dwell for a moment on the presence of God
around me, in every part of my body,
and deep within my being.

Freedom

"In these days, God taught me
as a schoolteacher teaches a pupil." (St. Ignatius)
I remind myself that there are things God has to teach me yet,
and ask for the grace to hear them and let them change me.

Consciousness

How do I find myself today?
Where am I with God? With others?
Do I have something to be grateful for? Then I give thanks.
Is there something I am sorry for? Then I ask forgiveness.

The Word

I read the Word of God slowly, a few times over, and I listen to what God is saying to me. (Please turn to your scripture on the following pages. Inspiration points are there should you need them. When you are ready, return here to continue.)

Conversation

Sometimes I wonder what I might say
if I were to meet you in person, Lord.
I might say "Thank you, Lord" for always being there for me.
I know with certainty there were times when you carried me,
when through your strength I got through the dark times in my life.

Conclusion

Glory be to the Father, and to the Son, and to the Holy Spirit,
As it was in the beginning, is now, and ever shall be,
World without end. Amen

Sunday 9th January,
The Baptism of the Lord **Matthew 3:13–17**

Then Jesus came from Galilee to John at the Jordan, to be baptized by him. John would have prevented him, saying, "I need to be baptized by you, and do you come to me?" But Jesus answered him, "Let it be so now; for it is proper for us in this way to fulfill all righteousness." Then he consented. And when Jesus had been baptized, just as he came up from the water, suddenly the heavens were opened to him and he saw the Spirit of God descending like a dove and alighting on him. And a voice from heaven said, "This is my Son, the Beloved, with whom I am well pleased."

- At any baptism there is the prayer and anointing to protect from evil. Baptism was Jesus immersing himself in the call of the Baptist to walk with his people on the way of God through the evil and sinfulness of the world.
- The oil of baptism gives strength and protects us from evil like suntan oil protects the body from the sun; the water of God gives life like the water of a well or a river gives life to the body.
- Protect me, Lord, from anything that leads me away.

Monday 10th January **Mark 1:14–20**

Now after John was arrested, Jesus came to Galilee, proclaiming the good news of God, and saying, "The time is fulfilled, and the kingdom of God has come near; repent, and believe in the good news." As Jesus passed along the Sea of Galilee, he saw Simon and his brother Andrew casting a net into the sea—for they were fishermen. And Jesus said to them, "Follow me and I will make you fish for people." And immediately they left their nets and followed him. As he went a little farther, he saw James son of Zebedee and his brother John, who were in their boat mending the nets. Immediately he called them; and they left their father Zebedee in the boat with the hired men, and followed him.

- The lives of the disciples were changed the day they followed Jesus: fishing would be over, and the world would be their home. The apostles would travel far with the memory and the story of Jesus and would die in his name.
- Let us give thanks for their generosity and trust.

Tuesday 11th January **Mark 1:21–28**

Jesus entered the synagogue and taught. They were astounded at his teaching, for he taught them as one having authority, and not as the scribes. Just then there was in their synagogue a man with an unclean spirit, and he cried out, "What have you to do with us, Jesus of Nazareth? Have you come to destroy us? I know who you are, the Holy One of God." But Jesus rebuked him, saying, "Be silent, and come out of him!" And the unclean spirit, convulsing him and crying with a loud voice, came out of him. They were all amazed, and they kept on asking one another, "What is this? A new teaching—with authority! He commands even the unclean spirits, and they obey him." At once his fame began to spread throughout the surrounding region of Galilee.

- Evil doesn't want to share life with goodness. Goodness can be too strong for evil. We see this often in the life of Jesus. The worst of the world recognized the goodness and godliness in him. Evil knows that goodness can eventually win.
- In the darkness of life and of the world, prayer can be a beacon of light, the light of heaven reaching the darkness of earth.

Wednesday 12th January **Mark 1:29–31**

As soon as they left the synagogue, they entered the house of Simon and Andrew, with James and John. Now Simon's mother-in-law was in bed with a fever, and they told him about her at once. He came and took her by the hand and lifted her up. Then the fever left her, and she began to serve them.

- Can I imagine for a moment Jesus lifting up Simon's unnamed mother-in-law? She is the representative of every man and woman who came into Jesus' life.
- Jesus' word and healing power lifts us up, even to resurrection.
- Today, let me lift myself up to God, in heart and mind.

Thursday 13th January **Mark 1:40–45**

A leper came to Jesus begging him, and kneeling he said to him, "If you choose, you can make me clean." Moved with pity, Jesus stretched out his hand and touched him, and said to him, "I do choose. Be made clean!" Immediately the leprosy left him, and he was made clean. After sternly warning him he sent him away at once, saying to him, "See that you say nothing to anyone; but go, show yourself to the priest, and offer for your cleansing what Moses commanded, as a testimony to them." But he went out and began to proclaim it freely, and to spread the word, so that Jesus could no longer go into a town openly, but stayed out in the country; and people came to him from every quarter.

- Jesus was outcast because he touched a leper. It put him outside the community and popular opinion, like those today who might campaign to protect migrant workers or unwanted refugees. But people still came to him.
- Something about Jesus broke through conventions and people went out to meet someone who touched a leper.

Friday 14th January **Mark 2:3–7**

Then some people came, bringing to him a paralyzed man, carried by four of them. And when they could not bring him to Jesus because of the crowd, they removed the roof above him; and after having dug through it, they let down the mat on which the paralytic lay. When Jesus saw their faith, he said to the paralytic, "Son, your sins are forgiven." Now some of the scribes were sitting there, questioning in their hearts, "Why does this fellow speak in this way? It is blasphemy! Who can forgive sins but God alone?"

- Jesus was challenged on his identity when he forgave sins. People said, "Only God can do this." The miracle that followed gave credibility to the forgiveness of the paralyzed man's sins.
- In sacrament and in prayer, God comes nearer to us than ever when our sins are forgiven. Maybe when we forgive each other's sins we are closest in our lives to the heart of God.

Saturday 15th January **Mark 2:13–17**

Jesus went out again beside the sea; the whole crowd gathered around him, and he taught them. As he was walking along, he saw Levi son of Alphaeus sitting at the tax booth, and he said to him, "Follow me." And he got up and followed him. And as he sat at dinner in Levi's house, many tax collectors and sinners were also sitting with Jesus and his disciples—for there were many who followed him. When the scribes of the Pharisees saw that he was eating with sinners and tax collectors, they said to his disciples, "Why does he eat with tax collectors and sinners?" When Jesus heard this, he said to them, "Those who are well have no need of a physician, but those who are sick; I have come to call not the righteous but sinners."

- I wonder how he said the words, "Follow me." Like an order, an invitation, a whisper, a definite challenge?
- Can I allow Jesus to address me in my prayer today? How do I hear his call to "follow"—as a gentle invitation, an urgent word?
- Can I ask for the gift of generosity and allow the words "Follow me" to echo like a mantra in my heart and mind?

january 16–22

Something to think and pray about each day this week:

Making Space

What is it in us that takes a simple notion like "making space for God," and surrounds it with laws? In Jesus' lifetime, keeping the sabbath had become a major worry. All work was forbidden, and work was classified under thirty-nine different headings. Time and again, Jesus ran into trouble with the scribes and Pharisees over keeping the sabbath. For the rabbis this was a matter of deadly sin and of life and death. When Jesus and his disciples plucked and ate ears of corn on the sabbath as they wandered through the cornfields, the rabbis saw them as guilty of four different offences: reaping, winnowing, threshing, and preparing a meal. All of these were forbidden on the sabbath. When the Pharisees threw this accusation at Jesus, he came back with a memorable phrase, "The sabbath was made for humankind, and not humankind for the sabbath" (Mark 2:27). Human beings were there before any regulations or laws, and human need overrides any law. The sabbath meets a human need, for space and a break from work.

The Presence of God
As I sit here, God is present,
breathing life into me and into everything around me.
For a few moments, I sit silently,
and become aware of God's loving presence.

Freedom
If God were trying to tell me something, would I know?
If God were reassuring me or challenging me, would I notice?
I ask for the grace to be free of my own preoccupations
and open to what God may be saying to me.

Consciousness
In God's loving presence I unwind the past day,
starting from now and looking back, moment by moment.
I gather in all the goodness and light, in gratitude.
I attend to the shadows and what they say to me,
seeking healing, courage, forgiveness.

The Word
I take my time to read the Word of God, slowly, a few times, allowing myself to dwell on anything that strikes me. (Please turn to your scripture on the following pages. Inspiration points are there should you need them. When you are ready, return here to continue.)

Conversation
What is stirring in me as I pray?
Am I consoled, troubled, left cold?
I imagine Jesus himself standing or sitting at my side,
and share my feelings with him.

Conclusion
Glory be to the Father, and to the Son, and to the Holy Spirit,
As it was in the beginning, is now, and ever shall be,
World without end. Amen

Sunday 16th January,
Second Sunday in Ordinary Time **John 1:29–34**

The next day John saw Jesus coming toward him and declared, "Here is the Lamb of God who takes away the sin of the world! This is he of whom I said, 'After me comes a man who ranks ahead of me because he was before me.' I myself did not know him; but I came baptizing with water for this reason, that he might be revealed to Israel." And John testified, "I saw the Spirit descending from heaven like a dove, and it remained on him. I myself did not know him, but the one who sent me to baptize with water said to me, 'He on whom you see the Spirit descend and remain is the one who baptizes with the Holy Spirit.' And I myself have seen and have testified that this is the Son of God."

- Somehow John the Baptist realized that this Jesus is the one to come. In the guidance of the Spirit, John has come to make Jesus known, and in Jesus' baptism John realized—he knew in his deepest being—that this was the Son of God.
- What we know and discover in prayer, in our hearts, is often difficult to share or prove to another. Today, allow yourself to open your heart to what the Spirit of God teaches in prayer.

Monday 17th January **Mark 2:18–22**

Now John's disciples and the Pharisees were fasting; and people came and said to him, "Why do John's disciples and the disciples of the Pharisees fast, but your disciples do not fast?" Jesus said to them, "The wedding-guests cannot fast while the bridegroom is with them, can they? As long as they have the bridegroom with them, they cannot fast. The days will come when the bridegroom is taken away from them, and then they will fast on that day. No one sews a piece of unshrunk cloth on an old cloak; otherwise, the patch pulls away from it, the new from the old, and a worse tear is made. And no one puts new wine into old wineskins; otherwise, the wine will burst the skins, and the wine is lost, and so are the skins; but one puts new wine into fresh wineskins."

- You can rise from prayer a "new person." All prayer opens us to the Holy Spirit. All prayer renews us.
- We need to freshen up the soul; to get rid of bitterness and old hurts; to find fresh skin so we can be a new creation in Christ.

Tuesday 18th January **Mark 2:23–28**

One sabbath Jesus was going through the grainfields; and as they made their way his disciples began to pluck heads of grain. The Pharisees said to him, "Look, why are they doing what is not lawful on the sabbath?" And he said to them, "Have you never read what David did when he and his companions were hungry and in need of food? He entered the house of God, when Abiathar was high priest, and ate the bread of the Presence, which it is not lawful for any but the priests to eat, and he gave some to his companions." Then he said to them, "The sabbath was made for humankind, and not humankind for the sabbath; so the Son of Man is lord even of the sabbath."

- For many people religion is about what we do, rules to be kept, rituals observed. But they may be empty. If our rituals are empty, our hearts may be empty of God too. Jesus revolutionizes the way we relate to God: the focus shifts from what we do to who we are.
- Be content to relax into the mystery of being loved. Goodness will flow from that realization and practice.

Wednesday 19th January **Mark 3:1–6**

Again he entered the synagogue, and a man was there who had a withered hand. They watched him to see whether he would cure him on the sabbath, so that they might accuse him. And he said to the man who had the withered hand, "Come forward." Then he said to them, "Is it lawful to do good or to do harm on the sabbath, to save life or to kill?" But they were silent. He looked around at them with anger; he was grieved at their hardness of heart and said to the man, "Stretch out your hand." He stretched it out, and his hand was restored. The Pharisees went out and immediately conspired with the Herodians against him, how to destroy him.

- Jesus' anger "got him going." He did not focus it on himself. He was angry because of their hardness of heart towards the sick man. His anger came from his love and urgent desire to heal and to bring us into a real relationship with God.
- His anger flowed into compassion and the sick man was healed.

Thursday 20th January **Mark 3:7–12**

Jesus departed with his disciples to the sea, and a great multitude from Galilee followed him; hearing all that he was doing, they came to him in great numbers from Judea, Jerusalem, Idumea, beyond the Jordan, and the region around Tyre and Sidon. He told his disciples to have a boat ready for him because of the crowd, so that they would not crush him; for he had cured many, so that all who had diseases pressed upon him to touch him. Whenever the unclean spirits saw him, they fell down before him and shouted, "You are the Son of God!" But he sternly ordered them not to make him known.

- Jesus needed a boat for his journey. He needs you and me, all of us today, for his journey in our times. The boat in the gospel is a sign of the self. To make a boat ready today means "make yourself ready."

- In prayer we are ready to meet with and hear God's call to do God's will. We are all part of the divine plan to love and save the universe.

Friday 21st January **Mark 3:13–19**

He went up the mountain and called to him those whom he wanted, and they came to him. And he appointed twelve, whom he also named apostles, to be with him, and to be sent out to proclaim the message, and to have authority to cast out demons. So he appointed the twelve: Simon (to whom he gave the name Peter); James son of Zebedee and John the brother of James (to whom he gave the name Boanerges, that is, Sons of Thunder); and Andrew, and Philip, and Bartholomew, and Matthew, and Thomas, and James son of Alphaeus, and Thaddaeus, and Simon the Cananaean, and Judas Iscariot, who betrayed him.

- We can put our name in that list. Say it aloud to yourself or silently. You are there, called by the Lord because he wants you.
- The gospel will reach some people only because of your words and your life. Ask for help, and give thanks.

Saturday 22nd January **Mark 3:20–21**

And the crowd came together again, so that they could not even eat. When his family heard it, they went out to restrain him, for people were saying, "He has gone out of his mind."

- Sometimes it's good to go out of our minds, like Jesus seemed to be. We go out of our own concerns and plans to find the mind of God. The journey of prayer is to put on the mind and heart of Christ.
- We all have different qualities of Jesus which we admire and like: his compassion, love, conviction, faithfulness, and many more.
- What are my Christ-qualities? Can I become more like Christ who became like us?

january 23–29

Something to think and pray about each day this week:

Embracing Aloneness

What a struggle we have, to keep the reality of our aloneness at bay! We use background music, phones, and earpieces like umbilical cords to distract us from the dread sense of isolation. Cities are full of people talking into phones to keep some sense of communion. Most of our talk does not really breach our loneliness. When Jesus had been with the crowds all day, talking to them, laying hands on the sick, he felt the urgent need to be alone and pray. On the hillside the Holy Spirit linked him to his Father. The same spirit dwells in us, as St. Paul describes: "The Spirit helps us in our weakness; for we do not know how to pray as we ought, but that very Spirit intercedes with sighs too deep for words" (Romans 8:26).

The Presence of God

As I sit here with my book, God is here.
Around me, in my sensations, in my thoughts and deep within me.
I pause for a moment,
and become aware of God's life-giving presence.

Freedom

I need to close out the noise, to rise above the noise;
The noise that interrupts, that separates,
the noise that isolates. I need to listen to God again.

Consciousness

I remind myself that I am in the presence of the Lord.
I will take refuge in his loving heart.
He is my strength in times of weakness.
He is my comforter in times of sorrow.

The Word

God speaks to each one of us individually. I need to listen to what he is saying to me. (Please turn to your scripture on the following pages. Inspiration points are there should you need them. When you are ready, return here to continue.)

Conversation

Do I notice myself reacting as I pray with the Word of God?
Do I feel challenged, comforted, angry?
Imagining Jesus sitting or standing by me,
I speak out my feelings, as one trusted friend to another.

Conclusion

Glory be to the Father, and to the Son, and to the Holy Spirit,
As it was in the beginning, is now, and ever shall be,
World without end. Amen

Sunday 23rd January,
Third Sunday in Ordinary Time **Matthew 4:12–17**

Now when Jesus heard that John had been arrested, he withdrew to Galilee. He left Nazareth and made his home in Capernaum by the sea, in the territory of Zebulun and Naphtali, so that what had been spoken through the prophet Isaiah might be fulfilled: "Land of Zebulun, land of Naphtali, on the road by the sea, across the Jordan, Galilee of the Gentiles—the people who sat in darkness have seen a great light, and for those who sat in the region and shadow of death light has dawned." From that time Jesus began to proclaim, "Repent, for the kingdom of heaven has come near."

- Faith is born in us from others and for others. It is not a matter of me and God, me and Jesus, or just me—and God inside me. Jesus called his apostles in community, and the same with us: religion is to be personal and not private; personal and communal. We light the candle of faith for each other.
- Let me pray for all those who are co-workers in the gospel-field of Jesus and give thanks for those whose faith has brought us into our own following of Jesus.

Monday 24th January **Mark 3:22–30**

And the scribes who came down from Jerusalem said, "He has Beelzebul, and by the ruler of the demons he casts out demons." And he called them to him, and spoke to them in parables, "How can Satan cast out Satan? If a kingdom is divided against itself, that kingdom cannot stand. And if a house is divided against itself, that house will not be able to stand. And if Satan has risen up against himself and is divided, he cannot stand, but his end has come. But no one can enter a strong man's house and plunder his property without first tying up the strong man; then indeed the house can be plundered. Truly I tell you, people will be forgiven for their sins and whatever blasphemies they utter; but whoever blasphemes against the Holy Spirit can never have forgiveness, but is guilty of an eternal sin"—for they had said, "He has an unclean spirit."

- With perverse venom, these scribes, educated religious men, decided to attack Jesus. He counters them first with cold, logical argument, then with a warning. By distorting the truth, Jesus warns, you warp your own heart and remain apart from God.
- Do I make hasty judgments? Am I blind to the goodness of others? Do I gossip? Lord, open my eyes to the Spirit in those around me.

Tuesday 25th January,
Conversion of St. Paul, Apostle **Acts 22:4–11**

Paul said: "I persecuted this Way up to the point of death by binding both men and women and putting them in prison, as the high priest and the whole council of elders can testify about me. From them I also received letters to the brothers in Damascus, and I went there in order to bind those who were there and to bring them back to Jerusalem for punishment. While I was on my way and approaching Damascus, about noon a great light from heaven suddenly shone about me. I fell to the ground and heard a voice saying to me, 'Saul, Saul, why are you persecuting me?' I answered, 'Who are you, Lord?' Then he said to me, 'I am Jesus of Nazareth whom you are persecuting.' Now those who were with me saw the light but did not hear the voice of the one who was speaking to me. I asked, 'What am I to do, Lord?' The Lord said to me, 'Get up and go to Damascus; there you will be told everything that has been assigned to you to do.' Since I could not see because of the brightness of that light, those who were with me took my hand and led me to Damascus."

- Paul's conversion was an inner experience, not just an idea, not information received from a friend. Afterwards, he knew.
- Each of us has to come to God, though perhaps not with the drama Paul experienced. Conversion changes our very identity. Afterwards, God is truly, deeply with us.
- Lord, open my mind to your immensity.

Wednesday 26th January **Mark 4:1–8**

Again he began to teach beside the sea. Such a very large crowd gathered around him that he got into a boat on the sea and sat there, while the whole crowd was beside the sea on the land. He began to teach them many things in parables, and in his teaching he said to them: "Listen! A sower went out to sow. And as he sowed, some seed fell on the path, and the birds came and ate it up. Other seed fell on rocky ground, where it did not have much soil, and it sprang up quickly, since it had no depth of soil. And when the sun rose, it was scorched; and since it had no root, it withered away. Other seed fell among thorns, and the thorns grew up and choked it, and it yielded no grain. Other seed fell into good soil and brought forth grain, growing up and increasing and yielding thirty and sixty and a hundredfold."

- The human heart is like a field that can, at different times, be open or closed. The Word of God comes to us as we are, with our faults and failings, our gifts and talents.
- It is God's word that is sown in us and, even in strange ways, it is God who gives the increase.

Thursday 27th January **Mark 4:21–25**

He said to them, "Is a lamp brought in to be put under the bushel basket, or under the bed, and not on the lampstand? For there is nothing hidden, except to be disclosed; nor is anything secret, except to come to light. Let anyone with ears to hear listen!" And he said to them, "Pay attention to what you hear; the measure you give will be the measure you get, and still more will be given you. For to those who have, more will be given; and from those who have nothing, even what they have will be taken away."

- The lamp to be placed on the lampstand is Jesus. He is the new revelation of God, replacing the lampstands of traditional religion. The prophet is a lamp to the people.
- In our words and actions, the lamp of Jesus is still alight. We offer to God in prayer the light of our minds and the love of our hearts. We acknowledge all the complexities that go with being human—the light and the dark.

Friday 28th January,
St. Thomas Aquinas **Matthew 23:8–12**

Jesus said to the crowds, "But you are not to be called rabbi, for you have one teacher, and you are all students. And call no one your father on earth, for you have one Father—the one in heaven. Nor are you to be called instructors, for you have one instructor, the Messiah. The greatest among you will be your servant. All who exalt themselves will be humbled, and all who humble themselves will be exalted."

- Thomas Aquinas, the Dominican, and his Franciscan counterpart Bonaventure brought great energy to the dialogue between faith and reason and to the growth of medieval universities.
- I cannot choose between being intelligent and being a person of faith. I give glory to God by being fully the person I am.

Saturday 29th January **Mark 4:35–41**

On that day, when evening had come, he said to them, "Let us go across to the other side." And leaving the crowd behind, they took him with them in the boat, just as he was. Other boats were with him. A great windstorm arose, and the waves beat into the boat, so that the boat was already being swamped. But he was in the stern, asleep on the cushion; and they woke him up and said to him, "Teacher, do you not care that we are perishing?" He woke up and rebuked the wind, and said to the sea, "Peace! Be still!" Then the wind ceased, and there was a dead calm. He said to them, "Why are you afraid? Have you still no faith?" And they were filled with great awe and said to one another, "Who then is this, that even the wind and the sea obey him?"

- Things are never too bad for Jesus. He goes through the storm with the disciples, protecting them though they do not know it.
- We may feel that things are too bad in our world for God even to be interested! With the corruption and violence and injustices we know so well, would God not have given up on us?
- God never gives up on me; God is always with me.

january 30–february 5

Something to think and pray about each day this week:

The Unknown God

St. Paul noticed an altar in Athens dedicated, "To an unknown God." That is you, Lord. I do not know you but I seek you. I have glimpses of you in the face of Christ. Sometimes I feel close to you in the sacraments and in prayer. I know you in dark times too: when I am in utter desolation, my heart tells me, "There must be something beyond this." These glimpses are always a gift, a grace, a promise, a momentary lifting of the veil. Saint John of the Cross mistrusted whatever removes a soul from the obscure faith where the understanding must be left behind in order to go to God by love.

The Presence of God
At any time of the day or night we can call on Jesus.
He is always waiting, listening for our call.
What a wonderful blessing.
No phone needed, no emails, just a whisper.

Freedom
I will ask God's help,
to be free from my own preoccupations,
to be open to God in this time of prayer,
to come to love and serve him more.

Consciousness
How am I really feeling? Light-hearted? Heavy-hearted?
I may be very much at peace, happy to be here
Equally, I may be frustrated, worried, or angry.
I acknowledge how I really am. It is the real me that the Lord loves.

The Word
I read the Word of God slowly, a few times over, and I listen to what God is saying to me. (Please turn to your scripture on the following pages. Inspiration points are there should you need them. When you are ready, return here to continue.)

Conversation
Remembering that I am still in God's presence,
I imagine Jesus himself standing or sitting beside me,
and say whatever is on my mind, whatever is in my heart,
speaking as one friend to another.

Conclusion
Glory be to the Father, and to the Son, and to the Holy Spirit,
As it was in the beginning, is now, and ever shall be,
World without end. Amen

Sunday 30th January,
Fourth Sunday in Ordinary Time **Matthew 5:1–12**

When Jesus saw the crowds, he went up the mountain; and after he sat down, his disciples came to him. Then he began to speak, and taught them, saying: "Blessed are the poor in spirit, for theirs is the kingdom of heaven. Blessed are those who mourn, for they will be comforted. Blessed are the meek, for they will inherit the earth. Blessed are those who hunger and thirst for righteousness, for they will be filled. Blessed are the merciful, for they will receive mercy. Blessed are the pure in heart, for they will see God. Blessed are the peacemakers, for they will be called children of God. Blessed are those who are persecuted for righteousness' sake, for theirs is the kingdom of heaven. Blessed are you when people revile you and persecute you and utter all kinds of evil against you falsely on my account. Rejoice and be glad, for your reward is great in heaven, for in the same way they persecuted the prophets who were before you."

- Each of the "blesseds" is a statement about something important in the Christian life. They are an ideal of how to live and how to find God close to us.
- We can ask for the grace to live by this vision of life, which was at the root of how Jesus lived.

Monday 31st January **Psalm 31:21–24**

Blessed be the Lord, for he has wondrously shown his steadfast love to me when I was beset as a city under siege. I had said in my alarm, "I am driven far from your sight." But you heard my supplications when I cried out to you for help. Love the Lord, all you his saints. The Lord preserves the faithful, but abundantly repays the one who acts haughtily. Be strong, and let your heart take courage, all you who wait for the Lord.

- The psalmist looks back and gives thanks to God that the crisis is past. God has been his refuge, his rescuer in a time of distress.
- "Be strong, and let your heart take courage." Can I face my own trials, can I encourage others with the power of this prayer?

Tuesday 1st February **Mark 5:21–24, 35–43**

When Jesus had crossed again in the boat to the other side, a great crowd gathered around him; and he was by the sea. Then one of the leaders of the synagogue named Jairus came and, when he saw him, fell at his feet and begged him repeatedly, "My little daughter is at the point of death. Come and lay your hands on her, so that she may be made well, and live." So he went with him. And a large crowd followed him and pressed in on him. While he was still speaking, some people came from the leader's house to say, "Your daughter is dead. Why trouble the teacher any further?" But overhearing what they said, Jesus said to the leader of the synagogue, "Do not fear, only believe." He allowed no one to follow him except Peter, James, and John, the brother of James. When they came to the house of the leader of the synagogue, he saw a commotion, people weeping and wailing loudly. When he had entered, he said to them, "Why do you make a commotion and weep? The child is not dead but sleeping." And they laughed at him. Then he put them all outside, and took the child's father and mother and those who were with him, and went in where the child was. He took her by the hand and said to her, "Talitha cum," which means, "Little girl, get up!" And immediately the girl got up and began to walk about (she was twelve years of age). At this they were overcome with amazement. He strictly ordered them that no one should know this, and told them to give her something to eat.

- The faith of the synagogue leader seems strong, the faith that brought him to Jesus in the first place. He accompanies Jesus to his daughter, despite the news of her death, and the girl revived.
- Cure and recovery come in God's time, not ours. It is often the same for us as we follow Jesus.

Wednesday 2nd February,
Presentation of the Lord **Luke 2:25–33**

Now there was a man in Jerusalem whose name was Simeon; this man was righteous and devout, looking forward to the consolation of Israel, and the Holy Spirit rested on him. It had been revealed to him by the Holy Spirit that he would not see death before he had seen the Lord's Messiah. Guided by the Spirit, Simeon came into the temple; and when the parents brought in the child Jesus, to do for him what was customary under the law, Simeon took him in his arms and praised God, saying, "Master, now you are dismissing your servant in peace, according to your word; for my eyes have seen your salvation, which you have prepared in the presence of all peoples, a light for revelation to the Gentiles and for glory to your people Israel." And the child's father and mother were amazed at what was being said about him.

- Life never got dull for Simeon. Old age didn't contract his hope and his openness to new faith and new belief. His prayer and life until now had somehow prepared him to welcome the unexpected at any age of his life.
- Am I, like Simeon, open to the surprises of God?

Thursday 3rd February **Mark 6:7–11**

Jesus called the twelve and began to send them out two by two, and gave them authority over the unclean spirits. He ordered them to take nothing for their journey except a staff; no bread, no bag, no money in their belts; but to wear sandals and not to put on two tunics. He said to them, "Wherever you enter a house, stay there until you leave the place. If any place will not welcome you and they refuse to hear you, as you leave, shake off the dust that is on your feet as a testimony against them."

- The message of the Lord is to travel light in the journey of life. Wealth, desire for recognition, and personal pride can stunt our desire for God and our freedom to love and to do good.
- We are just passing through our world for a short time; Jesus advises us to make the most of it for ourselves and for others.

Friday 4th February **Hebrews 13:1–8**

Let mutual love continue. Do not neglect to show hospitality to strangers, for by doing that some have entertained angels without knowing it. Remember those who are in prison, as though you were in prison with them; those who are being tortured, as though you yourselves were being tortured. Let marriage be held in honor by all, and let the marriage bed be kept undefiled; for God will judge fornicators and adulterers. Keep your lives free from the love of money, and be content with what you have; for he has said, "I will never leave you or forsake you." So we can say with confidence, "The Lord is my helper; I will not be afraid. What can anyone do to me?" Remember your leaders, those who spoke the word of God to you; consider the outcome of their way of life, and imitate their faith. Jesus Christ is the same yesterday and today and for ever.

- The letter to the Hebrews concludes with moral exhortations, reminding us of our day-to-day duties as Christians.
- Each day we must seek Jesus, in the sure hope that he is always with us—yesterday, today, and forever.

Saturday 5th February **Mark 6:30–34**

The apostles gathered around Jesus, and told him all that they had done and taught. He said to them, "Come away to a deserted place all by yourselves and rest a while." For many were coming and going, and they had no leisure even to eat. And they went away in the boat to a deserted place by themselves. Now many saw them going and recognized them, and they hurried there on foot from all the towns and arrived ahead of them. As he went ashore, he saw a great crowd; and he had compassion for them, because they were like sheep without a shepherd; and he began to teach them many things.

- This is a gospel story for people busy with caring for others. It strikes a special chord for parents and people in helping professions.
- We need rest and time to recharge the energy and love of the heart; but at times the needs of others will take over. Prayer can unite both—the prayer of our action and the prayer of love.

february 6–12

Something to think and pray about each day this week:

Staying Sharp

Jesus uses contrasting metaphors for Christian life—they apply at different times in each person's life and in the life of the Church. Sometimes we are put in the spotlight, and we have our fifteen minutes of fame: briefly we are the light of the world, and we can pray that when we are in such focus, we may be worthy of our Christian vocation. Most of the time we are more like salt or leaven (Matthew 5:13–16), working for good even when unseen. Salt is a less attractive image than light. If there is anything of the exhibitionist in us, this image will discover it.

Let me put aside the bad press that salt has received from dieticians, and remember why it has always been prized. It gives flavour to what is bland and lifts the everyday to something interesting. In the same way a new baby brings a family together; a visit from an old friend banishes my boredom and restores my zest for living; a leader gives a sense of purpose to a whole community. Yet I can lose my saltiness by my self-indulgence or sin or being centered totally on myself. Lord, may I always have other people with whom I can engage.

The Presence of God

I pause for a moment
and think of the love and the grace that God showers on me,
creating me in his image and likeness, making me his temple.

Freedom

Lord, grant me the grace to be free from the excesses of this life.
Let me not get caught up with the desire for wealth.
Keep my heart and mind free to love and serve you.

Consciousness

In the presence of my loving Creator,
I look honestly at my feelings over the last day,
the highs, the lows, and the level ground.
Can I see where the Lord has been present?

The Word

God speaks to each one of us individually. I need to listen to what he is saying to me. (Please turn to your scripture on the following pages. Inspiration points are there should you need them. When you are ready, return here to continue.)

Conversation

Sometimes I wonder what I might say
if I were to meet you in person, Lord.
I might say "Thank you, Lord" for always being there for me.
I know with certainty there were times when you carried me.
When through your strength I got through the dark times in my life.

Conclusion

Glory be to the Father, and to the Son, and to the Holy Spirit,
As it was in the beginning, is now, and ever shall be,
World without end. Amen

Sunday 6th February,
Fifth Sunday in Ordinary Time **Matthew 5:13**

Jesus said to the crowds, "You are the salt of the earth; but if salt has lost its taste, how can its saltiness be restored? It is no longer good for anything, but is thrown out and trampled under foot."

- The word "salt" pervades the English language and its phrases; it is found in most parts of the human body; it is essential to the health of the planet and its creatures. It is vital and everywhere.
- Jesus sets the bar high. As his followers, we are called to draw others to the love of God, to stay alert despite the distractions and even opposition of those around us. Lord, keep me refreshed.

Monday 7th February **Mark 6:53–56**

When Jesus and the disciples had crossed over, they came to land at Gennesaret and moored the boat. When they got out of the boat, people at once recognized him, and rushed about that whole region and began to bring the sick on mats to wherever they heard he was. And wherever he went, into villages or cities or farms, they laid the sick in the marketplaces, and begged him that they might touch even the fringe of his cloak; and all who touched it were healed.

- Sick people can recognize goodness and sincerity when they see it. Maybe that's why they went in crowds to Jesus, as well as hoping for a cure. Something of the divine went out from him, something that can lift us to hope and courage in bad times.
- Let me bring my "sick" side and weak side to God, knowing he is never untouched by prayer.

Tuesday 8th February **Mark 7:1–2, 5–8**

Now when the Pharisees and some of the scribes who had come from Jerusalem gathered around him, they noticed that some of his disciples were eating with defiled hands, that is, without washing them. So the Pharisees and the scribes asked him, "Why do your disciples not live according to the tradition of the elders, but eat with defiled hands?" He said to them, "Isaiah prophesied rightly about you hypocrites, as it is written, 'This people honors me with their lips, but their hearts are far from me; in vain do they worship me, teaching human precepts as doctrines.' You abandon the commandment of God and hold to human tradition."

- Prayer is time given to God, and this is good in itself. But not the end of the story!
- We know whether prayer is fruitful or sincere by the way we live our lives.

Wednesday 9th February **Mark 7:20–23**

Then Jesus said to the disciples, "It is what comes out of a person that defiles. For it is from within, from the human heart, that evil intentions come: fornication, theft, murder, adultery, avarice, wickedness, deceit, licentiousness, envy, slander, pride, folly. All these evil things come from within, and they defile a person."

- Jesus directs our focus to what is inside us. We find good and evil inside our hearts. Harsh judgments, retaining of past hurts, thoughts of greed, and misuse of others are part of the human heart as well as the love that dwells there.
- Prayer purifies the thoughts and desires of the heart as we allow the love of God in Jesus Christ to flood our personalities.

Thursday 10th February **Mark 7:24–30**

From there Jesus set out and went away to the region of Tyre. He entered a house and did not want anyone to know he was there. Yet he could not escape notice, but a woman whose little daughter had an unclean spirit immediately heard about him, and she came and bowed down at his feet. Now the woman was a Gentile, of Syrophoenician origin. She begged him to cast the demon out of her daughter. He said to her, "Let the children be fed first, for it is not fair to take the children's food and throw it to the dogs." But she answered him, "Sir, even the dogs under the table eat the children's crumbs." Then he said to her, "For saying that, you may go—the demon has left your daughter." So she went home, found the child lying on the bed, and the demon gone.

- The woman kept pressing Jesus to cure her daughter. We can understand that—how a mother would move heaven and earth to help and care for a daughter.
- Was it her faith or love that moved Jesus to grant her request? Lord, teach me to be wholehearted in prayer and in all I do.

Friday 11th February **Mark 7:31–37**

Then Jesus returned from the region of Tyre, and went by way of Sidon towards the Sea of Galilee, in the region of the Decapolis. They brought to him a deaf man who had an impediment in his speech; and they begged him to lay his hand on him. He took him aside in private, away from the crowd, and put his fingers into his ears, and he spat and touched his tongue. Then looking up to heaven, he sighed and said to him, "Ephphatha," that is, "Be opened." And immediately his ears were opened, his tongue was released, and he spoke plainly. Then Jesus ordered them to tell no one; but the more he ordered them, the more zealously they proclaimed it. They were astounded beyond measure, saying, "He has done everything well; he even makes the deaf to hear and the mute to speak."

- Jesus had a reputation as a healer, so that people flocked to him as they do today to healers—because they need him.
- We know from the weakness of our bodies and the fragility of our hearts that we need God. Prayer is the time we come in need to God knowing that he always gives strength of mind, body, or soul when we place ourselves in God's loving presence.

Saturday 12th February **Genesis 3:9–13**

But the Lord God called to the man, and said to him, "Where are you?" He said, "I heard the sound of you in the garden, and I was afraid, because I was naked; and I hid myself." He said, "Who told you that you were naked? Have you eaten from the tree of which I commanded you not to eat?" The man said, "The woman whom you gave to be with me, she gave me fruit from the tree, and I ate." Then the Lord God said to the woman, "What is this that you have done?" The woman said, "The serpent tricked me, and I ate."

- This may be a familiar story, but it is not a simple story about a man, a woman, an apple and a serpent. It is a meditation on our humanity, its limitations, and our proper relationship with God. Where do we find true wisdom: in the serpent—human wisdom—or in God?
- Do I tend to put my trust in human ingenuity, energy, and technology, and push God to one side? Or do I strive to see my life and my efforts as gifts of a generous God?

february 13–19

Something to think and pray about each day this week:

Embracing Life

Some years ago at the Western Wall in Jerusalem, I watched Jewish families celebrating the Bar Mitzvah of their sons. The vast courtyard looked chaotic at first, with dozens of groups clustered round tables where relatives and rabbis sang, hugged their children, broadcast sweets for the little ones to scramble for, and cheered as each Bar Mitzvah boy strapped on his phylacteries and read the scriptures.

The singing was liturgical, old and happy chants to celebrate the coming of age. The boys clutched and kissed the great ornate scrolls that contained the scriptures, climbed on their fathers' shoulders, and processed in a singing, dancing triumph into the synagogue. It was not a rehearsed or studied ritual, but an outpouring of happiness in God's house. Afterwards the drums came out, and families danced together in the sunshine—grandchildren, parents and grandparents.

There was no alcohol to dull their senses, and no guilt or inhibitions to tone down the hugging, kissing, and physical affection that marked the families, sisters with brothers, parents with children. Coming from Jesus' own race, it was a lesson in what Jesus offered: that we may have life and have it more abundantly.

The Presence of God
As I sit here with my book, God is here.
Around me, in my sensations, in my thoughts and deep within me.
I pause for a moment, and become aware
of God's life-giving presence.

Freedom
A thick and shapeless tree-trunk would never believe
that it could become a statue, admired as a miracle of sculpture,
and would never submit itself to the chisel of the sculptor,
who sees by her genius what she can make of it. (St. Ignatius)
I ask for the grace to let myself be shaped by my loving Creator.

Consciousness
How am I really feeling? Light-hearted? Heavy-hearted?
I may be very much at peace, happy to be here.
Equally, I may be frustrated, worried, or angry.
I acknowledge how I really am. It is the real me that the Lord loves.

The Word
God speaks to each one of us individually. I need to listen to what he is saying to me. (Please turn to your scripture on the following pages. Inspiration points are there should you need them. When you are ready, return here to continue.)

Conversation
Do I notice myself reacting as I pray with the Word of God?
Do I feel challenged, comforted, angry?
Imagining Jesus sitting or standing by me,
I speak out my feelings, as one trusted friend to another.

Conclusion
Glory be to the Father, and to the Son, and to the Holy Spirit,
As it was in the beginning, is now, and ever shall be,
World without end. Amen

Sunday 13th February,
Sixth Sunday in Ordinary Time **1 Corinthians 2:6–10**

Yet among the mature we do speak wisdom, though it is not a wisdom of this age or of the rulers of this age, who are doomed to perish. But we speak God's wisdom, secret and hidden, which God decreed before the ages for our glory. None of the rulers of this age understood this; for if they had, they would not have crucified the Lord of glory. But, as it is written, "What no eye has seen, nor ear heard, nor the human heart conceived, what God has prepared for those who love him"—these things God has revealed to us through the Spirit; for the Spirit searches everything, even the depths of God.

- God's wisdom does not necessarily match up with what humans value, such as intellectual prowess, prestige, or business success.
- Lord, teach me to look beyond any human achievements and to make the Spirit my centre, to lead me always towards you.

Monday 14th February,
Sts. Cyril and Methodius **Luke 10:1–6**

After this the Lord appointed seventy others and sent them on ahead of him in pairs to every town and place where he himself intended to go. He said to them, "The harvest is plentiful, but the laborers are few; therefore ask the Lord of the harvest to send out laborers into his harvest. Go on your way. See, I am sending you out like lambs into the midst of wolves. Carry no purse, no bag, no sandals; and greet no one on the road. Whatever house you enter, first say, 'Peace to this house!' And if anyone is there who shares in peace, your peace will rest on that person; but if not, it will return to you."

- Can I imagine myself in this story? How would I have felt—tense, anxious, confident, uncertain, frightened, fearless?

- "Peace to this house!" How do I proclaim this in my life?

Tuesday 15th February **Mark 8:14–17**

Now the disciples had forgotten to bring any bread; and they had only one loaf with them in the boat. And he cautioned them, saying, "Watch out—beware of the yeast of the Pharisees and the yeast of Herod." They said to one another, "It is because we have no bread." And becoming aware of it, Jesus said to them, "Why are you talking about having no bread? Do you still not perceive or understand?"

- The one loaf was all that was necessary. They had forgotten that Jesus could feed the many with the one bread. He cautions them to depend on him in life. The one loaf also looks ahead to the Eucharist. Jesus will identify himself then with a loaf of bread.
- Our prayer gives us time to allow the mystery of Jesus, the one thing necessary in life, to sink into the depths of our being.

Wednesday 16th February **Mark 8:22–26**

They came to Bethsaida. Some people brought a blind man to Jesus and begged him to touch him. He took the blind man by the hand and led him out of the village; and when he had put saliva on his eyes and laid his hands on him, he asked him, "Can you see anything?" And the man looked up and said, "I can see people, but they look like trees, walking." Then Jesus laid his hands on his eyes again; and he looked intently and his sight was restored, and he saw everything clearly. Then he sent him away to his home, saying, "Do not even go into the village."

- The saliva brings partial healing to a blind man. He can see something but not very clearly. The touch of Jesus on his eyes brings total healing.

- Jesus is different; his healing is from within himself. The disciples may recall later that growth in their knowledge of Jesus only comes bit by bit.
- I learn slowly. In prayer I learn the lessons of the heart of Jesus.

Thursday 17th February **Mark 8:27–33**

Jesus went on with his disciples to the villages of Caesarea Philippi; and on the way he asked his disciples, "Who do people say that I am?" And they answered him, "John the Baptist; and others, Elijah; and still others, one of the prophets." He asked them, "But who do you say that I am?" Peter answered him, "You are the Messiah." And he sternly ordered them not to tell anyone about him. Then he began to teach them that the Son of Man must undergo great suffering, and be rejected by the elders, the chief priests, and the scribes, and be killed, and after three days rise again. He said all this quite openly. And Peter took him aside and began to rebuke him. But turning and looking at his disciples, he rebuked Peter and said, "Get behind me, Satan! For you are setting your mind not on divine things but on human things."

- The Lord wants our faith in our prayer. Jesus asks us in many ways the same question: "Who do you say that I am?"
- How would you answer? You are God? the poor? the hungry? the need in every person I meet?
- Let his words of who he is echo in your prayer: "I am life, joy, and whatever you do for others, you do for me."

Friday 18th February **Mark 8:34–9:1**

Jesus called the crowd with his disciples, and said to them, "If any want to become my followers, let them deny themselves and take up their cross and follow me. For those who want to save their life will lose it, and those who lose their life for my sake, and for the sake of the gospel, will save it. For what will it profit them to gain the whole world and forfeit their life? Indeed, what can they give in return for their life? Those who are ashamed of me and of my words in this adulterous and sinful generation, of them the Son of Man will also be ashamed when he comes in the glory of his Father with the holy angels." And he said to them, "Truly I tell you, there are some standing here who will not taste death until they see that the kingdom of God has come with power."

- Discipleship has a cost. There are times when the call of Jesus will go against other desires and values, personal and cultural.
- Following Christ may make us feel foolish in front of others. We need the support of like-minded people. Our endurance will bring forth the kingdom in ways we may not expect.

Saturday 19th February **Mark 9:2–8**

Six days later, Jesus took with him Peter and James and John, and led them up a high mountain apart, by themselves. And he was transfigured before them, and his clothes became dazzling white, such as no one on earth could bleach them. And there appeared to them Elijah with Moses, who were talking with Jesus. Then Peter said to Jesus, "Rabbi, it is good for us to be here; let us make three dwellings, one for you, one for Moses, and one for Elijah." He did not know what to say, for they were terrified. Then a cloud overshadowed them, and from the cloud there came a voice, "This is my Son, the Beloved; listen to him!" Suddenly when they looked around, they saw no one with them any more, but only Jesus.

- This incident on the mountain gets us to look forward either to the resurrection of Jesus or the glory of the second coming. Peter's reaction also gets us to look forward to life with God, so that we will say in eternity, "It is good for us to be here."
- The transfiguration was for the benefit of the disciples, for their faith and confidence in the lasting glory of Jesus at bad times. It can be the same for each of us in prayer.

february 20–26

Something to think and pray about each day this week:

Knowing Ourselves

Jesus is quoted as telling us to gouge out our eye if it scandalizes us. It is a graphic Hebrew way of telling us to recognize the occasions of sin and what have been called our predominant passions. What is my fatal flaw? Sometimes it takes a close friend or one of the family to reveal to us the weakness that is most likely to lead us astray. Some fail through lack of self control, but some fail by wanting too much control, making others' lives a misery for the sake of tidiness and order. In its own way, that can be the eye scandalizing you—when you cannot bear the sight of a full ashtray. Jesus is saying, "Be aware of your weak point." It may be the eye, lustful, envious, or critical; or the greedy or cruel hand; or the caustic or deceitful tongue. It may be the love of money—Saint James is strong on that. It may be our sexuality which God calls us to transform into a vehicle of love, not to root it out. Jesus tells us to know ourselves in our weaknesses as in our strengths. No two of us are alike.

The Presence of God

"I stand at the door and knock," says the Lord.
What a wonderful privilege
that the Lord of all creation desires to come to me.
I welcome his presence.

Freedom

Lord, grant me the grace to be free from the excesses of this life.
Let me not get caught up with the desire for wealth.
Keep my heart and mind free to love and serve you.

Consciousness

"There is a time and place for everything," as the saying goes.
Lord, grant that I may always desire
to spend time in your presence. To hear your call.

The Word

God speaks to each one of us individually. I need to listen to what he is saying to me. (Please turn to your scripture on the following pages. Inspiration points are there should you need them. When you are ready, return here to continue.)

Conversation

The gift of speech is a wonderful gift.
May I use this gift with kindness.
May I be slow to utter harsh words,
hurtful words, and words spoken in anger.

Conclusion

Glory be to the Father, and to the Son, and to the Holy Spirit,
As it was in the beginning, is now, and ever shall be,
World without end. Amen

Sunday 20th February,
Seventh Sunday in Ordinary Time **Matthew 5:43–48**

Jesus said to his disciples, "You have heard that it was said, 'You shall love your neighbor and hate your enemy.' But I say to you, Love your enemies and pray for those who persecute you, so that you may be children of your Father in heaven; for he makes his sun rise on the evil and on the good, and sends rain on the righteous and on the unrighteous. For if you love those who love you, what reward do you have? Do not even the tax-collectors do the same? And if you greet only your brothers and sisters, what more are you doing than others? Do not even the Gentiles do the same? Be perfect, therefore, as your heavenly Father is perfect."

- How do I respond to these teachings in the Sermon on the Mount? Dismiss them as idealistic, impractical, too radical? How do I face the challenge they offer?
- Here is the lesson of the Cross in front of me. When I see things in the transforming light of Jesus, lifted up on the Cross, some things are reversed, but all things are different.

Monday 21st February **Mark 9:17–24**

Someone from the crowd answered Jesus, "Teacher, I brought you my son; he has a spirit that makes him unable to speak; and whenever it seizes him, it dashes him down; and he foams and grinds his teeth and becomes rigid; and I asked your disciples to cast it out, but they could not do so." Jesus said: "Bring him to me." And they brought the boy to him. When the spirit saw him, immediately it convulsed the boy, and he fell on the ground and rolled about, foaming at the mouth. Jesus asked the father, "How long has this been happening to him?" And he said, "From childhood. It has often cast him into the fire and into the water, to destroy him; but if you are able to do anything, have pity on us and help us." Jesus said to him, "If you are able! All things can be done for the one who believes." Immediately the father of the child cried out, "I believe; help my unbelief!"

- The father of the sick boy here seems to have more faith than the disciples. His love of the boy and the need for a cure may have opened his heart to more faith in Jesus than his disciples had.
- Love can open the door to faith in God, for all love comes from God. Parental love is one of the closest loves to the love of God for all God's children.

Tuesday 22nd February,
Chair of St. Peter, Apostle **Matthew 16:13–19**

Now when Jesus came into the district of Caesarea Philippi, he asked his disciples, "Who do people say that the Son of Man is?" And they said, "Some say John the Baptist, but others Elijah, and still others Jeremiah or one of the prophets." He said to them, "But who do you say that I am?" Simon Peter answered, "You are the Messiah, the Son of the living God." And Jesus answered him, "Blessed are you, Simon son of Jonah! For flesh and blood has not revealed this to you, but my Father in heaven. And I tell you, you are Peter, and on this rock I will build my church, and the gates of Hades will not prevail against it. I will give you the keys of the kingdom of heaven, and whatever you bind on earth will be bound in heaven, and whatever you loose on earth will be loosed in heaven."

- When we think of "church," it is often of the externals—buildings, bishops and dioceses, schools and hospitals. And we may be disappointed with what we see and experience.
- But the Church is much more; it is a living organism, infused with the life of the Spirit. It is a community in which we live, always called to the mission Jesus handed on.
- "Who do you say that I am?" Lord, lead me deeper still into this community of faith, to confess my response with Peter.

Wednesday 23rd February **Mark 9:38–40**

John said to Jesus, "Teacher, we saw someone casting out demons in your name, and we tried to stop him, because he was not following us." But Jesus said, "Do not stop him; for no one who does a deed of power in my name will be able soon afterwards to speak evil of me. Whoever is not against us is for us."

- "Whoever is not against us is for us." In modern parlance, John is "protecting the brand name," wanting to make sure Jesus' name is not misused. But Jesus has a different, wider view.
- Do I look with suspicion on others who work for good but belong to a party, a community, or a tribe that is different from mine? I will try to know them by their fruits, not by their labels. I will seek to focus on common ground, not on barriers.

Thursday 24th February **Mark 9:45–50**

Jesus said to his disciples, "If your foot causes you to stumble, cut it off; it is better for you to enter life lame than to have two feet and to be thrown into hell. And if your eye causes you to stumble, tear it out; it is better for you to enter the kingdom of God with one eye than to have two eyes and to be thrown into hell, where their worm never dies, and the fire is never quenched. For everyone will be salted with fire. Salt is good; but if salt has lost its saltiness, how can you season it? Have salt in yourselves, and be at peace with one another."

- These strong words are challenging for most of us who have little exposure to such apocalyptic images. But Jesus' message is clear; life in the kingdom of God stands above all else.
- Each of us has the responsibility to work hard for our own salvation and the salvation of others. How do I measure up?

Friday 25th February **Ecclesiasticus 6:5–6, 14–17**

Pleasant speech multiplies friends, and a gracious tongue multiplies courtesies. Let those who are friendly with you be many, but let your advisers be one in a thousand. Faithful friends are a sturdy shelter: whoever finds one has found a treasure. Faithful friends are beyond price; no amount can balance their worth. Faithful friends are life-saving medicine; and those who fear the Lord will find them. Those who fear the Lord direct their friendship aright, for as they are, so are their neighbors also.

- "A faithful friend is the elixir of life." We never outgrow the need for friends, and our friendships need to be kept in good repair. I have lost friends, some by death, some by sheer inability to cross the street or pick up a phone.
- My friend is the one who knows all about me and still likes me. I thank you, Lord, for the friends I have: not to be taken for granted.

Saturday 26th February **Mark 10:13–16**

People were bringing little children to Jesus in order that he might touch them; and the disciples spoke sternly to them. But when Jesus saw this, he was indignant and said to them, "Let the little children come to me; do not stop them; for it is to such as these that the kingdom of God belongs. Truly I tell you, whoever does not receive the kingdom of God as a little child will never enter it." And he took them up in his arms, laid his hands on them, and blessed them.

- Not for the first time—or last—the disciples get it wrong. Jesus patiently instructs them again, and patiently helps me to understand his message today.
- "To such as these . . . the kingdom of God belongs." In Jesus' time, children were viewed as having little value; they could not earn or perform useful work, so anything they received was a gift. Jesus blessed them, not just with a touch but with a loving embrace.
- This kingdom is a gift of God, unearned, an act of pure love. Thank you, Lord. How can I repay you?

february 27–march 5

Something to think and pray about each day this week:

Finding Space

It was the Jews who taught us to observe the sabbath, though they kept it on what we call Saturday. The book of Genesis describes God as resting on the seventh day. That story at the beginning of the Bible is not history but myth, a picturesque way of conveying a vital truth: that God existed before the world or time, and is the creator of all. The notion of working hard and creatively for six days and then resting on the seventh has entered deep into human history. The sabbath, whether we celebrate it on Saturday or Sunday (or on Friday as the Muslims do), is not just a day of rest. It is also the Lord's day, when we give time to God.

That seems like a simple and cheering idea. The father of monasticism, Saint Benedict, had a lovely phrase for it: vacare Deo, or "finding space for God." It means changing the tempo of our lives, taking it easy, stopping after a week's work to see where we are going. For some people that means slowing down, if they have a demanding job on weekdays. For others, especially as we grow older, one day is much the same as another, and we do not need much slowing down.

The Presence of God

Dear Jesus, today I call on you in a special way.
Mostly I come asking for favors.
Today I'd like just to be in your presence.
Let my heart respond to your Love.

Freedom

"I am free."
When I look at these words in writing
They seem to create in me a feeling of awe.
Yes, a wonderful feeling of freedom.
Thank you, God.

Consciousness

Lord, you gave me the night to rest in sleep.
In my waking hours may I not forget your goodness to me.
Guide me to share your blessings with others.

The Word

I read the Word of God slowly, a few times over, and I listen to what God is saying to me. (Please turn to your scripture on the following pages. Inspiration points are there should you need them. When you are ready, return here to continue.)

Conversation

Dear Jesus, I can open up my heart to you.
I can tell you everything that troubles me.
I know you care about all the concerns in my life.
Teach me to live in the knowledge
that you who care for me today,
will care for me tomorrow and all the days of my life.

Conclusion

Glory be to the Father, and to the Son, and to the Holy Spirit,
As it was in the beginning, is now, and ever shall be,
World without end. Amen

Sunday 27th February,
Eighth Sunday in Ordinary Time **Matthew 6:25, 28–34**

Jesus said to his disciples, "I tell you, do not worry about your life, what you will eat or what you will drink, or about your body, what you will wear. Is not life more than food, and the body more than clothing? Consider the lilies of the field, how they grow; they neither toil nor spin, yet I tell you, even Solomon in all his glory was not clothed like one of these. But if God so clothes the grass of the field, which is alive today and tomorrow is thrown into the oven, will he not much more clothe you—you of little faith? Therefore do not worry, saying, 'What will we eat?' or 'What will we drink?' or 'What will we wear?' For it is the Gentiles who strive for all these things; and indeed your heavenly Father knows that you need all these things. But strive first for the kingdom of God and his righteousness, and all these things will be given to you as well. So do not worry about tomorrow, for tomorrow will bring worries of its own. Today's trouble is enough for today."

- In this well-loved text, Jesus is not trying to make a moral point about whether or not we should spend time buying food and clothes. He is appealing to the imagination to focus his followers on the kingdom of God, to encourage them (and us) to put God first.
- How much time and conversation do I spend on food, drink, and clothes? How much time do I spend speaking personally with the Lord, thinking about God's role in my life?
- I bring my priorities before God in prayer, asking if I have them properly sorted out. What might I do to change things around?

Monday 28th February **Mark 10:17–23**

As he was setting out on a journey, a man ran up and knelt before him, and asked him, "Good Teacher, what must I do to inherit eternal life?" Jesus said to him, "Why do you call me good? No one is good but God alone. You know the commandments: 'You shall not murder; You shall not commit adultery; You shall not steal; You shall not bear false witness; You shall not defraud; Honor your father and mother.'" He said to him, "Teacher, I have kept all these since my youth." Jesus, looking at him, loved him and said, "You lack one thing; go, sell what you own, and give the money to the poor, and you will have treasure in heaven; then come, follow me." When he heard this, he was shocked and went away grieving, for he had many possessions. Then Jesus looked around and said to his disciples, "How hard it will be for those who have wealth to enter the kingdom of God!"

- "What must I do to inherit eternal life?" Jesus does not give a simple answer but, as a good teacher would, leads the young man to a deeper understanding of his own question.
- Jesus, "looking at him, loved him," then invited him to take a further step, beyond what he "shall not" do to what he must become, to how he must be transformed. Step one is to let go of the securities of this life, but the young man falters.
- Lord, teach me to put my trust in the security of the "good" God.

Tuesday 1st March **Mark 10:28–30**

Peter began to say to him, "Look, we have left everything and followed you." Jesus said, "Truly I tell you, there is no one who has left house or brothers or sisters or mother or father or children or fields, for my sake and for the sake of the good news, who will not receive a hundredfold now in this age—houses, brothers and sisters, mothers and children, and fields, with persecutions—and in the age to come eternal life."

- In a society in which wealth was considered a sign of God's favour, the disciples have already made a leap forward; they have left everything to follow Jesus.
- Jesus assures us that life in the community of God our Father more than compensates for the loss of what we leave behind for the sake of the kingdom.
- This is a radical message. Let me sit with it for a while today.

Wednesday 2nd March **Ecclesiasticus 36:1, 15–17**

Take pity on us, Master, Lord of the universe, look at us, spread fear of yourself throughout all other nations. Give those who wait for you their reward, let your prophets be proved true. Grant, Lord, the prayer of your servants, in the terms of Aaron's blessing on your people, so that all the earth's inhabitants may acknowledge that you are the Lord, the everlasting God.

- "Grant, Lord, the prayer of your servants." While Jesus teaches me about a God who is loving father rather than a God of fearsome power, my stance as a believer is unchanged; I am a servant who seeks to acknowledge "the Lord, the everlasting God."
- Are we in service of our fellow human beings? Is my community, for example, a place where the Lord Jesus loves, lives, and serves through me?

Thursday 3rd March **Mark 10:46–52**

They came to Jericho. As he and his disciples and a large crowd were leaving Jericho, Bartimaeus son of Timaeus, a blind beggar, was sitting by the roadside. When he heard that it was Jesus of Nazareth, he began to shout out and say, "Jesus, Son of David, have mercy on me!" Many sternly ordered him to be quiet, but he cried out even more loudly, "Son of David, have mercy on me!" Jesus stood still and said, "Call him here." And they called the blind man, saying to him, "Take heart; get up, he is calling you." So throwing off his cloak, he sprang up and came to Jesus. Then Jesus said to him, "What do you want me to do for you?" The blind man said to him, "My teacher, let me see again." Jesus said to him, "Go; your faith has made you well." Immediately he regained his sight and followed him on the way.

- "What do you want me to do for you?" It may seem obvious that Bartimaeus wanted his sight restored, but Jesus still asked him.
- And he asks me too. Do I want to "see"? Do I want to be saved? Do I want to follow him? It is up to me to respond.

Friday 4th March **Mark 11:22–26**

Jesus answered them, "Have faith in God. Truly I tell you, if you say to this mountain, 'Be taken up and thrown into the sea,' and if you do not doubt in your heart, but believe that what you say will come to pass, it will be done for you. So I tell you, whatever you ask for in prayer, believe that you have received it, and it will be yours. Whenever you stand praying, forgive, if you have anything against anyone; so that your Father in heaven may also forgive you your trespasses."

- "Whenever you stand praying, forgive, if you have anything against anyone." How do I stand today? Am I ready to pray?

Saturday 5th March **Ecclesiasticus 51:12–13**

You saved me from destruction and rescued me in time of trouble. For this reason I thank you and praise you, and I bless the name of the Lord.

- It is a worthy prayer, to beg for wisdom all through life. Boethius defined the wise person as the one who savors everything as it really is: *Sapiens est cui omnia sapiunt sicuti sunt.*
- I think of how I have prayed for help in the past and consider how God has helped me. I give thanks.

march 6–12

Something to think and pray about each day this week:

Exploring Our Space

In our cities the social supports for the sabbath have disappeared. In commercial and social terms, a Sunday is barely different from a weekday. There can be a blessing in this change. Jesus constantly shifted the emphasis from law to love, and we can learn to do the same. We can learn to think of the sabbath as a time to find space for God rather than focus on the guilt of missing Mass or doing a job. Generations of parents have worried themselves sick over their children ignoring church laws, not unlike the rabbis in Jesus' time.

It might be more productive to focus first on making Sunday special in some way, and then on making space for God. Many German households still make the family meal on Sunday the highest priority of the week, more important than any sport or other distraction. Dublin, the seedbed of *Sacred Space*, sees a great population of ramblers take to the hills on Sunday: the pleasures of the hike, and the change of tempo from work or study, are balm to the soul as well as the body. We get in touch with God in different ways, through sitting with our family over a meal, through taking time out to stop and stare at God's creation, through joining the community of our neighbours in the ancient but simple shared worship of the Mass.

The Presence of God
As I sit here with my book, God is here.
Around me, in my sensations, in my thoughts and deep within me.
I pause for a moment, and become aware
of God's life-giving presence.

Freedom
A thick and shapeless tree-trunk would never believe
that it could become a statue, admired as a miracle of sculpture,
and would never submit itself to the chisel of the sculptor,
who sees by her genius what she can make of it. (St. Ignatius)
I ask for the grace to let myself be shaped by my loving Creator.

Consciousness
How am I really feeling? Light-hearted? Heavy-hearted?
I may be very much at peace, happy to be here.
Equally, I may be frustrated, worried, or angry.
I acknowledge how I really am. It is the real me that the Lord loves.

The Word
The Word of God comes down to us through the scriptures. May the Holy Spirit enlighten my mind and my heart to respond to the gospel teachings. (Please turn to your scripture on the following pages. Inspiration points are there should you need them. When you are ready, return here to continue.)

Conversation
Do I notice myself reacting as I pray with the Word of God?
Do I feel challenged, comforted, angry?
Imagining Jesus sitting or standing by me,
I speak out my feelings, as one trusted friend to another.

Conclusion
Glory be to the Father, and to the Son, and to the Holy Spirit,
As it was in the beginning, is now, and ever shall be,
World without end. Amen

Sunday 6th March,
Ninth Sunday in Ordinary Time **Matthew 7:21–27**

Not everyone who says to me, "Lord, Lord," will enter the kingdom of heaven, but only one who does the will of my Father in heaven. On that day many will say to me, "Lord, Lord, did we not prophesy in your name, and cast out demons in your name, and do many deeds of power in your name?" Then I will declare to them, "I never knew you; go away from me, you evil-doers." Everyone then who hears these words of mine and acts on them will be like a wise man who built his house on rock. The rain fell, the floods came, and the winds blew and beat on that house, but it did not fall, because it had been founded on rock. And everyone who hears these words of mine and does not act on them will be like a foolish man who built his house on sand. The rain fell, and the floods came, and the winds blew and beat against that house, and it fell—and great was its fall!

- One of the rocks of the Christian life is the Word of God. The word of God speaks for every occasion and for every anxiety. Let the Bible be an open book for us, and God will be an open book.
- Perhaps I did not grow up with much experience of the Bible's riches. Let me make the time to read it personally and to listen carefully when I hear it read.

Monday 7th March **Mark 12:1–12**

Then Jesus began to speak to them in parables. "A man planted a vineyard, put a fence around it, dug a pit for the wine press, and built a watchtower; then he leased it to tenants and went to another country. When the season came, he sent a slave to the tenants to collect from them his share of the produce of the vineyard. But they seized him, and beat him, and sent him away empty-handed. And again he sent another slave to them; this one they beat over the head and insulted. Then he sent another, and that one they killed. And so it was with many others; some they beat, and others they killed. He had still one other, a beloved son. Finally he sent him to them, saying, 'They will respect my son.' But those tenants said to one another, 'This is the heir; come, let us kill him, and the inheritance will be ours.' So they seized him, killed him, and threw him out of the vineyard. What then will the owner of the vineyard do? He will come and destroy the tenants and give the vineyard to others. Have you not read this scripture: 'The stone that the builders rejected has become the cornerstone; this was the Lord's doing, and it is amazing in our eyes'?" When they realized that he had told this parable against them, they wanted to arrest him, but they feared the crowd. So they left him and went away.

- Jesus and his message can be the cornerstone of our lives—the guiding truth that gives security and conviction to all of life.
- All love and goodness is created through him. The way we try to live by his gospel is the Lord's doing also. Life itself and love are gifts of God, the touchstone of God's continual creation of us all.

Tuesday 8th March **Mark 12:13–17**

Then they sent to Jesus some Pharisees and some Herodians to trap him in what he said. And they came and said to him, "Teacher, we know that you are sincere, and show deference to no one; for you do not regard people with partiality, but teach the way of God in accordance with truth. Is it lawful to pay taxes to the emperor, or not? Should we pay them, or should we not?" But knowing their hypocrisy, he said to them, "Why are you putting me to the test? Bring me a denarius and let me see it." And they brought one. Then he said to them, "Whose head is this, and whose title?" They answered, "The emperor's." Jesus said to them, "Give to the emperor the things that are the emperor's, and to God the things that are God's." And they were utterly amazed at him.

- Jesus had to have his wits about him. People were often trying to trap him with trick questions. He often asked, "Why put me to the test?" He knew the complexities of his opponents.
- He advised us to pray that we too would not be put to the test, or led into temptation. Jesus made decisions from the wisdom of his relationship with the Father.

Wednesday 9th March,
Ash Wednesday **Matthew 6:1–6**

Beware of practicing your piety before others in order to be seen by them; for then you have no reward from your Father in heaven. So whenever you give alms, do not sound a trumpet before you, as the hypocrites do in the synagogues and in the streets, so that they may be praised by others. Truly I tell you, they have received their reward. But when you give alms, do not let your left hand know what your right hand is doing, so that your alms may be done in secret; and your Father who sees in secret will reward you. And whenever you pray, do not be like the hypocrites; for they love to stand and pray in the synagogues and at the street corners, so that they may be seen by others. Truly I tell you, they have received their reward. But whenever you pray, go into your room and shut the door and pray to your Father who is in secret; and your Father who sees in secret will reward you.

- Lent is a time to recall the priority of God in our lives: that we come from and go to God, and that God is the companion of our lives. The focus of living faith and religious practice is not on us, but on God's place in our lives.

- Ash Wednesday 2011 means twelve years of the *Sacred Space* website. It may be good, in prayer, to think of the others who will pray there or with this book today. We are not alone as we pray.

Thursday 10th March **Luke 9:22–25**

Jesus said to his disciples: "The Son of Man must undergo great suffering, and be rejected by the elders, chief priests, and scribes, and be killed, and on the third day be raised." Then he said to them all, "If any want to become my followers, let them deny themselves and take up their cross daily and follow me. For those who want to save their life will lose it, and those who lose their life for my sake will save it. What does it profit them if they gain the whole world, but lose or forfeit themselves?"

- The big mystery of Lent is the death and resurrection of the Lord.
- As he carried a cross, we too carry crosses throughout our lives in the difficulties and weaknesses of body, mind, and spirit. We save our lives in giving ourselves away in love to God and to others.

Friday 11th March **Matthew 9:14–15**

Then the disciples of John came to him, saying, "Why do we and the Pharisees fast often, but your disciples do not fast?" And Jesus said to them, "The wedding guests cannot mourn as long as the bridegroom is with them, can they? The days will come when the bridegroom is taken away from them, and then they will fast."

- No matter what mystery of Jesus' life we go to in prayer, we can rejoice. Even in his suffering and death, he is with us, and we do not mourn. Without his presence in our lives, we would truly mourn the loss of something and someone really relevant and essential to our lives.
- Today, let me focus on the place of Jesus in my life.

Saturday 12th March **Luke 5:27–32**

After this he went out and saw a tax collector named Levi, sitting at the tax booth; and he said to him, "Follow me." And he got up, left everything, and followed him. Then Levi gave a great banquet for him in his house; and there was a large crowd of tax collectors and others sitting at the table with them. The Pharisees and their scribes were complaining to his disciples, saying, "Why do you eat and drink with tax collectors and sinners?" Jesus answered, "Those who are well have no need of a physician, but those who are sick; I have come to call not the righteous but sinners to repentance."

- Jesus mixed with the riff-raff, with people who were outcasts in the society of the time. We see the same when he speaks with and heals people with leprosy. His eye seems to find the person who most needs the look of love and the power of his healing.
- The eye of Jesus will look with love on that part of each of us which needs the power of his healing love. He surprises us.

march 13–19

Something to think and pray about each day this week:

A Lenten Resolution

As we move into Lent we might be wondering if fasting has any meaning for us today. It has. It is really asking us to look at our relationship to food and drink. Jesus loved to eat with his friends. Meals were important for him. For families too, meals are a time when children watch and listen to their parents and vice versa. But family meals are in danger of disappearing, what with fast food, the lure of electronic games, and TV that is sometimes left on even when the family is eating together. Like talking on the phone in company, it reduces our presence to one another. For many families a good Lenten resolution would be to have meals together at least once a week, and expose themselves to the need for listening, sitting at peace, knowing how the rest of the family is, and going for slow rather than fast food.

The Presence of God

Jesus waits silent and unseen to come into my heart.
I will respond to his call.
He comes with his infinite power and love
May I be filled with joy in his presence.

Freedom

I ask for the grace
to let go of my own concerns
and be open to what God is asking of me,
to let myself be guided and formed by my loving Creator.

Consciousness

Knowing that God loves me unconditionally,
I can afford to be honest about how I am.
How has the last day been, and how do I feel now?
I share my feelings openly with the Lord.

The Word

I read the Word of God slowly, a few times over, and I listen to what God is saying to me. (Please turn to your scripture on the following pages. Inspiration points are there should you need them. When you are ready, return here to continue.)

Conversation

Remembering that I am still in God's presence,
I imagine Jesus himself standing or sitting beside me,
and say whatever is on my mind, whatever is in my heart,
speaking as one friend to another.

Conclusion

Glory be to the Father, and to the Son, and to the Holy Spirit,
As it was in the beginning, is now, and ever shall be,
World without end. Amen

Sunday 13th March,
First Sunday of Lent **Matthew 4:1–10**

Then Jesus was led up by the Spirit into the wilderness to be tempted by the devil. He fasted forty days and forty nights, and afterwards he was famished. The tempter came and said to him, "If you are the Son of God, command these stones to become loaves of bread." But he answered, "It is written, 'One does not live by bread alone, but by every word that comes from the mouth of God.'" Then the devil took him to the holy city and placed him on the pinnacle of the temple, saying to him, "If you are the Son of God, throw yourself down; for it is written, 'He will command his angels concerning you,' and 'On their hands they will bear you up, so that you will not dash your foot against a stone.'" Jesus said to him, "Again it is written, 'Do not put the Lord your God to the test.'" Again, the devil took him to a very high mountain and showed him all the kingdoms of the world and their splendor; and he said to him, "All these I will give you, if you will fall down and worship me." Jesus said to him, "Away with you, Satan! for it is written, 'Worship the Lord your God, and serve only him.'"

- In our desire to follow Jesus, there will be temptations, as there were for him. He was tempted to abandon his chosen mission, to use all his power for himself, to trust in himself alone.
- Our temptations may be different, but the reality is the same. Attractions other than the way of Jesus will make demands on us.
- What are some of the temptations I often face? How do I respond to them? Can I ask for strength as I pray today, and each day?

Monday 14th March **Matthew 25:31–40**

"When the Son of Man comes in his glory, and all the angels with him, then he will sit on the throne of his glory. All the nations will be gathered before him, and he will separate people one from another as a shepherd separates the sheep from the goats, and he will put the sheep at his right hand and the goats at the left. Then the king will say to those at his right hand, 'Come, you that are blessed by my Father, inherit the kingdom prepared for you from the foundation of the world; for I was hungry and you gave me food, I was thirsty and you gave me something to drink, I was a stranger and you welcomed me, I was naked and you gave me clothing, I was sick and you took care of me, I was in prison and you visited me. Then the righteous will answer him, 'Lord, when was it that we saw you hungry and gave you food, or thirsty and gave you something to drink? And when was it that we saw you a stranger and welcomed you, or naked and gave you clothing? And when was it that we saw you sick or in prison and visited you?' And the king will answer them, 'Truly I tell you, just as you did it to one of the least of these who are members of my family, you did it to me.'"

- How and where do I find God? These questions are often raised today and were raised with Jesus too. He gives many answers, but a strong answer is that in the poorest of the poor, we find Jesus. What we do for them, we do for him.
- Does this parable surprise me? Do I "get it" yet? Can I pray about needy people I know and see in them the light and the need of Jesus Christ?

Tuesday 15th March **Matthew 6:7–8**

Jesus said, "When you are praying, do not heap up empty phrases as the Gentiles do; for they think that they will be heard because of their many words. Do not be like them, for your Father knows what you need before you ask him."

- Prayer engages us in praise of God, in desiring God's will to be done and God's kingdom to come on earth; in prayer we ask for what we need for the day, and for the grace of forgiveness for self and others, and to stay on the path of our love and convictions.
- Lord, teach me pray like this each day.

Wednesday 16th March **Luke 11:29–32**

When the crowds were increasing, he began to say, "This generation is an evil generation; it asks for a sign, but no sign will be given to it except the sign of Jonah. For just as Jonah became a sign to the people of Nineveh, so the Son of Man will be to this generation. The queen of the South will rise at the judgment with the people of this generation and condemn them, because she came from the ends of the earth to listen to the wisdom of Solomon, and see, something greater than Solomon is here! The people of Nineveh will rise up at the judgment with this generation and condemn it, because they repented at the proclamation of Jonah, and see, something greater than Jonah is here!"

- Jonah was a man of narrow religious beliefs and intolerant of God's gracious treatment of Nineveh's pagan people. Yet the people believed in God and ultimately did God's will.
- Jesus is saying to us that the people of this pagan city had greater faith than the people to whom he spoke. He asks us for at least as much wisdom in hearing his word as the people of Nineveh had in hearing Jonah.

Thursday 17th March,
St. Patrick **Matthew 13:31–33**

Jesus put before them another parable: "The kingdom of heaven is like a mustard seed that someone took and sowed in his field; it is the smallest of all the seeds, but when it has grown it is the greatest of shrubs and becomes a tree, so that the birds of the air come and make nests in its branches." He told them another parable: "The kingdom of heaven is like yeast that a woman took and mixed in with three measures of flour until all of it was leavened."

- May the Strength of God guide us. May the Power of God preserve us. May the Wisdom of God instruct us. May the Hand of God protect us. May the Way of God direct us. May the Shield of God defend us. May the Angels of God guard us against the snares of the evil one.
- May Christ be with us! May Christ be before us! May Christ be in us! May Christ be in us, Christ be over all! May Thy Grace, Lord, Always be ours, This day, O Lord, and forevermore. Amen.

Friday 18th March **Matthew 5:20–24**

Jesus said to his disciples, "For I tell you, unless your righteousness exceeds that of the scribes and Pharisees, you will never enter the kingdom of heaven. You have heard that it was said to those of ancient times, 'You shall not murder'; and 'whoever murders shall be liable to judgment.' But I say to you that if you are angry with a brother or sister, you will be liable to judgment; and if you insult a brother or sister, you will be liable to the council; and if you say, 'You fool,' you will be liable to the hell of fire. So when you are offering your gift at the altar, if you remember that your brother or sister has something against you, leave your gift there before the altar and go; first be reconciled to your brother or sister, and then come and offer your gift."

- We can get stuck in our prayer, dwelling on those who have hurt us: the abusers, the unjust, those we struggle to forgive.
- Jesus knows this. The effect in prayer can be to allow grace to flow into the past, and know that God in Jesus is accompanying us in our hurt. We may ask the grace to forgive sometime, if not now.

Saturday 19th March,
St. Joseph **Matthew 1:18–25**

Now the birth of Jesus the Messiah took place in this way. When his mother Mary had been engaged to Joseph, but before they lived together, she was found to be with child from the Holy Spirit. Her husband Joseph, being a righteous man and unwilling to expose her to public disgrace, planned to dismiss her quietly. But just when he had resolved to do this, an angel of the Lord appeared to him in a dream and said, "Joseph, son of David, do not be afraid to take Mary as your wife, for the child conceived in her is from the Holy Spirit. She will bear a son, and you are to name him Jesus, for he will save his people from their sins." All this took place to fulfill what had been spoken by the Lord through the prophet: "Look, the virgin shall conceive and bear a son, and they shall name him Emmanuel," which means, "God is with us." When Joseph awoke from sleep, he did as the angel of the Lord commanded him; he took her as his wife, but had no marital relations with her until she had borne a son; and he named him Jesus.

- Joseph is the patron of carers—in love, and work he cared for his dearest ones. He was a man of faith who learned from the angels of God what was needed of him, and did the same. Jesus did as he did, and found some of the best qualities in his life from the people he grew up with, Joseph and Mary.
- Can I pray today for those who cared for me as I grew into faith and love?

march 20–26

Something to think and pray about each day this week:

A Fast for Today

Fasting has changed because food has changed. In the Western world it is rare for anyone to die of starvation, though plenty of people suffer from malnutrition—through eating too much fat, sugar, or salt. Food has changed its meaning, from being just an essential for survival to being a source of pleasure, temptation, and bargaining between children and their parents. In our culture, weight and eating habits are a highly charged topic, to be approached with sensitivity. But for each of us, Lent can offer energy and opportunity to move towards a happier use of food and drink. It is only when we try to change our habits that we discover how free or how shackled we are.

The Presence of God
For a few moments, I think of God's veiled presence in things:
in the elements, giving them existence;
in plants, giving them life; in animals, giving them sensation;
and finally, in me, giving me all this and more,
making me a temple, a dwelling-place of the Spirit.

Freedom
God is not foreign to my freedom.
Instead the Spirit breathes life into my most intimate desires,
gently nudging me towards all that is good.
I ask for the grace to let myself be enfolded by the Spirit.

Consciousness
Knowing that God loves me unconditionally,
I can afford to be honest about how I am.
How has the last day been, and how do I feel now?
I share my feelings openly with the Lord.

The Word
The Word of God comes down to us through the scriptures. May the Holy Spirit enlighten my mind and my heart to respond to the gospel teachings. (Please turn to your scripture on the following pages. Inspiration points are there should you need them. When you are ready, return here to continue.)

Conversation
How has God's Word moved me? Has it left me cold?
Has it consoled me or moved me to act in a new way?
I imagine Jesus standing or sitting beside me,
I turn and share my feelings with him.

Conclusion
Glory be to the Father, and to the Son, and to the Holy Spirit,
As it was in the beginning, is now, and ever shall be,
World without end. Amen

Sunday 20th March,
Second Sunday of Lent **Matthew 17:1–9**

Six days later, Jesus took with him Peter and James and his brother John and led them up a high mountain, by themselves. And he was transfigured before them, and his face shone like the sun, and his clothes became dazzling white. Suddenly there appeared to them Moses and Elijah, talking with him. Then Peter said to Jesus, "Lord, it is good for us to be here; if you wish, I will make three dwellings here, one for you, one for Moses, and one for Elijah." While he was still speaking, suddenly a bright cloud overshadowed them, and from the cloud a voice said, "This is my Son, the Beloved; with him I am well pleased; listen to him!" When the disciples heard this, they fell to the ground and were overcome by fear. But Jesus came and touched them, saying, "Get up and do not be afraid." And when they looked up, they saw no one except Jesus himself alone. As they were coming down the mountain, Jesus ordered them, "Tell no one about the vision until after the Son of Man has been raised from the dead."

- Transfiguration is about Jesus and about us. When we are with him, we are with the divine. When he is with us, he is with the human. His love, grace, sacraments, peace, and compassion can transfigure us.
- May we be present in prayer to light and brightness, allow light to invade us, and know that the light of Jesus given in baptism is never extinguished.

Monday 21st March **Luke 6:36–38**

Jesus said to his disciples, "Be merciful, just as your Father is merciful. Do not judge, and you will not be judged; do not condemn, and you will not be condemned. Forgive, and you will be forgiven; give, and it will be given to you. A good measure, pressed down, shaken together, running over, will be put into your lap; for the measure you give will be the measure you get back."

- A generous heart and mind is an immense reward that comes from God. Even in human terms we are enhanced by our qualities of mercy, forgiveness, and tolerance.
- Let us allow prayer to give us the energy of love to burn away some of the bitterness and grudges that are part of every life.

Tuesday 22nd March **Matthew 23:1–12**

Then Jesus said to the crowds and to his disciples, "The scribes and the Pharisees sit on Moses' seat; therefore, do whatever they teach you and follow it; but do not do as they do, for they do not practice what they teach. They tie up heavy burdens, hard to bear, and lay them on the shoulders of others; but they themselves are unwilling to lift a finger to move them. They do all their deeds to be seen by others; for they make their phylacteries broad and their fringes long. They love to have the place of honor at banquets and the best seats in the synagogues, and to be greeted with respect in the marketplaces, and to have people call them rabbi. But you are not to be called rabbi, for you have one teacher, and you are all students. And call no one your father on earth, for you have one Father—the one in heaven. Nor are you to be called instructors, for you have one instructor, the Messiah. The greatest among you will be your servant. All who exalt themselves will be humbled, and all who humble themselves will be exalted."

- We can easily think of people who are puffed up with their own praise and a sort of pomposity about themselves. We don't like that in others; there may be a bit in each of us.
- To realize that we are totally dependent on God for life and love is a humbling realization. Prayer at its best keeps us humble, calmed by the warmth of God's love.

Wednesday 23rd March **Matthew 20:25–28**

But Jesus called them to him and said, "You know that the rulers of the Gentiles lord it over them, and their great ones are tyrants over them. It will not be so among you; but whoever wishes to be great among you must be your servant, and whoever wishes to be first among you must be your slave; just as the Son of Man came not to be served but to serve, and to give his life as a ransom for many."

- Greatness with Jesus has little to do with success; it has to do with being like a slave, at the service of master or mistress.
- But a slave in those times also was an honoured member of the family. We are glad to be slaves in this sense—the ones who live for the service of God and are honoured by God in love.

Thursday 24th March **Luke 16:19–31**

Jesus said to the Pharisees, "There was a rich man who was dressed in purple and fine linen and who feasted sumptuously every day. And at his gate lay a poor man named Lazarus, covered with sores, who longed to satisfy his hunger with what fell from the rich man's table; even the dogs would come and lick his sores. The poor man died and was carried away by the angels to be with Abraham. The rich man also died and was buried. In

Hades, where he was being tormented, he looked up and saw Abraham far away with Lazarus by his side. He called out, 'Father Abraham, have mercy on me, and send Lazarus to dip the tip of his finger in water and cool my tongue; for I am in agony in these flames.' But Abraham said, 'Child, remember that during your lifetime you received your good things, and Lazarus in like manner evil things; but now he is comforted here, and you are in agony. Besides all this, between you and us a great chasm has been fixed, so that those who might want to pass from here to you cannot do so, and no one can cross from there to us.' He said, 'Then, father, I beg you to send him to my father's house—for I have five brothers—that he may warn them, so that they will not also come into this place of torment.' Abraham replied, 'They have Moses and the prophets; they should listen to them.' He said, 'No, father Abraham; but if someone goes to them from the dead, they will repent.' He said to him, 'If they do not listen to Moses and the prophets, neither will they be convinced even if someone rises from the dead.'"

- This story reminds us of the huge inequality of people in Jesus' time and still today. The parable invites us to see ourselves as richer in the goods of the world than many millions.
- This story challenges us to care for the needy in whatever way we can. Do I accept the challenge?

Friday 25th March,
Annunciation of the Lord **Luke 1:26–33**

In the sixth month the angel Gabriel was sent by God to a town in Galilee called Nazareth, to a virgin engaged to a man whose name was Joseph, of the house of David. The virgin's name was Mary. And he came to her and said, "Greetings, favored one! The Lord is with you." But she was much perplexed by his words and pondered what sort of greeting this might be. The angel said to her, "Do not be afraid, Mary, for you have found favor with God. And now, you will conceive in your womb and bear a son, and you will name him Jesus. He will be great, and will be called the Son of the Most High, and the Lord God will give to him the throne of his ancestor David. He will reign over the house of Jacob forever, and of his kingdom there will be no end."

- As with Mary, God announces to each of us that we are called to the work of the Son of God. Our vocation in life is first that we have found favour with God, and God is with us. Then we are asked to allow the life of God to reach deeply into our lives so that the Divine life and love reaches others through each of us.
- Each of us can be a part of the plan of God to love and save the world.

Saturday 26th March **Luke 15:22–24**

But the father said to his slaves, "Quickly, bring out a robe—the best one—and put it on him; put a ring on his finger and sandals on his feet. And get the fatted calf and kill it, and let us eat and celebrate; for this son of mine was dead and is alive again; he was lost and is found!"

- We probably know the Prodigal Son story well. It has been called the best short story ever written. It is more about the love of the father than about the sin of the son. It is about the celebration of a loved one's return to God and love.
- Nowhere is the son called to repentance or conversion—it's as if this will happen in the atmosphere of love and forgiveness.
- How can I respond in my life, today?

march 27–april 2

Something to think and pray about each day this week:

Best Practice

There was a time when church laws about fasting spelled out in detail the size and weight of what was allowed at main meals or snacks (collations as they were called). In our culture that makes no sense. Fasting, for us, means aiming to keep our personal freedom in face of ingrained habits, which may be habits of eating too much or too little or of eating the wrong sort of food or drink. There's plenty of room for resolutions still, but remember: a resolution becomes real not when we make it or write it down, but when we first put it into practice.

The Presence of God
For a few moments, I think of God's veiled presence in things:
in the elements, giving them existence;
in plants, giving them life; in animals, giving them sensation;
and finally, in me, giving me all this and more,
making me a temple, a dwelling-place of the Spirit.

Freedom
God is not foreign to my freedom.
Instead the Spirit breathes life into my most intimate desires,
gently nudging me towards all that is good.
I ask for the grace to let myself be enfolded by the Spirit.

Consciousness
Knowing that God loves me unconditionally,
I can afford to be honest about how I am.
How has the last day been, and how do I feel now?
I share my feelings openly with the Lord.

The Word
I take my time to read the Word of God, slowly, a few times, allowing myself to dwell on anything that strikes me. (Please turn to your scripture on the following pages. Inspiration points are there should you need them. When you are ready, return here to continue.)

Conversation
How has God's Word moved me? Has it left me cold?
Has it consoled me or moved me to act in a new way?
I imagine Jesus standing or sitting beside me,
I turn and share my feelings with him.

Conclusion
Glory be to the Father, and to the Son, and to the Holy Spirit,
As it was in the beginning, is now, and ever shall be,
World without end. Amen

Sunday 27th March,
Third Sunday of Lent **John 4:5–10**

Jesus came to a Samaritan city called Sychar, near the plot of ground that Jacob had given to his son Joseph. Jacob's well was there, and Jesus, tired out by his journey, was sitting by the well. It was about noon. A Samaritan woman came to draw water, and Jesus said to her, "Give me a drink." (His disciples had gone to the city to buy food.) The Samaritan woman said to him, "How is it that you, a Jew, ask a drink of me, a woman of Samaria?" (Jews do not share things in common with Samaritans.) Jesus answered her, "If you knew the gift of God, and who it is that is saying to you, 'Give me a drink', you would have asked him, and he would have given you living water."

- The Samaritan woman might have been angry or fled from this man who broke all the "rules" by speaking to her. Instead, she was astonished—and answered Jesus with a question of her own.
- She may not yet have come to belief, but by her response she laid herself open to something new which might change her life.
- Am I open to such a confronting, personal encounter with Jesus?

Monday 28th March **Luke 4:24–30**

And he said, "Truly I tell you, no prophet is accepted in the prophet's hometown. But the truth is, there were many widows in Israel in the time of Elijah, when the heaven was shut up three years and six months, and there was a severe famine over all the land; yet Elijah was sent to none of them except to a widow at Zarephath in Sidon. There were also many lepers in Israel in the time of the prophet Elisha, and none of them was cleansed except Naaman the Syrian." When they heard this, all in the synagogue were filled with rage. They got up, drove him out of the town, and led him to the brow of the hill on which their town was built, so that they might hurl him off the cliff. But he passed through the midst of them and went on his way.

- The people here were jealous of their community of faith. Jesus was including all nationalities in the care and the saving love of God. They were jealous of their own relationship with God, and used it in many ordinary ways to keep others out.
- Jesus is the one of universal welcome, his heart open in prayer and life to all, no matter their creed, nation, gender, or age.

Tuesday 29th March **Matthew 18:21–22**

Then Peter came and said to him, "Lord, if another member of the church sins against me, how often should I forgive? As many as seven times?" Jesus said to him, "Not seven times, but, I tell you, seventy-seven times."

- Jesus responds to Peter's generous benchmark of "seven times" by going even further—true forgiveness knows no limits at all.
- How do I express this in my own life; in my family, among my work colleagues, with my friends?

Wednesday 30th March **Matthew 5:17–19**

Jesus said to his disciples, "Do not think that I have come to abolish the law or the prophets; I have come not to abolish but to fulfill. For truly I tell you, until heaven and earth pass away, not one letter, not one stroke of a letter, will pass from the law until all is accomplished. Therefore, whoever breaks one of the least of these commandments, and teaches others to do the same, will be called least in the kingdom of heaven; but whoever does them and teaches them will be called great in the kingdom of heaven."

- Jesus is no destroyer of people's devotions and faith. He does not abolish the faith practice of a people or a person. All the goodness of our religion and our faith is precious to him. His grace is given to each personally.
- Each of us prays differently, or with a variety of times, places, and moods. Prayer is entering into the mystery of God's love.

Thursday 31st March **Psalm 95:6–9**

O come, let us worship and bow down. Let us kneel before the Lord, our Maker! For he is our God, and we are the people of his pasture, and the sheep of his hand. O that today you would listen to his voice! Do not harden your hearts, as at Meribah, as on the day at Massah in the wilderness, when your ancestors tested me, and put me to the proof, though they had seen my work.

- We all know the maxim, Do not put off until tomorrow what you can do today. Instead, *carpe diem*—seize the moment, seize the day, do what needs to be done while you are still able, live like a hopeful person.
- Let me think about "today," and how I live. Am I putting off my response to Jesus, pushing it back until tomorrow?

Friday 1st April **Mark 12:28–31**

One of the scribes came near and heard them disputing with one another, and seeing that he answered them well, he asked him, "Which commandment is the first of all?" Jesus answered, "The first is, 'Hear, O Israel: the Lord our God, the Lord is one; you shall love the Lord your God with all your heart, and with all your soul, and with all your mind, and with all your strength.' The second is this, 'You shall love your neighbor as yourself.' There is no other commandment greater than these."

- When we are committed to love, we are not far from the kingdom of God. It's like the open door to the kingdom.
- Our need for love sometimes brings us to darker places, so we need the help of God to bring us closer and closer to the sincerity and purity of love in God's kingdom.

Saturday 2nd April **Luke 18:9–14**

He also told this parable to some who trusted in themselves that they were righteous and regarded others with contempt: "Two men went up to the temple to pray, one a Pharisee and the other a tax collector. The Pharisee, standing by himself, was praying thus, 'God, I thank you that I am not like other people: thieves, rogues, adulterers, or even like this tax collector. I fast twice a week; I give a tenth of all my income.' But the tax collector, standing far off, would not even look up to heaven, but was beating his breast and saying, 'God, be merciful to me, a sinner!' I tell you, this man went down to his home justified rather than the other; for all who exalt themselves will be humbled, but all who humble themselves will be exalted."

- The tax collector seems a more attractive person, despite his job which was looked down on at the time, than the externally holy Pharisee. It is a grace of God to know we need his mercy.
- Prayer is our time to relax into the merciful love of God, whose compassion and understanding of each of us is greater than anything else in him.

april 3–9

Something to think and pray about each day this week:

Staying the Course

Long-term commitment—whether in marriage, religious life, or in any relationship—is harder these days because of change. The loved one changes, and we change ourselves with time, so our relationships change. We cannot live our whole lives at concert pitch. But when the tune changes, it need not be the end of the concert. It often is. In some countries, half the marriages end in divorce. What is there in us that can survive the changes of time, and the up-and-down of living relationships? As we look back at an anniversary or jubilee to celebrate twenty-five, forty, or even fifty years, we see our commitment is at once richer and more painful than when we started. Faithfulness is a bit of a mystery and a marvel; it has a value in itself. Faithful love builds up the one to whom we are faithful, expresses our hope in them. It is a grace, a gift: not so much what we do for God as what God does for us. It should make us feel humble—in spite of all our inadequacies, we stayed with it.

The Presence of God
I pause for a moment
and think of the love and the grace that God showers on me,
creating me in his image and likeness, making me his temple.

Freedom
Everything has the potential to draw forth from me a fuller love and life.
Yet my desires are often fixed, caught, on illusions of fulfillment.
I ask that God, through my freedom, may orchestrate
my desires in a vibrant loving melody rich in harmony.

Consciousness
In the presence of my loving Creator,
I look honestly at my feelings over the last day,
the highs, the lows, and the level ground.
Can I see where the Lord has been present?

The Word
God speaks to each one of us individually. I need to listen to what he is saying to me. (Please turn to your scripture on the following pages. Inspiration points are there should you need them. When you are ready, return here to continue.)

Conversation
What feelings are rising in me
as I pray and reflect on God's Word?
I imagine Jesus himself sitting or standing beside me,
and open my heart to him.

Conclusion
Glory be to the Father, and to the Son, and to the Holy Spirit,
As it was in the beginning, is now, and ever shall be,
World without end. Amen

Sunday 3rd April,
Fourth Sunday of Lent **John 9:1, 6–9, 13–17**

As Jesus walked along, he saw a man blind from birth. He spat on the ground and made mud with the saliva and spread the mud on the man's eyes, saying to him, "Go, wash in the pool of Siloam" (which means Sent). Then he went and washed and came back able to see. The neighbors and those who had seen him before as a beggar began to ask, "Is this not the man who used to sit and beg?" Some were saying, "It is he." Others were saying, "No, but it is someone like him." He kept saying, "I am the man." They brought to the Pharisees the man who had formerly been blind. Now it was a sabbath day when Jesus made the mud and opened his eyes. Then the Pharisees also began to ask him how he had received his sight. He said to them, "He put mud on my eyes. Then I washed, and now I see." Some of the Pharisees said, "This man is not from God, for he does not observe the sabbath." But others said, "How can a man who is a sinner perform such signs?" And they were divided. So they said again to the blind man, "What do you say about him? It was your eyes he opened." He said, "He is a prophet."

- Jesus' miracles cost him his life because he was claiming to be one with God. The leaders—religious, political—only wanted a savior on their terms.
- After many a healing he disappeared, to get out of sight. Maybe we can do the same: allow ourselves time for faith to grow, to be grateful for our spirituality, and be joyful that we can do something good in the love of our lives for others.

Monday 4th April **John 4:46–50**

Then he came again to Cana in Galilee where he had changed the water into wine. Now there was a royal official whose son lay ill in Capernaum. When he heard that Jesus had come from Judea to Galilee, he went and begged him to come down and heal his son, for he was at the point of death. Then Jesus said to him, "Unless you see signs and wonders you will not believe." The official said to him, "Sir, come down before my little boy dies." Jesus said to him, "Go; your son will live." The man believed the word that Jesus spoke to him and started on his way.

- Jesus' healing power seemed to be activated only by faith. With the faith of the royal official, maybe one of a group hostile to him, Jesus healed the son a day's walk away. The new era, announced with the Cana mystery of the water into wine, takes even more human meaning now as a dying young man is healed.
- Our faith and our prayer activate the energy in Jesus which heals and strengthens our spirits.

Tuesday 5th April **John 5:1–3, 5–9**

After this there was a festival of the Jews, and Jesus went up to Jerusalem. Now in Jerusalem by the Sheep Gate there is a pool, called in Hebrew Beth-zatha, which has five porticoes. In these lay many invalids—blind, lame, and paralyzed. One man was there who had been ill for thirty-eight years. When Jesus saw him lying there and knew that he had been there a long time, he said to him, "Do you want to be made well?" The sick man answered him, "Sir, I have no one to put me into the pool when the water is stirred up; and while I am making my way, someone else steps down ahead of me." Jesus said to him, "Stand up, take your mat and walk." At once the man was made well, and he took up his mat and began to walk.

- Memories come back at prayer—hurts that happened years ago, grief, losses, and bereavements, all the turmoil of the heart. This is just human, and we're like the man ill for thirty-eight years, sitting alongside the pool of Bethesda.
- All Jesus wants me to know is that if I take a step forward, his healing grace and love will lead me so that I walk through life a little bit freer.

Wednesday 6th April **Psalm 145:8–9, 13–14**

The Lord is gracious and merciful, slow to anger and abounding in steadfast love. The Lord is good to all, and his compassion is over all that he has made. Your kingdom is an everlasting kingdom, and your dominion endures throughout all generations. The Lord is faithful in all his words, and gracious in all his deeds. The Lord upholds all who are falling, and raises up all who are bowed down.

- The psalmists put their trust in the loving God of Israel, their king, their rock, their refuge, their shepherd. This is not a god of wrath, but the God of compassion, love, and forgiveness.
- In whom do I trust? Is it in a loving, forgiving God?

Thursday 7th April **John 5:31–36**

Jesus said to the Jews "If I testify about myself, my testimony is not true. There is another who testifies on my behalf, and I know that his testimony to me is true. You sent messengers to John, and he testified to the truth. Not that I accept such human testimony, but I say these things so that you may be saved. He was a burning and shining lamp, and you were willing to rejoice for a while in his light. But I have a testimony greater than John's."

- Can each of us be a "burning and shining light" like John the Baptist? Our call is to bring forth the life of God like Mary and, like John, to announce Jesus in word and deed.

Friday 8th April **John 7:25–30**

Now some of the people of Jerusalem were saying, "Is not this the man whom they are trying to kill? And here he is, speaking openly, but they say nothing to him! Can it be that the authorities really know that this is the Messiah? Yet we know where this man is from; but when the Messiah comes, no one will know where he is from." Then Jesus cried out as he was teaching in the temple, "You know me, and you know where I am from. I have not come on my own. But the one who sent me is true, and you do not know him. I know him, because I am from him, and he sent me." Then they tried to arrest him, but no one laid hands on him, because his hour had not yet come.

- Jesus lived all his public life under the danger of death. He lived in that awareness of mortal danger.
- But he seems to be the one in control, even though powers of evil and death surrounded him. He would choose his hour.

Saturday 9th April **John 7:40–47**

When they heard these words, some in the crowd said, "This is really the prophet." Others said, "This is the Messiah." But some asked, "Surely the Messiah does not come from Galilee, does he? Has not the scripture said that the Messiah is descended from David and comes from Bethlehem, the village where David lived?" So there was a division in the crowd because of him. Some of them wanted to arrest him, but no one laid hands on him. Then the temple police went back to the chief priests and Pharisees, who asked them, "Why did you not arrest him?" The police answered, "Never has anyone spoken like this!" Then the Pharisees replied, "Surely you have not been deceived too, have you?"

- Many were amazed at the power of the words of Jesus. They whispered to each other that nobody else spoke like him. His authority both influenced them and challenged them. Many tried to put him down for where he came from, but their disbelief doesn't influence everyone else. He was a sign of contradiction.

april 10–16

Something to think and pray about each day this week:

Slowing Down

These weeks leading to Good Friday can have a special poignancy as we grow older, a regret that Jesus never lived to middle or old age, but died when he was thirty-three, at the height of his powers. We do not know from the Gospels how he would have coped with sickness, accidents, the loss of friends, failure in work, the slowing of the mind, the lapses of memory, the aching limbs, the sense that life has passed its peak. All these things happened to him suddenly, in twenty-four hours, from Thursday evening to Friday afternoon. To us they happen slowly, with more time for us to accept them well or badly. They are, more than any individual tragedy, our crucifixion, our share in Jesus' fate.

The Presence of God
I reflect for a moment on God's presence around me and in me.
Creator of the universe, the sun and the moon, the earth,
every molecule, every atom, everything that is:
God is in every beat of my heart. God is with me, now.

Freedom
A thick and shapeless tree-trunk would never believe
that it could become a statue, admired as a miracle of sculpture,
and would never submit itself to the chisel of the sculptor,
who sees by her genius what she can make of it. (St. Ignatius)
I ask for the grace to let myself be shaped by my loving Creator.

Consciousness
Knowing that God loves me unconditionally,
I look honestly over the last day, its events and my feelings.
Do I have something to be grateful for? Then I give thanks.
Is there something I am sorry for? Then I ask forgiveness.

The Word
I read the Word of God slowly, a few times over, and I listen to what God is saying to me. (Please turn to your scripture on the following pages. Inspiration points are there should you need them. When you are ready, return here to continue.)

Conversation
What is stirring in me as I pray?
Am I consoled, troubled, left cold?
I imagine Jesus himself standing or sitting at my side,
and share my feelings with him.

Conclusion
Glory be to the Father, and to the Son, and to the Holy Spirit,
As it was in the beginning, is now, and ever shall be,
World without end. Amen

Sunday 10th April,
Fifth Sunday of Lent **John 11:41–45**

Jesus looked upwards and said, "Father, I thank you for having heard me. I knew that you always hear me, but I have said this for the sake of the crowd standing here, so that they may believe that you sent me." When he had said this, he cried with a loud voice, "Lazarus, come out!" The dead man came out, his hands and feet bound with strips of cloth, and his face wrapped in a cloth. Jesus said to them, "Unbind him, and let him go." Many of the Jews therefore, who had come with Mary and had seen what Jesus did, believed in him.

- Prayer brings us in touch with the body of Christ, of Jesus risen from death, and of Jesus present in all his people. Prayer affects the lives of others; in that way it is political, affecting how we live together, asking to be unbound and live in freedom like Lazarus.
- Knowing that others pray with *Sacred Space* can help my life of prayer.

Monday 11th April **John 8:2–11**

Early in the morning Jesus came again to the temple. All the people came to him and he sat down and began to teach them. The scribes and the Pharisees brought a woman who had been caught in adultery; and making her stand before all of them, they said to him, "Teacher, this woman was caught in the very act of committing adultery. Now in the law Moses commanded us to stone such women. Now what do you say?" They said this to test him, so that they might have some charge to bring against him. Jesus bent down and wrote with his finger on the ground. When they kept on questioning him, he straightened up and said to them, "Let anyone among you who is without sin be the first to throw a stone at her." And once again he bent down and wrote on the ground. When they heard it, they went away, one by one, beginning with the elders; and Jesus was left alone with the woman standing before him. Jesus straightened up and said to her, "Woman, where are they? Has no one condemned you?" She said, "No one, sir." And Jesus said, "Neither do I condemn you. Go your way, and from now on do not sin again."

- Jesus is the one who never condemns, even when we are most condemnatory of ourselves. The look of Jesus to this condemned woman saved her, the look of divine and everlasting love.
- In prayer we can bring all the shame and guilt of our lives to this story of forgiveness and hear words spoken to each of us—"I do not condemn you."

Tuesday 12th April **John 8:28–30**

Jesus said to the Jews, "When you have lifted up the Son of Man, then you will realize that I am he, and that I do nothing on my own, but I speak these things as the Father instructed me. And the one who sent me is with me; he has not left me alone, for I always do what is pleasing to him." As he was saying these things, many believed in him.

- Jesus had a sense in his life that he was not left alone. Even on the cross he did not seem alone, crying out, "My God, my God, why have you forsaken me?"
- In Jesus we are all loved by the Father, and in our lives, even in the most extreme moments, are never left alone.

Wednesday 13th April **John 8:31–32**

Then Jesus said to the Jews who had believed in him, "If you continue in my word, you are truly my disciples; and you will know the truth, and the truth will make you free."

- We are invited to immerse ourselves in the meaning of the Word of God, to continue in his Word. The Word of God in the gospel leads us into the heart of God where we find love.
- The mystery of the Passion and death of Jesus is a mystery of love before it is a mystery of suffering. The suffering of the Passion of Christ is the suffering of love to the end, and of love for all.

Thursday 14th April **John 8:54–59**

Jesus said to the Jews, "If I glorify myself, my glory is nothing. It is my Father who glorifies me, he of whom you say, 'He is our God,' though you do not know him. But I know him; if I were to say that I do not know him, I would be a liar like you. But I do know him and I keep his word. Your ancestor Abraham rejoiced that he would see my day; he saw it and was glad." Then the Jews said to him, "You are not yet fifty years old, and have you seen Abraham?" Jesus said to them, "Very truly, I tell you, before Abraham was, I am." So they picked up stones to throw at him, but Jesus hid himself and went out of the temple.

- The Word of God has a powerful effect and leads us to life that is everlasting. The Word of God begins in heaven, lives on earth for a short time, and returns to heaven, promising us the same.
- The mystery of these weeks of the Passion and death of Jesus links heaven and earth in a wide and wonderful bond of love.

Friday 15th April **John 10:31–38**

The Jews took up stones again to stone him. Jesus replied, "I have shown you many good works from the Father. For which of these are you going to stone me?" The Jews answered, "It is not for a good work that we are going to stone you, but for blasphemy, because you, though only a human being, are making yourself God." Jesus answered, "Is it not written in your law, 'I said, you are gods'? If those to whom the word of God came were called 'gods'—and the scripture cannot be annulled—can you say that the one whom the Father has sanctified and sent into the world is blaspheming because I said, 'I am God's Son'? If I am not doing the works of my Father, then do not believe me. But if I do them, even though you do not believe me, believe the works, so that you may know and understand that the Father is in me and I am in the Father."

- The works of healing, teaching, and forgiveness were among other works of Jesus done in the name of God. All of Jesus leads us to his divine origin, the Son and Word of God. Something more than human seemed to touch others through him, as some believed and many did not.
- May I be led to an ever deeper faith in the Divine Son of God.

Saturday 16th April **John 11:47–52**

So the chief priests and the Pharisees called a meeting of the council, and said, "What are we to do? This man is performing many signs. If we let him go on like this, everyone will believe in him, and the Romans will come and destroy both our holy place and our nation." But one of them, Caiaphas, who was high priest that year, said to them, "You know nothing at all! You do not understand that it is better for you to have one man die for the people than to have the whole nation destroyed." He did not say this on his own, but being high priest that year he prophesied that Jesus was about to die for the nation, and not for the nation only, but to gather into one the dispersed children of God.

- Numerous men and women have been the one victim for many.
- In the eyes of the religious leaders of his time, Jesus signed his death warrant the day he said to a paralyzed man, "Your sins are forgiven," thus making claim to be God. We simply accompany him these days as he approaches death and torture.
- We remember people in our world today who still suffer torture.

april 17–23

Something to think and pray about each day this week:

The Triumph of Suffering

Holy Week, as it is called, marked the steepest learning curve in the lives of Jesus' disciples, and we might gear our prayer to the events and lessons of each day. It seemed to start well, with the Hosannas of Palm Sunday. Jesus, mounted on a donkey, entered Jerusalem in triumph (Luke 19:28). But he had no illusions. Approaching the city he wept over it, "If you had only understood the message of peace!" As we watch the Passion unfold, we can appreciate the verdict of Saint Peter Claver, who spent his life in the holds of slave-ships, ministering to African victims condemned to hopeless suffering: "The only book people should read is the Passion." Or Saint Thérèse of Lisieux, in the anguish of her last illness: "What does it mean to have written beautiful words about suffering. Nothing! Nothing! One must experience it to know what such effusions are worth." In prayer this week we need to live with the taste of pain and triumphant evil.

The Presence of God

In the silence of my innermost being,
in the fragments of my yearned-for wholeness,
can I hear the whispers of God's presence?
Can I remember when I felt God's nearness?
When we walked together and I let myself be embraced by God's love.

Freedom

There are very few people
who realize what God would make of them
if they abandoned themselves into his hands,
and let themselves be formed by his grace. (St. Ignatius)
I ask for the grace to trust myself totally to God's love.

Consciousness

Where am I with God? With others?
Do I have something to be grateful for? Then I give thanks.
Is there something I am sorry for? Then I ask forgiveness.

The Word

I take my time to read the Word of God, slowly, a few times, allowing myself to dwell on anything that strikes me. (Please turn to your scripture on the following pages. Inspiration points are there should you need them. When you are ready, return here to continue.)

Conversation

Do I notice myself reacting as I pray with the Word of God?
Do I feel challenged, comforted, angry?
I speak out my feelings, as one trusted friend to another.

Conclusion

Glory be to the Father, and to the Son, and to the Holy Spirit,
As it was in the beginning, is now, and ever shall be,
World without end. Amen

Sunday 17th April,
Palm Sunday of the Lord's Passion **Matthew 21:1–9**

When they had come near Jerusalem and had reached Bethphage, at the Mount of Olives, Jesus sent two disciples, saying to them, "Go into the village ahead of you, and immediately you will find a donkey tied, and a colt with her; untie them and bring them to me. If anyone says anything to you, just say this, 'The Lord needs them.' And he will send them immediately." This took place to fulfill what had been spoken through the prophet, saying, "Tell the daughter of Zion, Look, your king is coming to you, humble, and mounted on a donkey, and on a colt, the foal of a donkey." The disciples went and did as Jesus had directed them; they brought the donkey and the colt, and put their cloaks on them, and he sat on them. A very large crowd spread their cloaks on the road, and others cut branches from the trees and spread them on the road. The crowds that went ahead of him and that followed were shouting, "Hosanna to the Son of David! Blessed is the one who comes in the name of the Lord! Hosanna in the highest heaven!"

- Christ's death is like a bridge; he lay on the Cross and was crucified, and is the bridge between nations and also between ourselves. Jesus can be the bridge between us all because he knows everything human—even to death. He fulfills all these conditions! Jesus is like that.
- Holy Week is "The week of the bridge." That makes it holy. Any week we build bridges among people is holy week.

Monday 18th April **John 12:1–6**

Six days before the Passover Jesus came to Bethany, the home of Lazarus, whom he had raised from the dead. There they gave a dinner for him. Martha served, and Lazarus was one of those at the table with him. Mary took a pound of costly perfume made of pure nard, anointed Jesus' feet, and wiped them with her hair. The house was filled with the fragrance of the perfume. But Judas Iscariot, one of his disciples (the one who was about to betray him), said, "Why was this perfume not sold for three hundred denarii and the money given to the poor?" (He said this not because he cared about the poor, but because he was a thief; he kept the common purse and used to steal what was put into it.)

- The anointing of Jesus' feet may represent the generosity of Mary: she gave without holding back, without being constrained by the logic of thoughts like those of Judas.
- Lord, help me to pray with generosity, to give my time without mean-spirited thoughts about what else I might be doing.

Tuesday 19th April **John 13:31–33, 36–38**

When Judas had gone out, Jesus said, "Now the Son of Man has been glorified, and God has been glorified in him. If God has been glorified in him, God will also glorify him in himself and will glorify him at once. Little children, I am with you only a little longer. You will look for me; and as I said to the Jews so now I say to you, 'Where I am going, you cannot come.'" Simon Peter said to him, "Lord, where are you going?" Jesus answered, "Where I am going, you cannot follow me now; but you will follow afterwards." Peter said to him, "Lord, why can I not follow you now? I will lay down my life for you." Jesus answered, "Will you lay down your life for me? Very truly, I tell you, before the cock crows, you will have denied me three times."

- Peter hit deep points of his life here. His sureness in following Jesus was challenged by Jesus himself. He would later find himself weak and failing in this following.
- But this would not be the last word; even when Peter said later that he didn't know Jesus, there would be time for taking it back and speaking it with his life.
- We oscillate in our following of the Lord. These days let us know in the certainty of Jesus' love that there is always another day, another chance, another joy in our following of Jesus.

Wednesday 20th April **Matthew 26:14–16, 20–25**

Then one of the twelve, who was called Judas Iscariot, went to the chief priests and said, "What will you give me if I betray him to you?" They paid him thirty pieces of silver. And from that moment he began to look for an opportunity to betray him. When it was evening, Jesus took his place with the twelve; and while they were eating, he said, "Truly I tell you, one of you will betray me." And they became greatly distressed and began to say to him one after another, "Surely not I, Lord?" He answered, "The one who has dipped his hand into the bowl with me will betray me. The Son of Man goes as it is written of him, but woe to that one by whom the Son of Man is betrayed! It would have been better for that one not to have been born." Judas, who betrayed him, said, "Surely not I, Rabbi?" He replied, "You have said so."

- "Thirty pieces of silver" is a phrase that retains its currency today, describing the worst type of treachery. Jesus suffered this much in his passion.
- The man of suffering is the God who still suffers the pain, injustices, greed, and betrayal of his people today. God is not impervious to our suffering.

- Our prayer can be simply to be with him in his suffering, trying to feel as he felt, to think as he thought.

Thursday 21st April,
Holy Thursday **John 13:2–15**

During supper Jesus, knowing that the Father had given all things into his hands, and that he had come from God and was going to God, got up from the table, took off his outer robe, and tied a towel around himself. Then he poured water into a basin and began to wash the disciples' feet and to wipe them with the towel that was tied around him. He came to Simon Peter, who said to him, "Lord, are you going to wash my feet?" Jesus answered, "You do not know now what I am doing, but later you will understand." Peter said to him, "You will never wash my feet." Jesus answered, "Unless I wash you, you have no share with me." Simon Peter said to him, "Lord, not my feet only but also my hands and my head!" Jesus said to him, "One who has bathed does not need to wash, except for the feet, but is entirely clean. And you are clean, though not all of you." For he knew who was to betray him; for this reason he said, "Not all of you are clean." After Jesus had washed their feet, had put on his robe, and had returned to the table, he said to them, "Do you know what I have done to you? You call me Teacher and Lord— and you are right, for that is what I am. So if I, your Lord and Teacher, have washed your feet, you also ought to wash one another's feet. For I have set you an example, that you also should do as I have done to you."

- There's much in the gospel story or words of Jesus that we can't immediately understand. He says little about the meaning of the washing of the feet, except that it's about service, and then just that we should do it too.

- By doing something in the example or name of Jesus, we often find its meaning. Or by just listening to his word, it begins to make sense. This is heart-knowledge, and prayer-knowledge.

Friday 22nd April,
Good Friday **John 19:25–30**

Meanwhile, standing near the cross of Jesus were his mother, and his mother's sister, Mary the wife of Clopas, and Mary Magdalene. When Jesus saw his mother and the disciple whom he loved standing beside her, he said to his mother, "Woman, here is your son." Then he said to the disciple, "Here is your mother." And from that hour the disciple took her into his own home. After this, when Jesus knew that all was now finished, he said (in order to fulfill the scripture), "I am thirsty." A jar full of sour wine was standing there. So they put a sponge full of the wine on a branch of hyssop and held it to his mouth. When Jesus had received the wine, he said, "It is finished." Then he bowed his head and gave up his spirit.

- All of us will one day give up our spirit. All of us will one day say, either with words, breath, or gesture, that it is finished. It will not be like Jesus on a cross, but it may be in pain or in loneliness or in fear.
- We can offer our death to God; we can do so with Mary—"Holy Mary, mother of God, pray for us, sinners; now and at the hour of our death."

Saturday 23rd April,
Holy Saturday **Matthew 27:57–66**

When it was evening, there came a rich man from Arimathea, named Joseph, who was also a disciple of Jesus. He went to Pilate and asked for the body of Jesus; then Pilate ordered it to be given to him. So Joseph took the body and wrapped it in a clean linen cloth and laid it in his own new tomb, which he had hewn in the rock. He then rolled a great stone to the door of the tomb and went away. Mary Magdalene and the other Mary were there, sitting opposite the tomb. The next day, that is, after the day of Preparation, the chief priests and the Pharisees gathered before Pilate and said, "Sir, we remember what that impostor said while he was still alive, 'After three days I will rise again.' Therefore command that the tomb be made secure until the third day; otherwise his disciples may go and steal him away, and tell the people, 'He has been raised from the dead,' and the last deception would be worse than the first." Pilate said to them, "You have a guard of soldiers; go, make it as secure as you can." So they went with the guard and made the tomb secure by sealing the stone.

- The Saturday of Holy Week can be an empty day as we wait and wait for the evening of resurrection. Like the ones who had placed Jesus kindly in their tomb, we wait with him for something new. With Jesus there is always the hint of something new, and even at the tomb they were afraid he might rise.
- We pray in hope this day—the wood of the Cross had within it the sap of hope. It may look like a dead tree, but it is alive with expectation.

april 24–30

Something to think and pray about each day this week:

The Body of Life

On the first Easter morning, the apostles and the holy women did not see a ghost of Jesus. They saw him in the flesh, but in a different flesh, as the oak tree is different from the acorn that was its origin. We touch on the mystery of a body, not just Jesus' body but our own, which will express us at our best, will not blunt our spirit with weariness and rebellion, but express it with ease and joy. The Lord knows my name and my body. He sees my lived-in face, shaped by my history, showing the lines of love, indulgence, suffering, humour, gentleness. As the proverb says, "The face you have at forty is the face that you deserve." Teach me to love my face and body, my temple of the Holy Spirit. It will grow old and die with me, but that is not the end.

This is a mystery beyond our imagination, but it is the centre of our faith. As we grow older, nothing in our faith makes more sense than the Passion and the Resurrection, the certainty that our bodies, like Jesus', must suffer and die, and the certainty that we, in our bodies, have a life beyond death. When we wish one another a happy Easter, it is not just three days in an armchair, but also deep joy in the knowledge that the best part of us will cheat the grave. Our weary bones, heavy flesh, addled brains, already hold the seeds of that resurrection. We are none of us mortal.

The Presence of God

God is with me, but more,
God is within me, giving me existence.
Let me dwell for a moment on God's life-giving presence
in my body, my mind, my heart
and in the whole of my life.

Freedom

Many countries are at this moment suffering
the agonies of war.
I bow my head in thanksgiving for my freedom.
I pray for all prisoners and captives.

Consciousness

I remind myself that I am in the presence of the Lord.
I will take refuge in his loving heart.
He is my strength in times of weakness.
He is my comforter in times of sorrow.

The Word

I read the Word of God slowly, a few times over, and I listen to what God is saying to me. (Please turn to your scripture on the following pages. Inspiration points are there should you need them. When you are ready, return here to continue.)

Conversation

How has God's Word moved me? Has it left me cold?
Has it consoled me or moved me to act in a new way?
I imagine Jesus standing or sitting beside me,
I turn and share my feelings with him.

Conclusion

Glory be to the Father, and to the Son, and to the Holy Spirit,
As it was in the beginning, is now, and ever shall be,
World without end. Amen

Sunday 24th April,
Easter Sunday **John 20:1–9**

Early on the first day of the week, while it was still dark, Mary Magdalene came to the tomb and saw that the stone had been removed from the tomb. So she ran and went to Simon Peter and the other disciple, the one whom Jesus loved, and said to them, "They have taken the Lord out of the tomb, and we do not know where they have laid him." Then Peter and the other disciple set out and went toward the tomb. The two were running together, but the other disciple outran Peter and reached the tomb first. He bent down to look in and saw the linen wrappings lying there, but he did not go in. Then Simon Peter came, following him, and went into the tomb. He saw the linen wrappings lying there, and the cloth that had been on Jesus' head, not lying with the linen wrappings but rolled up in a place by itself. Then the other disciple, who reached the tomb first, also went in, and he saw and believed; for as yet they did not understand the scripture, that he must rise from the dead.

- Wherever we share compassion, justice, reconciliation, faith, and encourage each other to be people of hope, we are people of the Resurrection and ministers of the Resurrection.
- Jesus is raised from death each time we live his way of life. We do this in our various ways by showing care and concern for the lives and troubles of others.
- Lord, teach me to be a minister of the Resurrection.

Monday 25th April,
St. Mark, Evangelist **Mark 16:15–20**

And Jesus said to the disciples, "Go into all the world and proclaim the good news to the whole creation. The one who believes and is baptized will be saved; but the one who does not believe will be condemned. And these signs will accompany those who believe: by using my name they will cast out demons; they will speak in new tongues; they will pick up snakes in their hands, and if they drink any deadly thing, it will not hurt them; they will lay their hands on the sick, and they will recover." So then the Lord Jesus, after he had spoken to them, was taken up into heaven and sat down at the right hand of God. And they went out and proclaimed the good news everywhere, while the Lord worked with them and confirmed the message by the signs that accompanied it.

- Each of us is called into the ministry of Jesus in some way. We are called to be "other Christs," to be people who wish to make known and spread the love of God and his care for his people.
- We may never know how much we have done this; it is sufficient that we do what we can. In prayer we ask that we use our gifts and talents as best we can in God's service.

Tuesday 26th April **John 20:11–18**

But Mary stood weeping outside the tomb. As she wept, she bent over to look into the tomb; and she saw two angels in white, sitting where the body of Jesus had been lying, one at the head and the other at the feet. They said to her, "Woman, why are you weeping?" She said to them, "They have taken away my Lord, and I do not know where they have laid him." When she had said this, she turned around and saw Jesus standing there, but she did not know that it was Jesus. Jesus said to her, "Woman, why are you weeping? Whom are you looking for?" Supposing him to be the gardener, she said to him, "Sir, if you have carried him away, tell me where you have laid him, and I will take him away." Jesus said to her, "Mary!" She turned and said to him in Hebrew, "Rabbouni!" (which means Teacher). Jesus said to her, "Do not hold on to me, because I have not yet ascended to the Father. But go to my brothers and say to them, 'I am ascending to my Father and your Father, to my God and your God.'" Mary Magdalene went and announced to the disciples, "I have seen the Lord"; and she told them that he had said these things to her.

- Have you seen the Lord? Like Mary, seeing may not be physical. We see him in the light of love, the colour of care, the beauty of compassion. In all that is human, we see and sense the Lord.
- Mary's mood changed from tears to joy; all she needed was the presence of the Lord, now and always, raised from death.

Wednesday 27th April **Luke 24:13–19, 25–29**

Now on that same day two of them were going to a village called Emmaus, about seven miles from Jerusalem, and talking with each other about all these things that had happened. While they were talking and discussing, Jesus himself came near and went with them, but their eyes were kept from recognizing him. And he said to them, "What are you discussing with each other while you walk along?" They stood still, looking sad. Then one of them, whose name was Cleopas, answered him, "Are you the only stranger in Jerusalem who does not know the things that have taken place there in these days?" He asked them, "What things?" They replied, "The things about Jesus of Nazareth, who was a prophet mighty in deed and word before God and all the people, and how our chief priests and leaders handed him over to be condemned to death and crucified him. But we had hoped that he was the one to redeem Israel. Yes, and besides all this, it is now the third day since these things took place. Moreover, some women of our group astounded us. They were at the tomb early this morning, and when they did not find his body there, they came back and told us that they had indeed seen a vision of angels who said that he was alive. Some of those who were with us went to the tomb and found it just as the women had said; but they did not see him." Then he said to them, "Oh, how foolish you are, and how slow of heart to believe all that the prophets have declared! Was it not necessary that the Messiah should suffer these things and then enter into his glory?" Then beginning with Moses and all the prophets, he interpreted to them the things about himself in all the scriptures. As they came near the village to which they were going, he walked ahead as if he were going on. But they urged him strongly, saying, "Stay with us, because it is almost evening and the day is now nearly over." So he went in to stay with them.

- Our footsteps, all along the paths of our lives, are matched by the footsteps of Jesus. Hearts burned and tears were dried as the risen Lord made his way into the lives of his followers.
- Prayer gives time for his word to enter deeply into our hearts, burning away selfishness and fear, leaving only the flame of love.

Thursday 28th April **Luke 24:35–40**

The disciples of Jesus told what had happened on the road, and how he had been made known to them in the breaking of the bread. While they were talking about this, Jesus himself stood among them and said to them, "Peace be with you." They were startled and terrified, and thought that they were seeing a ghost. He said to them, "Why are you frightened, and why do doubts arise in your hearts? Look at my hands and my feet; see that it is I myself. Touch me and see; for a ghost does not have flesh and bones as you see that I have." And when he had said this, he showed them his hands and his feet.

- The common greeting of Jesus to his followers is the wish for peace. In prayer that is his word to us; he knocks at our door with these words: "Peace be with you." Prayer can bring peace in turmoil and troubled times.
- Jesus offers his peace and asks his followers to be people who make peace. Let peace be the word for our prayer today, peace received and peace prayed for.

Friday 29th April **John 21:4–14**

Just after daybreak, Jesus stood on the beach; but the disciples did not know that it was Jesus. Jesus said to them, "Children, you have no fish, have you?" They answered him, "No." He said to them, "Cast the net to the right side of the boat, and you will find some." So they cast it, and now they were not able to haul it in because there were so many fish. That disciple whom Jesus loved said to Peter, "It is the Lord!" When Simon Peter heard that it was the Lord, he put on some clothes, for he was naked, and jumped into the sea. But the other disciples came in the boat, dragging the net full of fish, for they were not far from the land, only about a hundred yards off. When they had gone ashore, they saw a charcoal fire there, with fish on it, and bread. Jesus said to them, "Bring some of the fish that you have just caught." So Simon Peter went aboard and hauled the net ashore, full of large fish, a hundred fifty-three of them; and though there were so many, the net was not torn. Jesus said to them, "Come and have breakfast." Now none of the disciples dared to ask him, "Who are you?" because they knew it was the Lord. Jesus came and took the bread and gave it to them, and did the same with the fish. This was now the third time that Jesus appeared to the disciples after he was raised from the dead.

- You might imagine yourself walking on a beach towards a group around a fire. The smell of breakfast is in the air. You realize that it is Jesus and his followers. He has been raised from death.
- As you come near the group, you notice Jesus turns towards you and you hear his invitation, "Come and have breakfast." Let that picture guide your prayer today.

Saturday 30th April **Mark 16:9–15**

Now after he rose early on the first day of the week, he appeared first to Mary Magdalene, from whom he had cast out seven demons. She went out and told those who had been with him, while they were mourning and weeping. But when they heard that he was alive and had been seen by her, they would not believe it. After this he appeared in another form to two of them, as they were walking into the country. And they went back and told the rest, but they did not believe them. Later he appeared to the eleven themselves as they were sitting at the table; and he upbraided them for their lack of faith and stubbornness, because they had not believed those who saw him after he had risen. And he said to them, "Go into all the world and proclaim the good news to the whole creation."

- Faith in the risen Christ came slowly to the apostles. It took a few occasions and apparitions to convince them that the Lord had risen from death.
- All faith has its ups and downs; prayer has its good times and tough times. Faith grows in a trust that God is always near, though it may not seem so. It is sometimes a dark love; and love in the darkness is what brings faith to life.

may 1–7

Something to think and pray about each day this week:

The Peace of Jesus

"Even though we once knew Christ from a human point of view, we know him no longer in that way" (2 Corinthians, 5:16).

In the period after the Resurrection, the little community of Christians grew round the presence of Jesus; but it was a mysterious sort of presence. He showed himself as one bringing peace, and that was his greeting. Given the humanly hopeless situation of the disciples, the notion of peace might seem like a vapid optimism—"hopefully things will turn out alright." Jesus' peace is not like that. He knows the score. His peace does not depend on politics or people or places or the weather, but on his infinitely compassionate, strong presence. It sometimes required time to recognize his presence: it was only after Jesus had left them that the disciples on the road to Emmaus realized how their hearts were burning. Lord, make me alert to your presence.

The Presence of God

To be present is to arrive as one is and open up to the other.
At this instant, as I arrive here, God is present waiting for me.
God always arrives before me, desiring to connect with me
even more than my most intimate friend.
I take a moment and greet my loving God.

Freedom

In these days, God taught me
as a schoolteacher teaches a pupil. (St. Ignatius)
I remind myself that there are things God has to teach me yet,
and ask for the grace to hear them and let them change me.

Consciousness

How am I really feeling? Light-hearted? Heavy-hearted?
I may be very much at peace, happy to be here.
Equally, I may be frustrated, worried, or angry.
I acknowledge how I really am. It is the real me that the Lord loves.

The Word

I take my time to read the Word of God, slowly, a few times, allowing myself to dwell on anything that strikes me. (Please turn to your scripture on the following pages. Inspiration points are there should you need them. When you are ready, return here to continue.)

Conversation

What feelings are rising in me
as I pray and reflect on God's Word?
I imagine Jesus himself sitting or standing beside me,
and open my heart to him.

Conclusion

Glory be to the Father, and to the Son, and to the Holy Spirit,
As it was in the beginning, is now, and ever shall be,
World without end. Amen

Sunday 1st May,
Second Sunday of Easter **John 20:24–29**

But Thomas (who was called the Twin), one of the twelve, was not with them when Jesus came. So the other disciples told him, "We have seen the Lord." But he said to them, "Unless I see the mark of the nails in his hands, and put my finger in the mark of the nails and my hand in his side, I will not believe." A week later his disciples were again in the house, and Thomas was with them. Although the doors were shut, Jesus came and stood among them and said, "Peace be with you." Then he said to Thomas, "Put your finger here and see my hands. Reach out your hand and put it in my side. Do not doubt but believe." Thomas answered him, "My Lord and my God!" Jesus said to him, "Have you believed because you have seen me? Blessed are those who have not seen and yet have come to believe."

- Thomas was a modern man, finding faith hard. He was let down by the others who ran away, the leader who denied Jesus; his trust had been abused. He didn't want much more to do with them. He wanted to believe but needed some proof.
- But faith grows within a community. We find growth in our faith through the community—in the Mass, sharing our faith in a group, a good spiritual book, sharing our doubts but never closing the door to Jesus, sharing our faith in thanks.

Monday 2nd May **John 3:1–8**

Now there was a Pharisee named Nicodemus, a leader of the Jews. He came to Jesus by night and said to him, "Rabbi, we know that you are a teacher who has come from God; for no one can do these signs that you do apart from the presence of God." Jesus answered him, "Very truly, I tell you, no one can see the kingdom of God without being born from above." Nicodemus said to him, "How can anyone be born after having grown old? Can one enter a second time into the mother's womb and be born?" Jesus answered, "Very truly, I tell you, no one can enter the kingdom of God without being born of water and Spirit. What is born of the flesh is flesh, and what is born of the Spirit is spirit. Do not be astonished that I said to you, 'You must be born from above.' The wind blows where it chooses, and you hear the sound of it, but you do not know where it comes from or where it goes. So it is with everyone who is born of the Spirit."

- When we put aside time to speak with the Lord, we allow cares—no matter how important to ourselves and others—to drift off for a while. We leave aside the phone and messages, and allow God to become real in our lives.
- This is our daily time to rekindle love in our lives.

Tuesday 3rd May,
Sts. Philip and James, Apostles 1 Corinthians 15:1–8

Now I should remind you, brothers and sisters, of the good news that I proclaimed to you, which you in turn received, in which also you stand, through which also you are being saved, if you hold firmly to the message that I proclaimed to you—unless you have come to believe in vain. For I handed on to you as of first importance what I in turn had received: that Christ died for our sins in accordance with the scriptures, and that he was buried, and that he was raised on the third day in accordance with the scriptures, and that he appeared to Cephas, then to the twelve. Then he appeared to more than five hundred brothers and sisters at one time, most of whom are still alive, though some have died. Then he appeared to James, then to all the apostles. Last of all, as to someone untimely born, he appeared also to me.

- This is what Christian faith rests on, reaching back to Jesus' life on earth. This is at the heart of the gospel preached by Philip, James, and the other apostles until their deaths.
- How might I make this my own confession of faith, my Christian mission statement?

Wednesday 4th May **John 3:16–17**

Jesus said to Nicodemus, "For God so loved the world that he gave his only Son, so that everyone who believes in him may not perish but may have eternal life. Indeed, God did not send the Son into the world to condemn the world, but in order that the world might be saved through him."

- Jesus speaks of his relationship with God his Father and the one who already has this life of his by faith.
- We live in the new world of God when we love; when we love others and love God.

Thursday 5th May **John 3:31–34**

John the Baptist said to his disciples, "The one who comes from above is above all; the one who is of the earth belongs to the earth and speaks about earthly things. The one who comes from heaven is above all. He testifies to what he has seen and heard, yet no one accepts his testimony. Whoever has accepted his testimony has certified this, that God is true. He whom God has sent speaks the words of God."

- Faith brings us into a new atmosphere of life; with faith in Jesus we already have eternal life.
- When we put aside time for prayer, we can say little and just listen, allowing the love and the life of God to flood our lives and hearts. Little needs to be said, only to be received.

Friday 6th May **John 6:1–13**

After this Jesus went to the other side of the Sea of Galilee, also called the Sea of Tiberias. A large crowd kept following him, because they saw the signs that he was doing for the sick. Jesus went up the mountain and sat down there with his disciples. Now the Passover, the festival of the Jews, was near. When he looked up and saw a large crowd coming toward him, Jesus said to Philip, "Where are we to buy bread for these people to eat?" He said this to test him, for he himself knew what he was going to do. Philip answered him, "Six months' wages would not buy enough bread for each of them to get a little." One of his disciples, Andrew, Simon Peter's brother, said to him, "There is a boy here who has five barley loaves and two fish. But what are they among so many people?" Jesus said, "Make the people sit down." Now there was a great deal of grass in the place; so they sat down, about five thousand in all. Then Jesus took the loaves, and when he had given thanks, he distributed them to those who were seated; so also the fish, as much as they wanted. When they were satisfied, he told his disciples, "Gather up the fragments left over, so that nothing may be lost." So they gathered them up, and from the fragments of the five barley loaves, left by those who had eaten, they filled twelve baskets.

- The boy had enough food only for himself; it was the food of the poor, the barley loaf. Given with love, it seemed to multiply.
- Whatever the meaning of this miracle, one of its lessons is that God can make much of what we offer. Our attempts to live in his love and follow him are nothing without him. We never know where our efforts to love, to support others may bear fruit.

Saturday 7th May **Acts 6:1–7**

Now during those days, when the disciples were increasing in number, the Hellenists complained against the Hebrews because their widows were being neglected in the daily distribution of food. And the twelve called together the whole community of the disciples and said, "It is not right that we should neglect the word of God in order to wait at tables. Therefore, friends, select from among yourselves seven men of good standing, full of the Spirit and of wisdom, whom we may appoint to this task, while we, for our part, will devote ourselves to prayer and to serving the word." What they said pleased the whole community, and they chose Stephen, a man full of faith and the Holy Spirit, together with Philip, Prochorus, Nicanor, Timon, Parmenas, and Nicolaus, a proselyte of Antioch. They had these men stand before the apostles, who prayed and laid their hands on them. The word of God continued to spread; the number of the disciples increased greatly in Jerusalem, and a great many of the priests became obedient to the faith.

- The early community of faith had to face its own internal conflicts based on different religious traditions and priorities. It is no surprise that these conflicts crystallized around the question of resources.
- The authority of the twelve was brought to bear, and they settled the issues wisely, encouraging diversity while working towards unity in the community, as well as the spread of the Word of God.
- How can I learn from this and apply it in my own parish community and in my dealings with others?

may 8–14

Something to think and pray about each day this week:

Through Mary's Eyes

During the weeks after the Resurrection of Jesus, his mother Mary would have been a central presence in the community of disciples. As we do today, they would have lingered on the stories of Jesus' life and death. God was there in all of them. We are accustomed to thinking of God as present in Jesus' passion and crucifixion. I doubt if Mary ever got used to that idea. She could never have seen a cross without a turning of her stomach, a spasm of total desolation such as most of us feel when prodded with memories of our personal Calvary. When later she talked with John and Peter, she would have loved to recall Jesus' parables, his walking on the water, healing the lepers and feeding the crowds, much as today we exchange news of our houses, our children's successes, our jobs and hobbies.

We do not have to linger on the times of suffering, yet we can thank the Lord for our crosses, and for being with us in the worst of times as well as the best. We are never good judges of when God is closest to us. Saint John (15:1) reminds us of the meaning of suffering: "God prunes every branch that does bear fruit, that it may bear even more."

The Presence of God

What is present to me is what has a hold on my becoming.
I reflect on the presence of God always there in love,
amidst the many things that have a hold on me.
I pause and pray that I may let God
affect my becoming in this precise moment.

Freedom

If God were trying to tell me something, would I know?
If God were reassuring me or challenging me, would I notice?
I ask for the grace to be free of my own preoccupations
and open to what God may be saying to me.

Consciousness

Knowing that God loves me unconditionally,
I can afford to be honest about how I am.
How has the last day been, and how do I feel now?
I share my feelings openly with the Lord.

The Word

God speaks to each one of us individually. I need to listen to what he is saying to me. (Please turn to your scripture on the following pages. Inspiration points are there should you need them. When you are ready, return here to continue.)

Conversation

What is stirring in me as I pray?
Am I consoled, troubled, left cold?
I imagine Jesus himself standing or sitting at my side,
and share my feelings with him.

Conclusion

Glory be to the Father, and to the Son, and to the Holy Spirit,
As it was in the beginning, is now, and ever shall be,
World without end. Amen

Sunday 8th May,
Third Sunday of Easter **Luke 24:13–35**

Now on that same day two of them were going to a village called Emmaus, about seven miles from Jerusalem, and talking with each other about all these things that had happened. While they were talking and discussing, Jesus himself came near and went with them, but their eyes were kept from recognizing him. And he said to them, "What are you discussing with each other while you walk along?" They stood still, looking sad. Then one of them, whose name was Cleopas, answered him, "Are you the only stranger in Jerusalem who does not know the things that have taken place there in these days?" He asked them, "What things?" They replied, "The things about Jesus of Nazareth, who was a prophet mighty in deed and word before God and all the people, and how our chief priests and leaders handed him over to be condemned to death and crucified him. But we had hoped that he was the one to redeem Israel. Yes, and besides all this, it is now the third day since these things took place. Moreover, some women of our group astounded us. They were at the tomb early this morning, and when they did not find his body there, they came back and told us that they had indeed seen a vision of angels who said that he was alive. Some of those who were with us went to the tomb and found it just as the women had said; but they did not see him." Then he said to them, "Oh, how foolish you are, and how slow of heart to believe all that the prophets have declared! Was it not necessary that the Messiah should suffer these things and then enter into his glory?" Then beginning with Moses and all the prophets, he interpreted to them the things about himself in all the scriptures. As they came near the village to which they were going, he walked ahead as if he were going on. But they urged him strongly, saying, "Stay with us, because it is almost evening and the day is now nearly over."

So he went in to stay with them. When he was at the table with them, he took bread, blessed and broke it, and gave it to them. Then their eyes were opened, and they recognized him; and he vanished from their sight. They said to each other, "Were not our hearts burning within us while he was talking to us on the road, while he was opening the scriptures to us?" That same hour they got up and returned to Jerusalem; and they found the eleven and their companions gathered together. They were saying, "The Lord has risen indeed, and he has appeared to Simon!" Then they told what had happened on the road, and how he had been made known to them in the breaking of the bread.

- Every table of the Eucharist is Emmaus; every moment of hearing the Scriptures is the road to Emmaus. We are always on that road, as Jesus speaks his word and breaks the bread of his love.
- The word and the bread sent them to the community and into the world with their story of how they had recognized him. Maybe the daily word and the daily bread can do the same for us.

Monday 9th May **John 6:22–27**

The next day the crowd that had stayed on the other side of the lake saw that there had been only one boat there. They also saw that Jesus had not got into the boat with his disciples, but that his disciples had gone away alone. Then some boats from Tiberias came near the place where they had eaten the bread after the Lord had given thanks. So when the crowd saw that neither Jesus nor his disciples were there, they themselves got into the boats and went to Capernaum looking for Jesus. When they found him on the other side of the lake, they said to him, "Rabbi, when did you come here?" Jesus answered them, "Very truly, I tell you, you are looking for me, not because you saw signs, but because you ate your fill of the loaves. Do not work for the food that perishes, but for the food that endures for eternal life, which the Son of Man will give you."

- We look to God for many things. Jesus notices that his disciples follow now to get more bread: they wanted to be fed and not to lack ordinary food.
- Jesus has more to give. He offers the food and the drink of eternal life. The food and drink of his love and the love of God which will never get stale or run dry.

Tuesday 10th May **John 6:30–35**

The crowd said to Jesus, "What sign are you going to give us then, so that we may see it and believe you? What work are you performing? Our ancestors ate the manna in the wilderness; as it is written, 'He gave them bread from heaven to eat.'" Then Jesus said to them, "Very truly, I tell you, it was not Moses who gave you the bread from heaven, but it is my Father who gives you the true bread from heaven. For the bread of God is that which comes down from heaven and gives life to the world." They said to him, "Sir, give us this bread always." Jesus said to them, "I am the bread of life. Whoever comes to me will never be hungry, and whoever believes in me will never be thirsty."

- The bread of Jesus is his own life. That's what he means in saying he gives us his body as real food. We receive this bread of life if we do something that is from faith, or love of him and of God.
- His love, to the death on the Cross, is always life-giving. Each day we live in that love, finding it especially at a time of prayer.

Wednesday 11th May **John 6:39–40**

Jesus said to them, "And this is the will of him who sent me, that I should lose nothing of all that he has given me, but raise it up on the last day. This is indeed the will of my Father, that all who see the Son and believe in him may have eternal life; and I will raise them up on the last day."

- Jesus, the complete expression of the Father's love, wants to save each and every one of us, that we may be raised to eternal life.
- Thanks be to God, our Father, for the many gifts he offers us.

Thursday 12th May **John 6:45–51**

Jesus said to the people: "It is written in the prophets: 'And they shall all be taught by God'; everyone who has heard and learned from the Father comes to me. Not that anyone has seen the Father except the one who is from God; he has seen the Father. Very truly, I tell you, whoever believes has eternal life. I am the bread of life. Your ancestors ate the manna in the wilderness, and they died. This is the bread that comes down from heaven, so that one may eat of it and not die. I am the living bread that came down from heaven. Whoever eats of this bread will live for ever; and the bread that I will give for the life of the world is my flesh."

- Jesus lives in the shadow of eternity and calls on our faith that we will live forever. The experience of love in life hints at something more than human, of a mystery totally linked to God.
- The bread of life is the gift of God's life on earth. In opening ourselves to the Word of God and the bread of God we are gifted and graced with the love that lasts forever.

Friday 13th May **John 6:52–57**

The Jews then disputed among themselves, saying, "How can this man give us his flesh to eat?" So Jesus said to them, "Very truly, I tell you, unless you eat the flesh of the Son of Man and drink his blood, you have no life in you. Those who eat my flesh and drink my blood have eternal life, and I will raise them up on the last day; for my flesh is true food and my blood is true drink. Those who eat my flesh and drink my blood abide in me, and I in them. Just as the living Father sent me, and I live because of the Father, so whoever eats me will live because of me."

- We absorb the energy of our daily food and drink; it becomes part of us. We become absorbed into Jesus when we eat his body and drink his blood—his profound way of giving us himself.
- When we receive him in this way we are brought into a deep union with him, so that we and Jesus share his life and the life of God. We are divine mysteries, each of us a tabernacle of the divine as we walk in God's world.

Saturday 14th May,
St. Matthias, Apostle **John 15:9–11**

Jesus said to his disciples, "As the Father has loved me, so I have loved you; abide in my love. If you keep my commandments, you will abide in my love, just as I have kept my Father's commandments and abide in his love. I have said these things to you so that my joy may be in you, and that your joy may be complete."

- These are words of Jesus at the Last Supper, so they are among his last words.

- The full place of love in the Christian life is highlighted. All else flows from the love of God and ourselves uniting us together. Love of this kind leads to joy. We see Jesus as one who gifts us with joy and with love.

may 15–21

Something to think and pray about each day this week:

Looking Deeper

Dominican Vincent McNabb said that one sign of real intelligence is the ability to recognize holiness. Sanctity is never labeled. It tends to hide itself, and it takes a discerning eye to see the working of God's spirit in a person's life. More than once in the Gospels Jesus asks the leaders of the people to look beyond language to the witness of his life. When Jesus was asked, "If you are the Messiah, tell us plainly," he answered, "I have told you, and you do not believe. The works that I do in my Father's name testify to me" (John 10:24–25). When John the Baptist's followers pressed the same question, Jesus replied: "Go back and tell John what you see and hear" (Matthew 11:4). Jesus pushes me to look at my own life. Protestations of faith matter little compared with the presence or absence of truth and justice and love in my daily living.

The Presence of God

At any time of the day or night we can call on Jesus.
He is always waiting, listening for our call.
What a wonderful blessing.
No phone needed, no emails, just a whisper.

Freedom

I need to close out the noise, to rise above the noise;
The noise that interrupts, that separates,
The noise that isolates.
I need to listen to God again.

Consciousness

Help me, Lord, to be more conscious of your presence.
Teach me to recognize your presence in others.
Fill my heart with gratitude for the times your love
has been shown to me through the care of others.

The Word

I read the Word of God slowly, a few times over, and I listen to what God is saying to me. (Please turn to your scripture on the following pages. Inspiration points are there should you need them. When you are ready, return here to continue.)

Conversation

Do I notice myself reacting as I pray with the Word of God?
Do I feel challenged, comforted, angry?
Imagining Jesus sitting or standing by me,
I speak out my feelings, as one trusted friend to another.

Conclusion

Glory be to the Father, and to the Son, and to the Holy Spirit,
As it was in the beginning, is now, and ever shall be,
World without end. Amen

Sunday 15th May,
Fourth Sunday of Easter **John 10:10**

Jesus said to the people, "The thief comes only to steal and kill and destroy. I came that they may have life, and have it abundantly."

- Jesus talks a lot about giving life and about the fullness of life. It's not just for hereafter. Eternal life is our faith in him and in his word.
- We are called to be life-givers, to facilitate the full life of justice, compassion, and peace. We are called to be ministers of life, serving the God who loves all life.

Monday 16th May **John 10:14–18**

Jesus said to the people, "I am the good shepherd. I know my own and my own know me, just as the Father knows me and I know the Father. And I lay down my life for the sheep. I have other sheep that do not belong to this fold. I must bring them also, and they will listen to my voice. So there will be one flock, one shepherd. For this reason the Father loves me, because I lay down my life in order to take it up again. No one takes it from me, but I lay it down of my own accord. I have power to lay it down, and I have power to take it up again. I have received this command from my Father."

- The true voice of Jesus tones in with the desires and hopes of the human heart—for love, justice, forgiveness, and fulfillment.
- Other sheep will hear his voice and they won't find it strange. He speaks the language of self-sacrificing and faithful love for all. His voice is heard now mainly through the words and lives of others.

Tuesday 17th May **John 10:22–30**

At that time the festival of the Dedication took place in Jerusalem. It was winter, and Jesus was walking in the temple, in the portico of Solomon. So the Jews gathered around him and said to him, "How long will you keep us in suspense? If you are the Messiah, tell us plainly." Jesus answered, "I have told you, and you do not believe. The works that I do in my Father's name testify to me; but you do not believe, because you do not belong to my sheep. My sheep hear my voice. I know them, and they follow me. I give them eternal life, and they will never perish. No one will snatch them out of my hand. What my Father has given me is greater than all else, and no one can snatch it out of the Father's hand. The Father and I are one."

- Sheep hear the voice of the shepherd and immediately go after the shepherd. They are true followers in the image of shepherd and sheep in the words of Jesus.
- The voice of Jesus is heard in prayer and in the reading of his word; it calls us to follow with love, knowing that we are totally safe in following him.

Wednesday 18th May **John 12:44–50**

Then Jesus cried aloud: "Whoever believes in me believes not in me but in him who sent me. And whoever sees me sees him who sent me. I have come as light into the world, so that everyone who believes in me should not remain in the darkness. I do not judge anyone who hears my words and does not keep them, for I came not to judge the world, but to save the world. The one who rejects me and does not receive my word has a judge; on the last day the word that I have spoken will serve as judge, for I have not spoken on my own, but the Father who sent me has himself given me a commandment about what to say and what to speak. And I know that his commandment is eternal life. What I speak, therefore, I speak just as the Father has told me."

- This is a sort of summary of the message of Jesus. No time or place is given for this speech. He speaks of our faith in God and that he is the light of the world. That we can accept or reject him, and that his word is the word of his Father—God.
- Let me take time to think about Jesus, the Father's word.

Thursday 19th May **John 13:12–20**

After he had washed their feet, had put on his robe, and had returned to the table, he said to them, "Very truly, I tell you, servants are not greater than their master, nor are messengers greater than the one who sent them. If you know these things, you are blessed if you do them. I am not speaking of all of you; I know whom I have chosen. But it is to fulfill the scripture, 'The one who ate my bread has lifted his heel against me.' I tell you this now, before it occurs, so that when it does occur, you may believe that I am he. Very truly, I tell you, whoever receives one whom I send receives me; and whoever receives me receives him who sent me."

- A theme of the Last Supper from which these words are taken is that of the relationship of servant and master. Jesus is the humble servant washing the feet of his disciples. It is his wish to be humbly close to them.
- He teaches by his actions so that the disciples and we may follow.

Friday 20th May **John 14:1–4**

Jesus said to his disciples, "Do not let your hearts be troubled. Believe in God, believe also in me. In my Father's house there are many dwelling places. If it were not so, would I have told you that I go to prepare a place for you? And if I go and prepare a place for you, I will come again and will take you to myself, so that where I am, there you may be also. And you know the way to the place where I am going."

- Whenever God meets or sees us, God's look is a look of love and welcome. We are at home with God whenever we are in the presence of Jesus.
- Maybe prayer is spending some time in God's home, and God's home is the heart of each man and woman.

Saturday 21st May **John 14:10–14**

Jesus said to his disciples, "The words that I say to you I do not speak on my own; but the Father who dwells in me does his works. Believe me that I am in the Father and the Father is in me; but if you do not, then believe me because of the works themselves. Very truly, I tell you, the one who believes in me will also do the works that I do and, in fact, will do greater works than these, because I am going to the Father. I will do whatever you ask in my name, so that the Father may be glorified in the Son. If in my name you ask me for anything, I will do it."

- One of the biggest mysteries in the life of Jesus is his relationship with his Father and the Holy Spirit. It is always presented in terms of deep closeness; they are "I" to each other. So that when we know and love Jesus, we know and love the Father and the Holy Spirit.
- We are immersed in a world of divine community and so are called to live in the world of human community.

may 22–28

Something to think and pray about each day this week:

Quietness

Saint Teresa of Avila describes the prayer of quietness: "What the soul must do during these seasons of quietness amounts to no more than proceeding gently and noiselessly in prayer. What I mean by noise is running about with the intellect, looking for many words and meanings so as to give thanks for this gift, and piling up one's sins and faults in order to see that the gift is unmerited. Everything is in motion and rush. The intellect is thinking hard and the memory is hurrying about in the past . . .

"Therefore, in such times of quietude, let the soul remain in its repose. Put aside learning. The time will come when learning will be useful for the Lord. Believe me, in the presence of infinite Wisdom, a little study of humility and one act of humility is worth all the knowledge of the world. For here there is no demand for reasoning, but simply for knowing what we are and that we are humbly in God's presence."

The Presence of God
As I sit here, the beating of my heart,
the ebb and flow of my breathing, the movements of my mind
are all signs of God's ongoing creation of me.
I pause for a moment, and become aware
of this presence of God within me.

Freedom
I will ask God's help,
to be free from my own preoccupations,
to be open to God in this time of prayer,
to come to love and serve him more.

Consciousness
Knowing that God loves me unconditionally,
I look honestly over the last day, its events and my feelings.
Do I have something to be grateful for? Then I give thanks.
Is there something I am sorry for? Then I ask forgiveness.

The Word
I take my time to read the Word of God, slowly, a few times, allowing myself to dwell on anything that strikes me. (Please turn to your scripture on the following pages. Inspiration points are there should you need them. When you are ready, return here to continue.)

Conversation
Remembering that I am still in God's presence,
I imagine Jesus himself standing or sitting beside me,
and say whatever is on my mind, whatever is in my heart,
speaking as one friend to another.

Conclusion
Glory be to the Father, and to the Son, and to the Holy Spirit,
As it was in the beginning, is now, and ever shall be,
World without end. Amen

Sunday 22nd May,
Fifth Sunday of Easter **John 14:1–7**

Jesus said to his disciples, "Do not let your hearts be troubled. Believe in God, believe also in me. In my Father's house there are many dwelling places. If it were not so, would I have told you that I go to prepare a place for you? And if I go and prepare a place for you, I will come again and will take you to myself, so that where I am, there you may be also. And you know the way to the place where I am going." Thomas said to him, "Lord, we do not know where you are going. How can we know the way?" Jesus said to him, "I am the way, and the truth, and the life. No one comes to the Father except through me. If you know me, you will know my Father also. From now on you do know him and have seen him."

- The gospel presents Jesus as the guide in life, as the "way, truth, and life." The Christian centre is the person of Christ. Our work for Jesus and our love for people, no matter what our calling in life may be, flow from this.
- This centre always holds, it cannot be unhinged. It is a deeply personal relationship. We are led by Jesus "one by one," known by name, not as just one of a group.

Monday 23rd May **John 14:21–26**

Jesus said to his disciples: "They who have my commandments and keep them are those who love me; and those who love me will be loved by my Father, and I will love them and reveal myself to them." Judas (not Iscariot) said to him, "Lord, how is it that you will reveal yourself to us, and not to the world?" Jesus answered him, "Those who love me will keep my word, and my Father will love them, and we will come to them and make our home with them. Whoever does not love me does not keep my words; and the word that you hear is not mine, but is from the Father who sent me. I have said these things to you while I am still with you. The Advocate, the Holy Spirit, whom the Father will send in my name, will teach you everything, and remind you of all that I have said to you."

- The image of "home" is strong in the gospel—Jesus would visit the house of Zacchaeus, visit the home of Peter, and others, and makes a home in each of us.
- Jesus knocks at the door and waits to be invited into our space and our lives. He is not a crowding visitor but one who accepts what he sees and enjoys our welcome. Let me welcome him.

Tuesday 24th May **John 14:27**

Jesus said to his disciples, "Peace I leave with you; my peace I give to you. I do not give to you as the world gives. Do not let your hearts be troubled, and do not let them be afraid."

- Peace can exist in the heart at times of great turmoil and trouble, pain, and illness. The peace of Christ sort of invades us gently and fills us when we are open to peace.
- It is the peace of healing and forgiveness, and the peace which comes from doing what we know to be our calling.

Wednesday 25th May **John 15:1–8**

Jesus said to his disciples, "I am the true vine, and my Father is the vine-grower. He removes every branch in me that bears no fruit. Every branch that bears fruit he prunes to make it bear more fruit. You have already been cleansed by the word that I have spoken to you. Abide in me as I abide in you. Just as the branch cannot bear fruit by itself unless it abides in the vine, neither can you unless you abide in me. I am the vine, you are the branches. Those who abide in me and I in them bear much fruit, because apart from me you can do nothing. Whoever does not abide in me is thrown away like a branch and withers; such branches are gathered, thrown into the fire, and burned. If you abide in me, and my words abide in you, ask for whatever you wish, and it will be done for you. My Father is glorified by this, that you bear much fruit and become my disciples."

- When we try to do good in our lives and live according to the Word of God and the gospel of Jesus, God helps us. With love and grace, God is creating each of us every day, growing us in love and service.
- We need just to allow ourselves to be reached by Jesus in prayer, and be touched in heart and soul by him each day.

Thursday 26th May **John 15:9–11**

Jesus said to his disciples, "As the Father has loved me, so I have loved you; abide in my love. If you keep my commandments, you will abide in my love, just as I have kept my Father's commandments and abide in his love. I have said these things to you so that my joy may be in you, and that your joy may be complete."

- To abide with Jesus is to become his friend, to make our home with him, and to let him make his home with us.
- We see Jesus as one who gifts us with joy and with love.

Friday 27th May **John 15:12–17**

Jesus said to his disciples: "This is my commandment, that you love one another as I have loved you. No one has greater love than this, to lay down one's life for one's friends. You are my friends if you do what I command you. I do not call you servants any longer, because the servant does not know what the master is doing; but I have called you friends, because I have made known to you everything that I have heard from my Father. You did not choose me but I chose you. And I appointed you to go and bear fruit, fruit that will last, so that the Father will give you whatever you ask him in my name. I am giving you these commands so that you may love one another."

- The love of Jesus is self-sacrificing love, seen on the Cross. Where better to see love than at Calvary? The love of Calvary is love for all, and wants and desires that we know and receive this love.
- In prayer we might imagine ourselves at Calvary and allow the love of Jesus Christ to be given to each of us.

Saturday 28th May **John 15:18–21**

Jesus said to his disciples: "If the world hates you, be aware that it hated me before it hated you. If you belonged to the world, the world would love you as its own. Because you do not belong to the world, but I have chosen you out of the world—therefore the world hates you. Remember the word that I said to you, 'Servants are not greater than their master.' If they persecuted me, they will persecute you; if they kept my word, they will keep yours also. But they will do all these things to you on account of my name, because they do not know him who sent me."

- Not everyone accepts Jesus, which was his experience from the start. Opposition to him took him to death, and love took him from death to resurrection. Persecution and similar opposition is the experience of many of his followers.
- Goodness sometimes offends people; evil can seem for a while to be stronger than love, but the message of Jesus is that love conquers all.

may 29–june 4

Something to think and pray about each day this week:

Moving Forward

A.E. Housman wrote of the generation slaughtered in World War I:

> Here dead we lie because we did not choose
> To live and shame the land from which we sprung.
> Life, to be sure, is nothing much to lose;
> But young men think it is, and we were young.

It is not only the young who find it hard to let go of life. People in later life hang on tenaciously, wondering what lies beyond. Scripture gives glimpses, as in 1 John 3:2: "We are God's children now; what we will be has not yet been revealed. What we do know is this: when he is revealed, we will be like him, for we will see him as he is." Or Saint Paul in his first letter to the Corinthians, "For now we see in a mirror, dimly, but then we will see face to face. Now I know only in part; then I will know fully, even as I have been fully known" (13:12). We will move from this cloud of unknowing to a state of being known and loved such as we seldom experience in this life.

The Presence of God

Dear Jesus, today I call on you in a special way.
Mostly I come asking for favours.
Today I'd like just to be in your presence.
Let my heart respond to your Love.

Freedom

"I am free."
When I look at these words in writing,
They seem to create in me a feeling of awe.
Yes, a wonderful feeling of freedom.
Thank you, God.

Consciousness

Lord, you gave me the night to rest in sleep.
In my waking hours may I not forget your goodness to me.
Guide me to share your blessings with others.

The Word

I read the Word of God slowly, a few times over, and I listen to what God is saying to me. (Please turn to your scripture on the following pages. Inspiration points are there should you need them. When you are ready, return here to continue.)

Conversation

Dear Jesus, I can open up my heart to you.
I can tell you everything that troubles me.
I know you care about all the concerns in my life.
Teach me to live in the knowledge
that you who care for me today,
will care for me tomorrow and all the days of my life.

Conclusion

Glory be to the Father, and to the Son, and to the Holy Spirit,
As it was in the beginning, is now, and ever shall be,
World without end. Amen

Sunday 29th May,
Sixth Sunday of Easter **John 14:15–18**

Jesus said to his disciples, "If you love me, you will keep my commandments. And I will ask the Father, and he will give you another Advocate, to be with you forever. This is the Spirit of truth, whom the world cannot receive, because it neither sees him nor knows him. You know him, because he abides with you, and he will be in you. I will not leave you orphaned; I am coming to you."

- Jesus speaks about being still alive even after his death. Mostly we find Jesus to be alive for us in the love of others.
- There is an energy of love that is connected to the energy of God, for God is love. This is the working of the Spirit of God, alive in love, care, and compassion, and in all other good works.

Monday 30th May **John 15:26–16:4**

Jesus said to his disciples, "When the Advocate comes, whom I will send to you from the Father, the Spirit of truth who comes from the Father, he will testify on my behalf. You also are to testify because you have been with me from the beginning. I have said these things to you to keep you from stumbling. They will put you out of the synagogues. Indeed, an hour is coming when those who kill you will think that by doing so they are offering worship to God. And they will do this because they have not known the Father or me. But I have said these things to you so that when their hour comes you may remember that I told you about them. I did not say these things to you from the beginning, because I was with you."

- Jesus taught his disciples with his word and prepared them for life when he would no longer be with them. He knew that there would be opposition to them and danger to their lives. Banishment from their places of worship would bring them to remember what he told them.
- Prayer is listening over and over again to the Word of God so that it becomes part of us like our daily food and daily bread.

Tuesday 31st May, Visitation of the Virgin Mary — Luke 1:39–47

In those days Mary set out and went with haste to a Judean town in the hill country, where she entered the house of Zechariah and greeted Elizabeth. When Elizabeth heard Mary's greeting, the child leaped in her womb. And Elizabeth was filled with the Holy Spirit and exclaimed with a loud cry, "Blessed are you among women, and blessed is the fruit of your womb. And why has this happened to me, that the mother of my Lord comes to me? For as soon as I heard the sound of your greeting, the child in my womb leaped for joy. And blessed is she who believed that there would be a fulfillment of what was spoken to her by the Lord." And Mary said, "My soul magnifies the Lord, and my spirit rejoices in God my Savior."

- This scene can lead us towards a deeper understanding of love, care, kinship, and friendship. These two women meet in the midst of a doubting, pragmatic, and cynical world; the humanly impossible has happened to each of them.
- We need to visit each other often, to offer each other a safe place to celebrate our freedom and our gifts.

Wednesday 1st June **John 16:12–15**

Jesus said to his disciples, "I still have many things to say to you, but you cannot bear them now. When the Spirit of truth comes, he will guide you into all the truth; for he will not speak on his own, but will speak whatever he hears, and he will declare to you the things that are to come. He will glorify me, because he will take what is mine and declare it to you. All that the Father has is mine. For this reason I said that he will take what is mine and declare it to you."

- Jesus does not abandon the one who followed him. Earthly death does not confine his word to the era of the first century. Jesus, through his Spirit, is still our guide and our way, truth, and life.
- The Spirit unites heaven and earth, God and humanity, within each person and within each community of Jesus Christ.

Thursday 2nd June **John 16:19–20**

Jesus said to his disciples, "Are you discussing among yourselves what I meant when I said, 'A little while, and you will no longer see me, and again a little while, and you will see me'? Very truly, I tell you, you will weep and mourn, but the world will rejoice; you will have pain, but your pain will turn into joy."

- Pain turning into joy is part of the human condition. A grain of wheat falls, dies in the ground and then becomes a rich harvest.
- Loss and pain can bring us close—to God and to each other. It may not. Prayer can be a time of noticing the good in everything and of praying that pain will turn into joy.

Friday 3rd June **John 16:20–23**

Very truly, I tell you, you will weep and mourn, but the world will rejoice; you will have pain, but your pain will turn into joy. When a woman is in labor, she has pain, because her hour has come. But when her child is born, she no longer remembers the anguish because of the joy of having brought a human being into the world. So you have pain now; but I will see you again, and your hearts will rejoice, and no one will take your joy from you. On that day you will ask nothing of me. Very truly, I tell you, if you ask anything of the Father in my name, he will give it to you.

- Pain and life's difficulties need not be the final word for Jesus' followers. Pain often turns to joy, and in every small "death" in life is the hope of rising into a deeper life with Jesus.
- Human experience teaches us that problems we encounter can be on a path to growth, especially in the context of love; they may also be a cul-de-sac, blocking any future development and joy.
- With Jesus we walk always with the "Alleluia" on our lips and in our hearts.

Saturday 4th June **John 16:23–24**

Jesus said to his disciples, "Very truly, I tell you, if you ask anything of the Father in my name, he will give it to you. Until now you have not asked for anything in my name. Ask and you will receive, so that your joy may be complete."

- We ask often in prayer and sometimes prayer is answered very directly. Even when this appears not to happen, no prayer, like no act in love, is wasted.
- The true gift of prayer is always the Father's love, given to us no matter what we ask for. We are always gifted with the Spirit of Jesus, alive in our lives and in our love.

june 5–11

Something to think and pray about each day this week:

Professing Love

One encounter with the risen Jesus has been described with exquisite care by the author of the fourth Gospel. The story of John 21 can be seen as a powerful image of the apostolic efforts of the first generation of Christians, and therefore a link between Jesus and his disciples, the risen Lord and the early Christian community, and between Jesus and ourselves. The text is unique in the New Testament in that it makes Peter's profession of his deep personal love for Jesus the condition for being given responsibility and leadership. Secondly, Jesus makes Peter profess his love for him by reminding him of his earlier betrayal, perhaps in order to purify Peter's love completely from any trace of pride, conceit, and vanity. Jesus wants nothing less than a wholly committed, transparent, and unselfish Peter who does not trust in his own strength and power but is aware of his recent betrayal and failure, and therefore trusts only in the risen Lord who gives him that responsibility and leadership: "Simon, son of John, do you love me, do you love me more than these?" (John 21:15).

Nowhere else in the New Testament is a person asked so directly and insistently whether he or she loves Jesus. For Christians, that personal love is central.

The Presence of God

"I stand at the door and knock," says the Lord.
What a wonderful privilege
that the Lord of all creation desires to come to me.
I welcome his presence.

Freedom

Lord, grant me the grace to be free from the excesses of this life.
Let me not get caught up with the desire for wealth.
Keep my heart and mind free to love and serve you.

Consciousness

"There is a time and place for everything," as the saying goes.
Lord, grant that I may always desire
to spend time in your presence. To hear your call.

The Word

God speaks to each one of us individually. I need to listen to what he is saying to me. (Please turn to your scripture on the following pages. Inspiration points are there should you need them. When you are ready, return here to continue.)

Conversation

The gift of speech is a wonderful gift.
May I use this gift with kindness.
May I be slow to utter harsh words,
hurtful words, and words spoken in anger.

Conclusion

Glory be to the Father, and to the Son, and to the Holy Spirit,
As it was in the beginning, is now, and ever shall be,
World without end. Amen

Sunday 5th June,
Ascension of the Lord **Matthew 28:16–20**

Now the eleven disciples went to Galilee, to the mountain to which Jesus had directed them. When they saw him, they worshipped him; but some doubted. And Jesus came and said to them, "All authority in heaven and on earth has been given to me. Go therefore and make disciples of all nations, baptizing them in the name of the Father and of the Son and of the Holy Spirit, and teaching them to obey everything that I have commanded you. And remember, I am with you always, to the end of the age."

- A man went out on a starry night and shook his fist at the heavens yelling, "Oh, God, what a lousy, rotten world you've made. I could have done much better." Then a voice boomed from the clouds saying, "That's why I put you there. Get busy."
- The feast of the Ascension marks the time when Jesus puts us in charge of his mission and of his work, promising to be always with us.
- Let me talk to the Lord, to discover where I can do his work.

Monday 6th June **John 16:29–33**

The disciples said to Jesus, "Yes, now you are speaking plainly, not in any figure of speech! Now we know that you know all things, and do not need to have anyone question you; by this we believe that you came from God." Jesus answered them, "Do you now believe? The hour is coming, indeed it has come, when you will be scattered, each one to his home, and you will leave me alone. Yet I am not alone because the Father is with me. I have said this to you, so that in me you may have peace. In the world you face persecution. But take courage; I have conquered the world!"

- We are brought back to the events which would result in the crucifixion. To remember this central mystery is life-giving as it gives hope and courage to the disciples in times of persecution.

- The conviction that the Father is with Jesus always is shared with all of us—God is always with us, always near, always on our side.

Tuesday 7th June **John 17:1–3**

After Jesus had spoken these words, he looked up to heaven and said, "Father, the hour has come; glorify your Son so that the Son may glorify you, since you have given him authority over all people, to give eternal life to all whom you have given him. And this is eternal life, that they may know you, the only true God, and Jesus Christ whom you have sent."

- Jesus wanted the Father to show some sign to his disciples before his death that God was with him, and that he was following the way of God even to the Cross.
- Later on they would hear a voice from heaven, glorifying the name of Jesus, giving security and hope to the disciples at the hour of Jesus' death.

Wednesday 8th June **John 17:11–15**

Jesus said to the disciples, "And now I am no longer in the world, but they are in the world, and I am coming to you. Holy Father, protect them in your name that you have given me, so that they may be one, as we are one. While I was with them, I protected them in your name that you have given me. I guarded them, and not one of them was lost except the one destined to be lost, so that the scripture might be fulfilled. But now I am coming to you, and I speak these things in the world so that they may have my joy made complete in themselves. I have given them your word, and the world has hated them because they do not belong to the world, just as I do not belong to the world. I am not asking you to take them out of the world, but I ask you to protect them from the evil one."

- Jesus' first prayer is for those who were with him in the Last Supper room. He prays that they always be in communion with God and for their protection from the evil that surrounds them every day.
- Like ourselves, they are to find closeness with God and protection from harm even in the midst of the world.

Thursday 9th June **John 17:20–23**

Jesus looked up to heaven and said, "Father, I ask not only on behalf of these, but also on behalf of those who will believe in me through their word, that they may all be one. As you, Father, are in me and I am in you, may they also be in us, so that the world may believe that you have sent me. The glory that you have given me I have given them, so that they may be one, as we are one, I in them and you in me, that they may become completely one, so that the world may know that you have sent me and have loved them even as you have loved me."

- Jesus' second prayer at the Last Supper is for future generations of believers, including ourselves. His prayer is that all of us will be united with God our Father and with him. He is to share with all of us what is deepest in his heart—the glory he had from the beginning of time.
- Love wants to share all that is best with the beloved.

Friday 10th June **John 21:15–17**

When they had finished breakfast, Jesus said to Simon Peter, "Simon son of John, do you love me more than these?" He said to him, "Yes, Lord; you know that I love you." Jesus said to him, "Feed my lambs." A second time he said to him, "Simon son of John, do you love me?" He said to him, "Yes, Lord; you know that I love you." Jesus said to him, "Tend my sheep." He said to him the third time, "Simon son of John, do you love me?" Peter felt hurt because he said to him the third time, "Do you love me?" And he said to him, "Lord, you know everything; you know that I love you." Jesus said to him, "Feed my sheep."

- At the end of all of Jesus' instructions to his followers, he asks the simple question which grounds all discipleship: whether we love him.
- We may sometimes wonder about the strength of our faith and our love. Like Peter, we just hope at times that the Lord knows we love him as we try to live out this love in our lives.

Saturday 11th June **John 21:20–25**

Peter turned and saw the disciple whom Jesus loved following them; he was the one who had reclined next to Jesus at the supper and had said, "Lord, who is it that is going to betray you?" When Peter saw him, he said to Jesus, "Lord, what about him?" Jesus said to him, "If it is my will that he remain until I come, what is that to you? Follow me!" So the rumor spread in the community that this disciple would not die. Yet Jesus did not say to him that he would not die, but, "If it is my will that he remain until I come, what is that to you?" This is the disciple who is testifying to these things and has written them, and we know that his testimony is true. But there are also many other things that Jesus did; if every one of them were written down, I suppose that the world itself could not contain the books that would be written.

- Not everything about Jesus is written down. The events and words in the gospel are for our faith, and propose the essentials of the message of Jesus in the different communities of the time.
- Jesus is still doing many things in the world, and now these are done through his followers and all who live by his gospel of faith, love, and justice. Each of us now is a living gospel for all to hear.

june 12–18

Something to think and pray about each day this week:

Silence of the Spirit

This week we celebrate Pentecost, the feast of the Holy Spirit. We speak of the Spirit guiding us. Quakers wait in silence for the Spirit to move them to speak. How does this work? The Holy Spirit does not normally work by telling us things we do not know, or by extraordinary revelations. The Holy Spirit introduces no new ideas, but improves and deepens my knowledge of what I already know. Jesus said, "The Paraclete, the Holy Spirit, whom the Father will send in my name, will teach you everything and remind you of all I have said to you" (John 14:26). We shall sometimes, but not always, be conscious of a special divine influence, and we may feel sure that the action we have received is from God. But God's action, though strong, is often quite imperceptible, for instance as the grace of fidelity in a time of great aridity.

The Presence of God

I remind myself that, as I sit here now,
God is gazing on me with love and holding me in being.
I pause for a moment and think of this.

Freedom

I need to close out the noise, to rise above the noise;
The noise that interrupts, that separates,
The noise that isolates.
I need to listen to God again.

Consciousness

In God's loving presence I unwind the past day,
starting from now and looking back, moment by moment.
I gather in all the goodness and light, in gratitude.
I attend to the shadows and what they say to me,
seeking healing, courage, forgiveness.

The Word

I take my time to read the Word of God, slowly, a few times, allowing myself to dwell on anything that strikes me. (Please turn to your scripture on the following pages. Inspiration points are there should you need them. When you are ready, return here to continue.)

Conversation

Do I notice myself reacting as I pray with the Word of God?
Do I feel challenged, comforted, angry?
Imagining Jesus sitting or standing by me,
I speak out my feelings, as one trusted friend to another.

Conclusion

Glory be to the Father, and to the Son, and to the Holy Spirit,
As it was in the beginning, is now, and ever shall be,
World without end. Amen

Sunday 12th June,
Pentecost **John 20:19–23**

When it was evening on that day, the first day of the week, and the doors of the house where the disciples had met were locked for fear of the Jews, Jesus came and stood among them and said, "Peace be with you." After he said this, he showed them his hands and his side. Then the disciples rejoiced when they saw the Lord. Jesus said to them again, "Peace be with you. As the Father has sent me, so I send you." When he had said this, he breathed on them and said to them, "Receive the Holy Spirit. If you forgive the sins of any, they are forgiven them; if you retain the sins of any, they are retained."

- Unity is not easy. It is not just similarity. Unity doesn't mean we all pretend all is well. It's living with, accepting, even enjoying differences.
- Some differences are too much for friendship or family, but we can still value the other. As unity demands tolerance, at times it will demand forgiveness and a desire for healing and freedom. At other times, if we are to get along, side by side, it means reconciliation and a new relationship.
- Pray for someone you are at odds with—believe that he or she has the Spirit of God like you. It helps! This is some of the Spirit of Pentecost.

Monday 13th June,
St. Anthony of Padua **Isaiah 61:1–3**

The spirit of the Lord God is upon me, because the Lord has anointed me; he has sent me to bring good news to the oppressed, to bind up the brokenhearted, to proclaim liberty to the captives, and release to the prisoners; to proclaim the year of the Lord's favor, and the day of vengeance of our God; to comfort all who mourn; to provide for those who mourn in Zion—to give them a garland instead of ashes, the oil of gladness instead of mourning, the mantle of praise instead of a faint spirit.

- Anthony of Padua's work included humble kitchen tasks as well as preaching and scholarship.
- "The Spirit of the Lord is upon me." This applies to me, as it did to Anthony. Am I open to the Spirit today?

Tuesday 14th June **Matthew 5:43–48**

Jesus said to the crowds, "You have heard that it was said, 'You shall love your neighbor and hate your enemy.' But I say to you, Love your enemies and pray for those who persecute you, so that you may be children of your Father in heaven; for he makes his sun rise on the evil and on the good, and sends rain on the righteous and on the unrighteous. For if you love those who love you, what reward do you have? Do not even the tax collectors do the same? And if you greet only your brothers and sisters, what more are you doing than others? Do not even the Gentiles do the same? Be perfect, therefore, as your heavenly Father is perfect."

- These words of Jesus can make us feel like we will never measure up. To forgive is one of the most difficult things to do in life.
- All we know is that the more we can forgive, the freer we become. The example of Jesus' love and forgiveness on the Cross can help us make small steps on the way of forgiveness in our lives.

Wednesday 15th June **Matthew 6:1–6, 16–18**

Jesus said to the disciples, "Beware of practicing your piety before others in order to be seen by them; for then you have no reward from your Father in heaven. Whenever you give alms, do not sound a trumpet before you, as the hypocrites do in the synagogues and in the streets, so that they may be praised by others.

Truly I tell you, they have received their reward. But when you give alms, do not let your left hand know what your right hand is doing, so that your alms may be done in secret; and your Father who sees in secret will reward you. And whenever you pray, do not be like the hypocrites; for they love to stand and pray in the synagogues and at the street corners, so that they may be seen by others. Truly I tell you, they have received their reward. But whenever you pray, go into your room and shut the door and pray to your Father who is in secret; and your Father who sees in secret will reward you. And whenever you fast, do not look dismal, like the hypocrites, for they disfigure their faces so as to show others that they are fasting. Truly I tell you, they have received their reward. But when you fast, put oil on your head and wash your face, so that your fasting may be seen not by others but by your Father who is in secret; and your Father who sees in secret will reward you."

- This piece of the gospel highlights three essential elements in religion: prayer, self-control, and giving to the needy.
- Each of these brings us in touch with God: prayer brings us into the mystery of God's love; fasting or self-control alerts us to our real dependency on the creation of God rather than on God; and giving to the needy is giving to God who lives and is poor in those in need.

Thursday 16th June **Matthew 6:7–15**

Jesus said to the crowds, "When you are praying, do not heap up empty phrases as the Gentiles do; for they think that they will be heard because of their many words. Do not be like them, for your Father knows what you need before you ask him. Pray then in this way: Our Father in heaven, hallowed be your name. Your kingdom come. Your will be done, on earth as it is in heaven. Give us this day our daily bread. And forgive us our debts, as we also have forgiven our debtors. And do not bring us to the time of trial, but rescue us from the evil one. For if you forgive others their trespasses, your heavenly Father will also forgive you; but if you do not forgive others, neither will your Father forgive your trespasses."

- Maybe we pray best when we say nothing at all! Our words can be sparing. Often we don't know what to say in our prayers, or we tire of saying the same things over and over.
- Maybe we can be silent before God, with each breath a grateful receiving of life and love; or just say some of the words of the *Our Father*, the prayer he uses to put words on our desire to pray.

Friday 17th June **Matthew 6:19–21**

Jesus said to his disciples, "Do not store up for yourselves treasures on earth, where moth and rust consume and where thieves break in and steal; but store up for yourselves treasures in heaven, where neither moth nor rust consumes and where thieves do not break in and steal. For where your treasure is, there your heart will be also."

- Nothing much has changed; we still lock away our valuables and take pride in our personal possessions today.
- Jesus is asking each of us: To what do I give my heart? What is my "treasure"? What do I think about?

Saturday 18th June **Matthew 6:24–34**

Jesus said to his disciples, "No one can serve two masters; for a slave will either hate the one and love the other, or be devoted to the one and despise the other. You cannot serve God and wealth. Therefore I tell you, do not worry about your life, what you will eat or what you will drink, or about your body, what you will wear. Is not life more than food, and the body more than clothing? Look at the birds of the air; they neither sow nor reap nor gather into barns, and yet your heavenly Father feeds them. Are you not of more value than they? And can any of you by worrying add a single hour to your span of life? And why do you worry about clothing? Consider the lilies of the field, how they grow; they neither toil nor spin, yet I tell you, even Solomon in all his glory was not clothed like one of these. But if God so clothes the grass of the field, which is alive today and tomorrow is thrown into the oven, will he not much more clothe you—you of little faith? Therefore do not worry, saying, 'What will we eat?' or 'What will we drink?' or 'What will we wear?' For it is the Gentiles who strive for all these things; and indeed your heavenly Father knows that you need all these things. But strive first for the kingdom of God and his righteousness, and all these things will be given to you as well. So do not worry about tomorrow, for tomorrow will bring worries of its own. Today's trouble is enough for today."

- Many of the phrases in this passage are well known. The message of Jesus is not to be worried about many things in life. He does not look down on concern for money, clothing, and the things we need every day, even telling us to pray for our daily bread.
- He alerts us to the futility of worry and anxiety which can take our minds and hearts off what is really essential in our lives.

june 19–25

Something to think and pray about each day this week:

The Promise of Life

In the week after the birth of John the Baptist, the neighbours gathered for the circumcision and naming of the baby, and as they saw Zechariah name the child John and recover his speech, they marveled, "What then will this child become?" (Luke 1:66). Lord, it is sobering for me to think back on a similar gathering around my cradle. Every newborn child is a beacon of promise and hope. Lawrence of Arabia once said that to be old and wise is to be tired and disappointed. Okay, tired perhaps, but rather disenchanted than disappointed. We would be rightly suspicious if somebody was able to look back on their life with total satisfaction and claim that all their promise was fulfilled. Our hearts are restless till they rest in God. Only there is our promise fulfilled and we are loved as we long to be.

The Presence of God

At any time of the day or night we can call on Jesus.
He is always waiting, listening for our call.
What a wonderful blessing.
No phone needed, no emails, just a whisper.

Freedom

Lord, grant me the grace to be free from the excesses of this life.
Let me not get caught up with the desire for wealth.
Keep my heart and mind free to love and serve you.

Consciousness

I exist in a web of relationships—links to nature, people, God.
I trace out these links, giving thanks for the life that flows through them.
Some links are twisted or broken: I may feel regret, anger, disappointment.
I pray for the gift of acceptance and forgiveness.

The Word

God speaks to each one of us individually. I need to listen to what he is saying to me. (Please turn to your scripture on the following pages. Inspiration points are there should you need them. When you are ready, return here to continue.)

Conversation

Remembering that I am still in God's presence,
I imagine Jesus himself standing or sitting beside me,
and say whatever is on my mind, whatever is in my heart,
speaking as one friend to another.

Conclusion

Glory be to the Father, and to the Son, and to the Holy Spirit,
As it was in the beginning, is now, and ever shall be,
World without end. Amen

Sunday 19th June,
The Holy Trinity **John 3:16–17**

Jesus said to Nicodemus, "For God so loved the world that he gave his only Son, so that everyone who believes in him may not perish but may have eternal life. Indeed, God did not send the Son into the world to condemn the world, but in order that the world might be saved through him."

- They looked down from heaven—the Father, Son, and Holy Spirit—with love for their people, for all of us. They could see men and women of all races, colours, ages, faiths. They could see their holiness and their sin. They knew help was needed for the human race and they waited a long time before the time was right.
- Prayer inserts us into our true space of belonging—into the community of the Trinity—and in that prayer we are called to bring this divine help to the human race.

Monday 20th June **Matthew 7:1–5**

Jesus said to the crowds, "Do not judge, so that you may not be judged. For with the judgment you make you will be judged, and the measure you give will be the measure you get. Why do you see the speck in your neighbor's eye, but do not notice the log in your own eye? Or how can you say to your neighbor, 'Let me take the speck out of your eye,' while the log is in your own eye? You hypocrite, first take the log out of your own eye, and then you will see clearly to take the speck out of your neighbor's eye."

- Our minds can be active in judging others and our words may follow. It is part of being human to judge, and to condemn. These words of Jesus highlight that none of us are perfect.

- Often what we criticize in others may be qualities we don't like in ourselves. Our relationship to God, which we share with everyone, can be an entry into the world of love where we know that all, even those whom we find hard to relate to, are loved by God.

Tuesday 21st June,
St. Aloysius Gonzaga **Mark 10:23–27**

Then Jesus looked around and said to his disciples, "How hard it will be for those who have wealth to enter the kingdom of God!" And the disciples were perplexed at these words. But Jesus said to them again, "Children, how hard it is to enter the kingdom of God! It is easier for a camel to go through the eye of a needle than for someone who is rich to enter the kingdom of God." They were greatly astounded and said to one another, "Then who can be saved?" Jesus looked at them and said, "For mortals it is impossible, but not for God; for God all things are possible."

- Born into a family of wealth and power, Aloysius left all that behind to follow Jesus, even to death. It set him free.
- What are the things I hold on to? What more can I do to be free, for Jesus' sake?

Wednesday 22nd June **Matthew 7:15–20**

Jesus told the crowds, "Beware of false prophets, who come to you in sheep's clothing but inwardly are ravenous wolves. You will know them by their fruits. Are grapes gathered from thorns, or figs from thistles? In the same way, every good tree bears good fruit, but the bad tree bears bad fruit. A good tree cannot bear bad fruit, nor can a bad tree bear good fruit. Every tree that does not bear good fruit is cut down and thrown into the fire. Thus you will know them by their fruits."

- "You will know them by their fruits." Jesus teaches us with direct words—wolves, fruit, thorns, figs, thistles, fire. We understand him. He warns us that religious display and power can deceive when in the hands of those hungry for things other than service of God.
- How does my inner life reveal itself to others? Am I concerned about how others see me? Is there a gap between what I say and what I do?

Thursday 23rd June **Matthew 7:24–27**

Jesus said to his disciples, "Everyone then who hears these words of mine and acts on them will be like a wise man who built his house on rock. The rain fell, the floods came, and the winds blew and beat on that house, but it did not fall, because it had been founded on rock. And everyone who hears these words of mine and does not act on them will be like a foolish man who built his house on sand. The rain fell, and the floods came, and the winds blew and beat against that house, and it fell—and great was its fall!"

- The Word of God is a constant of support and enlightenment in life. Jesus' wisdom is a rock of truth from which we can make decisions and commitments in life.
- To read slowly the Word of God in prayer each day is to place ourselves on that solid footing which will give us both insight and compassion in all we do in our lives.

Friday 24th June,
Birth of St. John the Baptist **Luke 1:57–66**

Now the time came for Elizabeth to give birth, and she bore a son. Her neighbors and relatives heard that the Lord had shown his great mercy to her, and they rejoiced with her. On the eighth day they came to circumcise the child, and they were going to name him Zechariah after his father. But his mother said, "No; he is to be called John." They said to her, "None of your relatives has this name." Then they began motioning to his father to find out what name he wanted to give him. He asked for a writing tablet and wrote, "His name is John." And all of them were amazed. Immediately his mouth was opened and his tongue freed, and he began to speak, praising God. Fear came over all their neighbors, and all these things were talked about throughout the entire hill country of Judea. All who heard them pondered them and said, "What then will this child become?" For, indeed, the hand of the Lord was with him.

- His parents did not know what this child, John, was to become. At every birth we are engaged in the mystery of another human being and don't know what our children will become.
- Now may be a time of prayer for the children in our lives and for whom we are responsible. Name them in prayer and in loving care give each to God.

Saturday 25th June **Matthew 8:5–13**

When he entered Capernaum, a centurion came to him, appealing to him and saying, "Lord, my servant is lying at home paralyzed, in terrible distress." And he said to him, "I will come and cure him." The centurion answered, "Lord, I am not worthy to have you come under my roof; but only speak the word, and my servant will be healed. For I also am a man under authority, with soldiers under me; and I say to one, 'Go,' and he goes, and to another, 'Come,' and he comes, and to my slave, 'Do this,' and the slave does it." When Jesus heard him, he was amazed and said to those who followed him, "Truly I tell you, in no one in Israel have I found such faith. I tell you, many will come from east and west and will eat with Abraham and Isaac and Jacob in the kingdom of heaven, while the heirs of the kingdom will be thrown into the outer darkness, where there will be weeping and gnashing of teeth." And to the centurion Jesus said, "Go; let it be done for you according to your faith." And the servant was healed in that hour.

- Faith has its results. The centurion's prayer was heard because of a strong faith.
- Our prayers may be heard in different ways, as all the time we pray in faith that God cares for us and knows us and grants us what is best. We may ask for one thing and get something better.

june 26–july 2

Something to think and pray about each day this week:

Service of Unity

The feast of the Body of Christ, which the church celebrates this week, recalls Jesus' gift of himself in the Eucharist. This was to be the symbol of unity—strangers sharing the one table, many grains making one loaf, many grapes making the shared wine. But it has become a source of division: there is no element of our religion about which Christians disagree more than about the Eucharist. In the fourth Gospel, Saint John, conscious of these divisions, introduced his account of the Last Supper not with the Eucharist but with Jesus washing the apostles' feet. If we cannot find unity in liturgy and sacraments, we can always find it in service, where we are moved, as Jesus was, not by theology but by our neighbour's needs. Meanwhile we pray, as Jesus did, that all his followers may eventually be united in the Eucharist as well.

The Presence of God
God is with me, but more,
God is within me, giving me existence.
Let me dwell for a moment on God's life-giving presence
in my body, my mind, my heart
and in the whole of my life.

Freedom
God is not foreign to my freedom.
Instead the Spirit breathes life into my most intimate desires,
gently nudging me towards all that is good.
I ask for the grace to let myself be enfolded by the Spirit.

Consciousness
How am I really feeling? Light-hearted? Heavy-hearted?
I may be very much at peace, happy to be here.
Equally, I may be frustrated, worried, or angry.
I acknowledge how I really am. It is the real me that the Lord loves.

The Word
I read the Word of God slowly, a few times over, and I listen to what God is saying to me. (Please turn to your scripture on the following pages. Inspiration points are there should you need them. When you are ready, return here to continue.)

Conversation
How has God's Word moved me? Has it left me cold?
Has it consoled me or moved me to act in a new way?
I imagine Jesus standing or sitting beside me,
I turn and share my feelings with him.

Conclusion
Glory be to the Father, and to the Son, and to the Holy Spirit,
As it was in the beginning, is now, and ever shall be,
World without end. Amen

Sunday 26th June,
Feast of the Body and Blood of Christ **John 6:51–56**

Jesus said to the crowd, "I am the living bread that came down from heaven. Whoever eats of this bread will live forever; and the bread that I will give for the life of the world is my flesh." The Jews then disputed among themselves, saying, "How can this man give us his flesh to eat?" So Jesus said to them, "Very truly, I tell you, unless you eat the flesh of the Son of Man and drink his blood, you have no life in you. Those who eat my flesh and drink my blood have eternal life, and I will raise them up on the last day; for my flesh is true food and my blood is true drink. Those who eat my flesh and drink my blood abide in me, and I in them."

- This is indeed a great mystery—the sacred power and presence of Christ in bread and wine, and the intimate meal offering food for the journey, for both saints and sinners. Little wonder that there is often tension and argument as we seek to understand the mystery of the Eucharist.
- As God does with us when we pray, so we are nourished in the closeness and intimacy of this feast. Let us pray.

Monday 27th June **Matthew 8:18–20**

Now when Jesus saw great crowds around him, he gave orders to go over to the other side. A scribe then approached and said, "Teacher, I will follow you wherever you go." And Jesus said to him, "Foxes have holes, and birds of the air have nests; but the Son of Man has nowhere to lay his head."

- Jesus is blunt—before you follow me, he warns the scribe, look at the cost. The disciple puts aside security for an unsettled life. The kingdom, Jesus says, takes priority; this is urgent.

- Where are my priorities falling? Is there urgency in how I live; in my decisions; in my prayer?

Tuesday 28th June **Matthew 8:23–27**

And when Jesus got into the boat, his disciples followed him. A windstorm arose on the sea, so great that the boat was being swamped by the waves; but he was asleep. And they went and woke him up, saying, "Lord, save us! We are perishing!" And he said to them, "Why are you afraid, you of little faith?" Then he got up and rebuked the winds and the sea; and there was a dead calm. They were amazed, saying, "What sort of man is this, that even the winds and the sea obey him?"

- This scene is often painted by artists and is a favourite for times of stress and of darkness. We may feel Jesus is asleep, not nearby. He woke when he was really needed and calmed the waters.
- In prayer he calms us too; maybe not immediately, but when we really need him he is there, a hand outstretched to save us from anxiety, darkness, and despair.

Wednesday 29th June,
Sts. Peter & Paul, Apostles **Matthew 16:13–19**

Now when Jesus came into the district of Caesarea Philippi, he asked his disciples, "Who do people say that the Son of Man is?" And they said, "Some say John the Baptist, but others Elijah, and still others Jeremiah or one of the prophets." He said to them, "But who do you say that I am?" Simon Peter answered, "You are the Messiah, the Son of the living God." And Jesus answered him, "Blessed are you, Simon son of Jonah! For flesh and blood has not revealed this to you, but my Father in heaven. And I tell you, you are Peter, and on this rock I will build my church, and the gates of Hades will not prevail against it. I will give you the keys of the kingdom of heaven, and whatever you bind on earth will be bound in heaven, and whatever you loose on earth will be loosed in heaven."

- Peter is praised today within the Church for his belief and faith in Jesus as the Son of the living God. This faith would lead him into times of doubt, unfaithfulness, and eventually to martyrdom.
- The first call in his following of Jesus was to grow in the faith that would sustain his life. May our faith do the same.

Thursday 30th June **Matthew 9:1–8**

And after getting into a boat he crossed the water and came to his own town. And just then some people were carrying a paralyzed man lying on a bed. When Jesus saw their faith, he said to the paralytic, "Take heart, son; your sins are forgiven." Then some of the scribes said to themselves, "This man is blaspheming." But Jesus, perceiving their thoughts, said, "Why do you think evil in your hearts? For which is easier, to say, 'Your sins are forgiven,' or to say, 'Stand up and walk'? But so that you may know that the Son of Man has authority on earth to forgive sins"—he then said to the paralytic—"Stand up, take your bed and go to your home." And he stood up and went to his home. When the crowds saw it, they were filled with awe, and they glorified God, who had given such authority to human beings.

- "Take heart . . . stand up . . . go home." Jesus' healing and words of forgiveness cheer us up. Contact with him brings us alive. We know that our home is everywhere because everywhere is his home, and he lives within us.

Friday 1st July,
Feast of the Sacred Heart of Jesus **Matthew 11:25–30**

At that time Jesus said, "I thank you, Father, Lord of heaven and earth, because you have hidden these things from the wise and the intelligent and have revealed them to infants; yes, Father, for such was your gracious will. All things have been handed over to me by my Father; and no one knows the Son except the Father, and no one knows the Father except the Son and anyone to whom the Son chooses to reveal him. Come to me, all you that are weary and are carrying heavy burdens, and I will give you rest. Take my yoke upon you, and learn from me; for I am gentle and humble in heart, and you will find rest for your souls. For my yoke is easy, and my burden is light."

- The invitation of God, "come to me," is always spoken, especially when we really need the peace, rest, protection, and love of God.
- Inside each of us is the space for the Divine, for the Trinity. From that deep interior space we are invited daily and consistently to come to God for what only God can give. Ask today for what you want and be open to what God wants to give.

Saturday 2nd July **Matthew 9:14–17**

Then the disciples of John came to him, saying, "Why do we and the Pharisees fast often, but your disciples do not fast?" And Jesus said to them, "The wedding guests cannot mourn as long as the bridegroom is with them, can they? The days will come when the bridegroom is taken away from them, and then they will fast. No one sews a piece of unshrunk cloth on an old cloak, for the patch pulls away from the cloak, and a worse tear is made. Neither is new wine put into old wineskins; otherwise, the skins burst, and the wine is spilled, and the skins are destroyed; but new wine is put into fresh wineskins, and so both are preserved."

- Jesus speaks here of the continuity of his message with the religious beliefs of the people. He respects their beliefs and practices but knows that something new and deeper is needed.
- He freshens their understanding of God's dealings with them over centuries and then gives his own new message.
- The map of our faith lives is made up of all that has happened in our lives and in our faith. Faith is always developing and dynamic, new truths building on the truths of the past.

july 3–9

Something to think and pray about each day this week:

Coming Closer

Examination of conscience is an ancient practice among Christians. During recent years "conscience" has been expanded to include consciousness. We look back on our day, focusing not so much on faults as on feelings, on what moved us. We look back on gifts as well as gaffes. There is a place for guilt, meaning a judgment that some things we did may have been stupid, self-indulgent, cowardly, or unfair. There is a bigger place for gratitude, for intimations of affection, and for the moments that lifted our hearts and helped us to sense God's closeness and the sweetness of being alive.

The Presence of God
To be present is to arrive as one is and open up to the other.
At this instant, as I arrive here, God is present waiting for me.
God always arrives before me, desiring to connect with me
even more than my most intimate friend.
I take a moment and greet my loving God.

Freedom
Everything has the potential to draw forth from me a fuller love and life.
Yet my desires are often fixed, caught, on illusions of fulfillment.
I ask that God, through my freedom, may orchestrate
my desires in a vibrant loving melody rich in harmony.

Consciousness
Knowing that God loves me unconditionally,
I can afford to be honest about how I am.
How has the last day been, and how do I feel now?
I share my feelings openly with the Lord.

The Word
I take my time to read the Word of God, slowly, a few times, allowing myself to dwell on anything that strikes me. (Please turn to your scripture on the following pages. Inspiration points are there should you need them. When you are ready, return here to continue.)

Conversation
What feelings are rising in me
as I pray and reflect on God's Word?
I imagine Jesus himself sitting or standing beside me,
and open my heart to him.

Conclusion
Glory be to the Father, and to the Son, and to the Holy Spirit,
As it was in the beginning, is now, and ever shall be,
World without end. Amen

Sunday 3rd July,
Fourteenth Sunday in Ordinary Time Matthew 11:28–30

Jesus said, "Come to me, all you that are weary and are carrying heavy burdens, and I will give you rest. Take my yoke upon you, and learn from me; for I am gentle and humble in heart, and you will find rest for your souls. For my yoke is easy, and my burden is light."

- These lines have been a consolation to many millions of people over the years. We all know the times of carrying heavy burdens of failure, pain, loss, shame, guilt, depression, hopelessness.
- We can all add to this list. All can be part of our prayer and relationship with God. Only in honestly admitting our big needs can we find the rest of soul which we need. A soul at rest can share with many the peace of God.

Monday 4th July Matthew 9:18–26

While Jesus was speaking, suddenly a leader of the synagogue came in and knelt before him, saying, "My daughter has just died; but come and lay your hand on her, and she will live." And Jesus got up and followed him, with his disciples. Then suddenly a woman who had been suffering from hemorrhages for twelve years came up behind him and touched the fringe of his cloak, for she said to herself, "If I only touch his cloak, I will be made well." Jesus turned, and seeing her he said, "Take heart, daughter; your faith has made you well." And instantly the woman was made well. When Jesus came to the leader's house and saw the flute players and the crowd making a commotion, he said, "Go away; for the girl is not dead but sleeping." And they laughed at him. But when the crowd had been put outside, he went in and took her by the hand, and the girl got up. And the report of this spread throughout that district.

- The gospel story remembers a woman who was suffering for a long time. She came in her need for healing; the journey was enlivened by her faith. Faith may not cure our ills and sicknesses; but over a long time of faith, we are healed and strengthened.
- Our prayer today might reach out to those whose suffering is long-term with little hope of healing.

Tuesday 5th July **Matthew 9:32–38**

After they had gone away, a demoniac who was mute was brought to Jesus. And when the demon had been cast out, the one who had been mute spoke; and the crowds were amazed and said, "Never has anything like this been seen in Israel." But the Pharisees said, "By the ruler of the demons he casts out the demons." Then Jesus went about all the cities and villages, teaching in their synagogues, and proclaiming the good news of the kingdom, and curing every disease and every sickness. When he saw the crowds, he had compassion for them, because they were harassed and helpless, like sheep without a shepherd. Then he said to his disciples, "The harvest is plentiful, but the laborers are few; therefore ask the Lord of the harvest to send out laborers into his harvest."

- Jesus saw people searching for meaning in their lives, for the truth that he spoke. He knows that this is part of life, and that people often look in the wrong place for meaning. We look for fullness in life and get caught into its superficiality. We look for faith and hope and get caught into trivialities.
- Jesus offers the way that guides our steps, the truth that enlightens our minds, and the life that gives love which lasts.

Wednesday 6th July **Matthew 10:1–7**

Then Jesus summoned his twelve disciples and gave them authority over unclean spirits, to cast them out, and to cure every disease and every sickness. These are the names of the twelve apostles: first, Simon, also known as Peter, and his brother Andrew; James son of Zebedee, and his brother John; Philip and Bartholomew; Thomas and Matthew the tax collector; James son of Alphaeus, and Thaddaeus; Simon the Cananaean, and Judas Iscariot, the one who betrayed him. These twelve Jesus sent out with the following instructions: "Go nowhere among the Gentiles, and enter no town of the Samaritans, but go rather to the lost sheep of the house of Israel. As you go, proclaim the good news, 'The kingdom of heaven has come near.'"

- The kingdom of heaven, or the reign of God, is near in the preaching and teaching of Jesus. It is near as something he brings, and as something we bring.
- We pray daily that his kingdom will come. How can I bring this reign of God alive in the world today?

Thursday 7th July **Matthew 10:7–14**

As you go, proclaim the good news, "The kingdom of heaven has come near." Cure the sick, raise the dead, cleanse the lepers, cast out demons. You received without payment; give without payment. Take no gold, or silver, or copper in your belts, no bag for your journey, or two tunics, or sandals, or a staff; for laborers deserve their food. Whatever town or village you enter, find out who in it is worthy, and stay there until you leave. As you enter the house, greet it. If the house is worthy, let your peace come upon it; but if it is not worthy, let your peace return to you. If anyone will not welcome you or listen to your words, shake off the dust from your feet as you leave that house or town.

- This is a sort of mission statement for the disciples. The central vision of the statement is to trust in God. The pilgrim puts no trust in home or money, in long-term contracts or in superficial welcomes.
- Our dependency on God and trust in God's care gives us a conviction about living in the love and service of God.

Friday 8th July **Matthew 10:16–20**

See, I am sending you out like sheep into the midst of wolves; so be wise as serpents and innocent as doves. Beware of them, for they will hand you over to councils and flog you in their synagogues; and you will be dragged before governors and kings because of me, as a testimony to them and the Gentiles. When they hand you over, do not worry about how you are to speak or what you are to say; for what you are to say will be given to you at that time; for it is not you who speak, but the Spirit of your Father speaking through you."

- Commitment to Jesus Christ is long term. In difficult times his help will be there, and our convictions about him may lead to conflict, even with those closest to us.
- We are compared to sheep—these find their way even among wolves if they follow the shepherd. We keep our eye on the Lord who guides our way.

Saturday 9th July **Matthew 10:29–31**

Jesus said to the Twelve: "Are not two sparrows sold for a penny? Yet not one of them will fall to the ground unperceived by your Father. And even the hairs of your head are all counted. So do not be afraid; you are of more value than many sparrows."

- "Do not be afraid" is said to be the most common phrase in scripture. Fear haunts us; we fear even fear itself.
- Yet Jesus tells us that the Father knows each one of us intimately, down to the hairs on our head. In the midst of our fear, God is with us each and every step of the way.

july 10–16

Something to think and pray about each day this week:

Making Room

In his letter to the Philippians (2:7), Paul wrote of Jesus emptying himself, voluntarily taking the form of a servant to conceal his divine glory. It is remarkable how much self-emptying we all experience as we grow older. If we have built ourselves up in the first half of our life, acquiring skills, family, possessions, lovers, reputation, or power—whether on a small domestic or on a larger scale—the time comes when we start to mislay or shed them. We lose those we have loved, find that our knowledge or skills become obsolete, or our memories unsure. Our reputation, our possessions, our power may slip away from us. Saint John of the Cross, writing *The Dark Night of the Soul*, saw God's action in all this: as ego recedes, God can fill our hearts.

Trop est avare á qui Dieu ne suffit. (You're too greedy if God is not enough for you.)

The Presence of God

What is present to me is what has a hold on my becoming.
I reflect on the presence of God always there in love,
amidst the many things that have a hold on me.
I pause and pray that I may let God
affect my becoming in this precise moment.

Freedom

There are very few people
who realize what God would make of them
if they abandoned themselves into his hands,
and let themselves be formed by his grace. (St. Ignatius)
I ask for the grace to trust myself totally to God's love.

Consciousness

In the presence of my loving Creator,
I look honestly at my feelings over the last day,
the highs, the lows, and the level ground.
Can I see where the Lord has been present?

The Word

God speaks to each one of us individually. I need to listen to what he is saying to me. (Please turn to your scripture on the following pages. Inspiration points are there should you need them. When you are ready, return here to continue.)

Conversation

What is stirring in me as I pray?
Am I consoled, troubled, left cold?
I imagine Jesus himself standing or sitting at my side,
and share my feelings with him.

Conclusion

Glory be to the Father, and to the Son, and to the Holy Spirit,
As it was in the beginning, is now, and ever shall be,
World without end. Amen

Sunday 10th July, Fifteenth Sunday in Ordinary Time — Matthew 13:3–9

And Jesus told them many things in parables, saying: "Listen! A sower went out to sow. And as he sowed, some seeds fell on the path, and the birds came and ate them up. Other seeds fell on rocky ground, where they did not have much soil, and they sprang up quickly, since they had no depth of soil. But when the sun rose, they were scorched; and since they had no root, they withered away. Other seeds fell among thorns, and the thorns grew up and choked them. Other seeds fell on good soil and brought forth grain, some a hundredfold, some sixty, some thirty. Let anyone with ears listen!"

- Each time we pray, the seeds of God's word and love are scattered. Each time we speak the kind word, do a kind deed, care for others in any way, the seed is bearing fruit. Our heart is the soil. Like a varied garden, the heart is many-sided. Our hurts, bitterness, and sins weaken and destroy good soil.
- God is the one who purifies the heart so that the Word of God takes effect.

Monday 11th July, St. Benedict — Matthew 19:27–29

Then Peter said in reply, "Look, we have left everything and followed you. What then will we have?" Jesus said to them, "Truly I tell you, at the renewal of all things, when the Son of Man is seated on the throne of his glory, you who have followed me will also sit on twelve thrones, judging the twelve tribes of Israel. And everyone who has left houses or brothers or sisters or father or mother or children or fields, for my name's sake, will receive a hundredfold, and will inherit eternal life."

- Jesus has turned upside down what the disciples were raised to believe, that wealth is a sign of God's favour.
- All of us, rich and poor, are called to detach ourselves from the goods of this earth. In light of this reversal we can understand the reward of the kingdom that Jesus promises. God alone saves.

Tuesday 12th July **Matthew 11:20–24**

Then Jesus began to reproach the cities in which most of his deeds of power had been done, because they did not repent. "Woe to you, Chorazin! Woe to you, Bethsaida! For if the deeds of power done in you had been done in Tyre and Sidon, they would have repented long ago in sackcloth and ashes. But I tell you, on the day of judgment it will be more tolerable for Tyre and Sidon than for you. And you, Capernaum, will you be exalted to heaven? No, you will be brought down to Hades. For if the deeds of power done in you had been done in Sodom, it would have remained until this day. But I tell you that on the day of judgment it will be more tolerable for the land of Sodom than for you."

- Jesus seems to expect results in his mission. So there is condemnation for the pride and arrogance which blocks people from hearing him.
- To human weakness and struggle Jesus shows compassion and a divine breadth of understanding; to pride and hypocrisy he speaks strongly, as in these few words to the cities he knew well.

Wednesday 13th July **Matthew 11:25–27**

At that time Jesus said, "I thank you, Father, Lord of heaven and earth, because you have hidden these things from the wise and the intelligent and have revealed them to infants; yes, Father, for such was your gracious will. All things have been handed over to me by my Father; and no one knows the Son except the

Father, and no one knows the Father except the Son and anyone to whom the Son chooses to reveal him."

- We have just read Jesus' hard words to the cities which rejected him. Now he turns to the ones who do accept him. They are the people of openness, sincerity, and humility—the "little ones."
- No matter what our learning, we are all children of the Father and students of Jesus always. Prayer can bring the truths of faith and life from the head to the heart; prayer opens the heart not only to God, but to all we meet.

Thursday 14th July **Matthew 11:28–30**

Jesus said, "Come to me, all you that are weary and are carrying heavy burdens, and I will give you rest. Take my yoke upon you, and learn from me; for I am gentle and humble in heart, and you will find rest for your souls. For my yoke is easy, and my burden is light."

- Jesus' invitation to "rest" is for this life and the next. Time spent with him refreshes the soul, mind, and body. Time spent in the company of Jesus is a time of well being.
- The psalms express our security: "my body and soul shall rest in safety" (Psalm 15). The invitation is for today and for eternity.

Friday 15th July **Matthew 12:1–8**

At that time Jesus went through the grainfields on the sabbath; his disciples were hungry, and they began to pluck heads of grain and to eat. When the Pharisees saw it, they said to him, "Look, your disciples are doing what is not lawful to do on the sabbath." He said to them, "Have you not read what David did when he and his companions were hungry? He entered the house of God and ate the bread of the Presence, which it was not lawful for him or his companions to eat, but only for the priests.

Or have you not read in the law that on the sabbath the priests in the temple break the sabbath and yet are guiltless? I tell you, something greater than the temple is here. But if you had known what this means, 'I desire mercy and not sacrifice,' you would not have condemned the guiltless. For the Son of Man is lord of the sabbath."

- Jesus highlights that a compassionate response to hunger and human need takes precedence over scrupulous observance of a ritual or a law. While the temple and all intuitional trappings of the gospel may have their relative importance, there are higher concerns.
- Jesus states that God—in this case, himself—and God's concerns are of higher value.

Saturday 16th July **Matthew 12:14–21**

But the Pharisees went out and conspired against him, how to destroy him. When Jesus became aware of this, he departed. Many crowds followed him, and he cured all of them, and he ordered them not to make him known. This was to fulfill what had been spoken through the prophet Isaiah: "Here is my servant, whom I have chosen, my beloved, with whom my soul is well pleased. I will put my Spirit upon him, and he will proclaim justice to the Gentiles. He will not wrangle or cry aloud, nor will anyone hear his voice in the streets. He will not break a bruised reed or quench a smoldering wick until he brings justice to victory. And in his name the Gentiles will hope."

- Jesus will always intervene on behalf of the weak, and do so in a way that is sensitive to them and takes the limelight off him. Justice is a major concern of Jesus, and this concern with justice will bring hope to all people.
- In prayer we often find the conviction and strength to do the work of justice.

july 17–23

Something to think and pray about each day this week:

The Unknown Ones

For a mother with a baby, the work is endless, respecting neither day nor night nor timetables. But even a mother's work seems easy compared with what is required to care for the old and incontinent. A mother is handling the precious, promising body of her baby. She is rewarded at least with trust and occasional smiles. But when we are old, our bodies fall apart, our controls slip and we are not easy to help. We are proud, ashamed, and angry at being so reduced. Smiles do not come easily. Yet across every country there are wives, husbands, and other carers whose daily existence centres round cleaning up for their loved ones. "Your Father who sees in secret will reward you" (Matthew 6:6).

It is an unfashionable doctrine. Thomas à Kempis (remember *The Imitation of Christ*?), urged us to, "Enjoy being unknown and regarded as nothing." He was praising the ability to persist through tedium, to survive without the oxygen of recognition, praise, and stroking, to do some good things every day that are seen only by God. Carers are among the world's most heroic people.

The Presence of God

Jesus waits silent and unseen to come into my heart.
I will respond to his call.
He comes with his infinite power and love
May I be filled with joy in his presence.

Freedom

A thick and shapeless tree-trunk would never believe
that it could become a statue, admired as a miracle of sculpture,
and would never submit itself to the chisel of the sculptor,
who sees by her genius what she can make of it. (St. Ignatius)
I ask for the grace to let myself be shaped by my loving Creator.

Consciousness

Knowing that God loves me unconditionally,
I look honestly over the last day, its events and my feelings.
Do I have something to be grateful for? Then I give thanks.
Is there something I am sorry for? Then I ask forgiveness.

The Word

I read the Word of God slowly, a few times over, and I listen to what God is saying to me. (Please turn to your scripture on the following pages. Inspiration points are there should you need them. When you are ready, return here to continue.)

Conversation

Do I notice myself reacting as I pray with the Word of God?
Do I feel challenged, comforted, angry?
Imagining Jesus sitting or standing by me,
I speak out my feelings, as one trusted friend to another.

Conclusion

Glory be to the Father, and to the Son, and to the Holy Spirit,
As it was in the beginning, is now, and ever shall be,
World without end. Amen

Sunday 17th July,
Sixteenth Sunday in Ordinary Time **Matthew 13:24–30**

Jesus put before them another parable: "The kingdom of heaven may be compared to someone who sowed good seed in his field; but while everybody was asleep, an enemy came and sowed weeds among the wheat, and then went away. So when the plants came up and bore grain, then the weeds appeared as well. And the slaves of the householder came and said to him, 'Master, did you not sow good seed in your field? Where, then, did these weeds come from?' He answered, 'An enemy has done this.' The slaves said to him, 'Then do you want us to go and gather them?' But he replied, 'No; for in gathering the weeds you would uproot the wheat along with them. Let both of them grow together until the harvest; and at harvest time I will tell the reapers, Collect the weeds first and bind them in bundles to be burned, but gather the wheat into my barn.'"

- We had a fellow on a team once who was reluctant to pass the ball—he liked to score the goals himself. When he did pass, we often scored; other times he didn't pass, and he didn't score. We took the good with the bad. Nothing is perfect.
- Jesus seems to be saying the same about the growth of the kingdom of God. Isn't it the same with all of us? There is a bit of the best in the worst of us and a bit of the worst in the best. Holiness is closeness to God, not perfection.

Monday 18th July **Matthew 12:38–42**

Then some of the scribes and Pharisees said to him, "Teacher, we wish to see a sign from you." But he answered them, "An evil and adulterous generation asks for a sign, but no sign will be given to it except the sign of the prophet Jonah. For just as Jonah was three days and three nights in the belly of the sea monster, so for three days and three nights the Son of Man will be in the heart of the earth. The people of Nineveh will rise up at the judgment with this generation and condemn it, because they repented at the proclamation of Jonah, and see, something greater than Jonah is here! The queen of the South will rise up at the judgment with this generation and condemn it, because she came from the ends of the earth to listen to the wisdom of Solomon, and see, something greater than Solomon is here!"

- When we hear of Jonah, we remember that he was a reluctant prophet. He was the one who resisted the call of the Lord to speak to the Gentiles, to enter into the world of the other, the foreigner, the ones who were not like him. But eventually he did it—he encountered the world of the other.
- Jesus encounters the other—he is one whose heart, words, love, and truth are for all.

Tuesday 19th July **Matthew 12:46–50**

While he was still speaking to the crowds, his mother and his brothers were standing outside, wanting to speak to him. Someone told him, "Look, your mother and your brothers are standing outside, wanting to speak to you." But to the one who had told him this, Jesus replied, "Who is my mother, and who are my brothers?" And pointing to his disciples, he said, "Here are my mother and my brothers! For whoever does the will of my Father in heaven is my brother and sister and mother."

- I wonder, what did his mother and family want to speak to him about? The evidence is that they were coming from home to take him back there. Jesus' teachings and challenges to established religion were embarrassing his family.
- His way of life would lead him into opposition with his own family, but also into fellowship with a new family.

Wednesday 20th July **Psalm 78:18–20**

They tested God in their heart by demanding the food they craved. They spoke against God, saying, "Can God spread a table in the wilderness?" Yet he commanded the skies above, and opened the doors of heaven; he rained down on them manna to eat, and gave them the grain of heaven.

- This psalm recalls Exodus 16, where the people complained about God even though they were fed manna and quail in the desert.
- When I speak to the Lord, do I demand what I want, and then complain when I don't receive it? Do I want a god in my own image, or do I want to know God?

Thursday 21st July **Matthew 13:10–13**

Then the disciples came and asked Jesus, "Why do you speak to them in parables?" He answered, "To you it has been given to know the secrets of the kingdom of heaven, but to them it has not been given. For to those who have, more will be given, and they will have an abundance; but from those who have nothing, even what they have will be taken away. The reason I speak to them in parables is that 'seeing they do not perceive, and hearing they do not listen, nor do they understand.'"

- The events of Jesus' ministry seem to go over the heads of some bystanders. They do not believe. So he will tell them stories that they might see behind the words to the true meaning of those stories.
- Every parable Jesus tells will throw some light on God, the world, and the self. Let me sit quietly with these stories.

Friday 22nd July,
St. Mary Magdalene **2 Corinthians 5:14–17**

For the love of Christ urges us on, because we are convinced that one has died for all; therefore all have died. And he died for all, so that those who live might live no longer for themselves, but for him who died and was raised for them. From now on, therefore, we regard no one from a human point of view; even though we once knew Christ from a human point of view, we know him no longer in that way. So if anyone is in Christ, there is a new creation: everything old has passed away; see, everything has become new!

- Paul reminds us that Christ's love for us leads us to new life, to a new creation: "everything has become new!"
- We are all invited to be "in Christ," to be God's children. How am I responding?

Saturday 23rd July,
St. Bridget **Galatians 2:19–20**

I have been crucified with Christ; and it is no longer I who live, but it is Christ who lives in me. And the life I now live in the flesh I live by faith in the Son of God, who loved me and gave himself for me.

- Teach me, Lord Jesus, what it is to live in you, and for you to live in me. It means being in love with you, being at ease with you, finding my strength in you, and being ready, when questioned, to explain to others what you are in my life.

july 24–30

Something to think and pray about each day this week:

God at Work

Saint Ignatius, whose feast is celebrated on 31 July, spoke of God dwelling and at work in all creatures, in all plant and animal life, and in us. The God of Ignatian spirituality is the God who "acts in the manner of one who is working." In a church in Germany there is a life-size crucifix, ordinary except for the fact that—a casualty of war—the body of Jesus has no arms. The parishioners decided to leave the crucifix in that truncated state as a reminder to onlookers that they are to become Christ's arms. God works through us.

The Presence of God
As I sit here, the beating of my heart,
the ebb and flow of my breathing, the movements of my mind
are all signs of God's ongoing creation of me.
I pause for a moment, and become aware
of this presence of God within me.

Freedom
I ask for the grace
to let go of my own concerns
and be open to what God is asking of me,
to let myself be guided and formed by my loving Creator.

Consciousness
How do I find myself today?
Where am I with God? With others?
Do I have something to be grateful for? Then I give thanks.
Is there something I am sorry for? Then I ask forgiveness.

The Word
I take my time to read the Word of God, slowly, a few times, allowing myself to dwell on anything that strikes me. (Please turn to your scripture on the following pages. Inspiration points are there should you need them. When you are ready, return here to continue.)

Conversation
Remembering that I am still in God's presence,
I imagine Jesus himself standing or sitting beside me,
and say whatever is on my mind, whatever is in my heart,
speaking as one friend to another.

Conclusion
Glory be to the Father, and to the Son, and to the Holy Spirit,
As it was in the beginning, is now, and ever shall be,
World without end. Amen

Sunday 24th July,
Seventeenth Sunday in Ordinary Time Matthew 13:44–46

Jesus said to the disciples, "The kingdom of heaven is like treasure hidden in a field, which someone found and hid; then in his joy he goes and sells all that he has and buys that field. Again, the kingdom of heaven is like a merchant in search of fine pearls; on finding one pearl of great value, he went and sold all that he had and bought it."

- Jesus' message is that the kingdom of God has come among us now. In him, God is very close to the world and to us.
- The marks of this kingdom are qualities like compassion, justice, love, mercy, peace of mind and heart, closeness to God. These are treasures of life; to live by them, we will give up other concerns.

Monday 25th July,
St. James, Apostle Matthew 20:20–23

Then the mother of the sons of Zebedee came to him with her sons, and kneeling before him, she asked a favor of him. And he said to her, "What do you want?" She said to him, "Declare that these two sons of mine will sit, one at your right hand and one at your left, in your kingdom." But Jesus answered, "You do not know what you are asking. Are you able to drink the cup that I am about to drink?" They said to him, "We are able." He said to them, "You will indeed drink my cup, but to sit at my right hand and at my left, this is not mine to grant, but it is for those for whom it has been prepared by my Father."

- The life and convictions of Jesus would lead him to drink the bitter cup of rejection, suffering, and death. Being close to him would mean something like this for his followers. He often reminded them of this.
- To live out the gospel makes its own demands on everyone's life. Prayer is a way of offering ourselves to share in this side of Jesus' life now and to meet the challenges of discipleship.

Tuesday 26th July **Matthew 13:36–43**

His disciples approached Jesus, saying, "Explain to us the parable of the weeds of the field." He answered, "The one who sows the good seed is the Son of Man; the field is the world, and the good seed are the children of the kingdom; the weeds are the children of the evil one, and the enemy who sowed them is the devil; the harvest is the end of the age, and the reapers are angels. Just as the weeds are collected and burned up with fire, so will it be at the end of the age. The Son of Man will send his angels, and they will collect out of his kingdom all causes of sin and all evildoers, and they will throw them into the furnace of fire, where there will be weeping and gnashing of teeth. Then the righteous will shine like the sun in the kingdom of their Father. Let anyone with ears listen!"

- Weeds and wheat all grow together and, at the harvest, are separated. In each of us strengths and weaknesses of personality exist together, as do our goodness and faults.
- God sees us whole, and looks on the total field. All are growing together and too much emphasis on faults means we may forget our goodness. Let us offer the good to God for strengthening, and what is weak for healing and forgiveness.

Wednesday 27th July **Matthew 13:44**

Jesus said to the disciples, "The kingdom of heaven is like treasure hidden in a field, which someone found and hid; then in his joy he goes and sells all that he has and buys that field."

- We treasure many things in life. We treasure some more than others. Our faith and love of God, the love of others and our care for them—these are treasures.
- Treasures give us joy and also challenge us to move out of narrow self-concern. Let us be grateful for what we really value in life, and ask God that we value highly our relationship with him.

Thursday 28th July **Matthew 13:47–53**

Jesus said, "Again, the kingdom of heaven is like a net that was thrown into the sea and caught fish of every kind; when it was full, they drew it ashore, sat down, and put the good into baskets but threw out the bad. So it will be at the end of the age. The angels will come out and separate the evil from the righteous and throw them into the furnace of fire, where there will be weeping and gnashing of teeth. Have you understood all this?" They answered, "Yes." And he said to them, "Therefore every scribe who has been trained for the kingdom of heaven is like the master of a household who brings out of his treasure what is new and what is old."

- There's a mixture of good and bad in all of us. The Church and our local communities are a mixture of good and bad also.
- We simply pray to respond to goodness in our desires and in our activities, and ask the forgiveness and help of Jesus where we fail.

Friday 29th July **Matthew 13:54–58**

Jesus came to his home town and began to teach the people in their synagogue, so that they were astounded and said, "Where did this man get this wisdom and these deeds of power? Is not this the carpenter's son? Is not his mother called Mary? And are not his brothers James and Joseph and Simon and Judas? And are not all his sisters with us? Where then did this man get all this?" And they took offense at him. But Jesus said to them, "Prophets are not without honor except in their own country and in their own house." And he did not do many deeds of power there, because of their unbelief.

- It is baffling to record that, for a period of thirty years, the Son of Man did not appear to be anything other than a man. Once people began to glimpse his divinity, like all creatures, Christ is transformed by the person who is attracted to him.
- Lord, open my eyes to see your true face.

Saturday 30th July **Matthew 14:1–12**

At that time Herod the ruler heard reports about Jesus; and he said to his servants, "This is John the Baptist; he has been raised from the dead, and for this reason these powers are at work in him." For Herod had arrested John, bound him, and put him in prison on account of Herodias, his brother Philip's wife, because John had been telling him, "It is not lawful for you to have her." Though Herod wanted to put him to death, he feared the crowd, because they regarded him as a prophet. But when Herod's birthday came, the daughter of Herodias danced before the company, and she pleased Herod so much that he promised on oath to grant her whatever she might ask. Prompted by her mother, she said, "Give me the head of John the Baptist here on a platter." The king was grieved, yet out of regard for his oaths and for the guests, he commanded it to be given; he sent and had John beheaded in the prison. The head was brought on a platter and given to the girl, who brought it to her mother. His disciples came and took the body and buried it; then they went and told Jesus.

- Death will be the fate of Jesus. In death and in life Jesus and the Baptist are intimately linked. Beheading, like crucifixion, was a shameful public death, a calculated insult.
- A shared meal that would be Jesus' gift to his followers, can also be the meal in which evil is done. The Baptist's life brought him often into high contrasts of good and evil, and he was praised always by Jesus—"no greater has been born of woman than John" (Matthew 11:11).

july 31–august 6

Something to think and pray about each day this week:

The Visible Sign

Some people bless themselves—make the Sign of the Cross—when they pass a church. What does it mean? Perhaps only God knows. It is a prayer, an invocation, a visible act of faith, a public yet personal gesture as you walk, cycle, bus, or drive past "God's house." It is a reminder of how precious and universal that gesture is: to bless yourself in the name of the Father and of the Son and of the Holy Spirit.

You see people blessing themselves in all sorts of situations: absent-mindedly on the way into church; solemnly at the end of Mass; in thankful delight, as with sports competitors; poignantly, in the case of mourners at a grave. In extreme sickness, when the brain can no longer form words and the only way we can turn to God may be with our feeble fingers, forming a cross. This sign can grow hurried and thoughtless through custom, but in moments of crisis and deep emotion, there are few gestures as rich in meaning as blessing ourselves. Perhaps this is the meaning today of Jesus' command. "Let your light shine before all . . ." Our Lord's words are not about coercing other people into religion but about doing good in a visible way "so that people, seeing your good works, may glorify your Father in heaven" (Matthew 5:16).

The Presence of God
I pause for a moment and reflect on God's life-giving presence in every part of my body, in everything around me, in the whole of my life.

Freedom
I ask for the grace to believe
in what I could be and do
if I only allowed God, my loving Creator,
to continue to create me, guide me and shape me.

Consciousness
In God's loving presence I unwind the past day,
starting from now and looking back, moment by moment.
I gather in all the goodness and light, in gratitude.
I attend to the shadows and what they say to me,
seeking healing, courage, forgiveness.

The Word
God speaks to each one of us individually. I need to listen to what he is saying to me. (Please turn to your scripture on the following pages. Inspiration points are there should you need them. When you are ready, return here to continue.)

Conversation
How has God's Word moved me? Has it left me cold?
Has it consoled me or moved me to act in a new way?
I imagine Jesus standing or sitting beside me,
I turn and share my feelings with him.

Conclusion
Glory be to the Father, and to the Son, and to the Holy Spirit,
As it was in the beginning, is now, and ever shall be,
World without end. Amen

Sunday 31st July,
Eighteenth Sunday in Ordinary Time Matthew 14:13–21

Now when Jesus heard of the death of John the Baptist, he withdrew from there in a boat to a deserted place by himself. But when the crowds heard it, they followed him on foot from the towns. When he went ashore, he saw a great crowd; and he had compassion for them and cured their sick. When it was evening, the disciples came to him and said, "This is a deserted place, and the hour is now late; send the crowds away so that they may go into the villages and buy food for themselves." Jesus said to them, "They need not go away; you give them something to eat." They replied, "We have nothing here but five loaves and two fish." And he said, "Bring them here to me." Then he ordered the crowds to sit down on the grass. Taking the five loaves and the two fish, he looked up to heaven, and blessed and broke the loaves, and gave them to the disciples, and the disciples gave them to the crowds. And all ate and were filled; and they took up what was left over of the broken pieces, twelve baskets full. And those who ate were about five thousand men, besides women and children.

- Think of the food left over. The twelve baskets seem a lot and we're not told what happened to them. The food had been the food of the poor—barley bread and sardines.
- In Jesus' mind, this meal feeds us today. Enough was left over to feed the souls of the world for all time. The apostles who fed the crowd still feed us today in the word of Jesus and in the Eucharist, and each time we receive the bread of the Eucharist.

Monday 1st August **Matthew 14:22–27**

Jesus made the disciples get into the boat and go on ahead to the other side, while he dismissed the crowds. And after he had dismissed the crowds, he went up the mountain by himself to pray. When evening came, he was there alone, but by this time the boat, battered by the waves, was far from the land, for the wind was against them. And early in the morning he came walking toward them on the sea. But when the disciples saw him walking on the sea, they were terrified, saying, "It is a ghost!" And they cried out in fear. But immediately Jesus spoke to them and said, "Take heart, it is I; do not be afraid."

- What causes deep darkness in life may not go away—the darkness of poor self-esteem, long-term illness, bereavement. Jesus may seem asleep. But in the friendship and love of God we find we can survive and even grow through them.
- The disciples found calm when they were in the middle of this storm. We will also find Jesus in the middle of our storms. We sit with him in prayer and let him know how we are, warts and all, and just allow his calm to come over us.

Tuesday 2nd August **Matthew 15:1–2, 10–14**

Then Pharisees and scribes came to Jesus from Jerusalem and said, "Why do your disciples break the tradition of the elders? For they do not wash their hands before they eat." Then he called the crowd to him and said to them, "Listen and understand: it is not what goes into the mouth that defiles a person, but it is what comes out of the mouth that defiles." Then the disciples approached and said to him, "Do you know that the Pharisees took offence when they heard what you said?" He answered, "Every plant that my heavenly Father has not planted will be uprooted.

Let them alone; they are blind guides of the blind. And if one blind person guides another, both will fall into a pit."

- These are harsh words about the Pharisees, who were, after all, the upholders of religion and law. They were not "bad people." Somehow they were righteous, moral, people of high standards.
- But Jesus always seems to look farther than people do; he looks to the heart. He looks to see if we nourish what his Father plants in us—care, compassion, openness, and union with the Father. On this we judge ourselves and others, if we judge at all.

Wednesday 3rd August **Matthew 15:21–28**

Jesus left that place and went away to the district of Tyre and Sidon. Just then a Canaanite woman from that region came out and started shouting, "Have mercy on me, Lord, Son of David; my daughter is tormented by a demon." But he did not answer her at all. And his disciples came and urged him, saying, "Send her away, for she keeps shouting after us." He answered, "I was sent only to the lost sheep of the house of Israel." But she came and knelt before him, saying, "Lord, help me." He answered, "It is not fair to take the children's food and throw it to the dogs." She said, "Yes, Lord, yet even the dogs eat the crumbs that fall from their masters' table." Then Jesus answered her, "Woman, great is your faith! Let it be done for you as you wish." And her daughter was healed instantly.

- "Dogs" was a name for the Gentiles—and in this story the woman plays on its meaning to get Jesus to feed the dogs and, in this way, care for her.
- Maybe this is a "change moment" for Jesus when he realizes through this poor woman that he is sent not only to his own lost ones; he realizes his mission is for the whole world.

Thursday 4th August **Psalm 95:1–2, 6**

O come, let us sing to the Lord; let us make a joyful noise to the rock of our salvation! Let us come into his presence with thanksgiving; let us make a joyful noise to him with songs of praise! O come, let us worship and bow down, let us kneel before the Lord, our Maker!

- Let me praise the Lord with joy for all that I receive each day.

Friday 5th August **Matthew 16:24–28**

Then Jesus told his disciples, "If any want to become my followers, let them deny themselves and take up their cross and follow me. For those who want to save their life will lose it, and those who lose their life for my sake will find it. For what will it profit them if they gain the whole world but forfeit their life? Or what will they give in return for their life? For the Son of Man is to come with his angels in the glory of his Father, and then he will repay everyone for what has been done. Truly I tell you, there are some standing here who will not taste death before they see the Son of Man coming in his kingdom."

- We look at the life of Jesus to understand the mystery of losing life. He lost it all, his last breath given away to God. But in losing his life in love he lost nothing worth keeping! All that is given in love is never lost; even life itself is raised in joy and beauty for the next generations.
- Think of Oscar Romero, killed at the altar in El Salvador more than thirty years ago. Has he ever died? He lives on in love and his courage remains.

Saturday 6th August,
Transfiguration of the Lord **Matthew 17:1–9**

Six days later, Jesus took with him Peter and James and his brother John and led them up a high mountain, by themselves. And he was transfigured before them, and his face shone like the sun, and his clothes became dazzling white. Suddenly there appeared to them Moses and Elijah, talking with him. Then Peter said to Jesus, "Lord, it is good for us to be here; if you wish, I will make three dwellings here, one for you, one for Moses, and one for Elijah." While he was still speaking, suddenly a bright cloud overshadowed them, and from the cloud a voice said, "This is my Son, the Beloved; with him I am well pleased; listen to him!" When the disciples heard this, they fell to the ground and were overcome by fear. But Jesus came and touched them, saying, "Get up and do not be afraid." And when they looked up, they saw no one except Jesus himself alone. As they were coming down the mountain, Jesus ordered them, "Tell no one about the vision until after the Son of Man has been raised from the dead."

- They saw him then as they had never seen him before. They were told that he is the one who is to come. They knew now they would listen to him, that his words were to be the rock of life.
- For the apostles, their faith was confirmed on this mount of Transfiguration. Prayer moments may often be transfiguration moments when we glimpse the beauty of Jesus Christ and we commit ourselves to "listen to him" as God invites.

august 7–13

Something to think and pray about each day this week:

Sharing with Jesus

Since 2008 and 2009, the petitions coming in to the Chapel of Intentions on the Sacred Space website have grown in intensity. Across the world people are feeling the general unease and insecurity that flow through after great economic upheavals, feelings reinforced by continuing military conflicts and natural disasters. Blame for serious financial mismanagement has been bandied about freely, and many people still feel angry and powerless, their future uncertain or even in tatters.

In times like these it can be reassuring to be on the Christian journey. No situation is more essentially Christ-like than that of the suffering victim, humiliated and helpless. This is a demanding prayer that costs: to look at Jesus on the Cross and say, "Thank you, Lord, for giving me a taste of what you went through for us."

The Presence of God

The world is charged with the grandeur of God. (Gerard Manley Hopkins)
I dwell for a moment on the presence of God
around me, in every part of my body,
and deep within my being.

Freedom

In these days, God taught me
as a schoolteacher teaches a pupil. (St. Ignatius)
I remind myself that there are things God has to teach me yet,
and ask for the grace to hear them and let them change me.

Consciousness

Help me, Lord, to be more conscious of your presence.
Teach me to recognize your presence in others.
Fill my heart with gratitude for the times your love
has been shown to me through the care of others.

The Word

I read the Word of God slowly, a few times over, and I listen to what God is saying to me. (Please turn to your scripture on the following pages. Inspiration points are there should you need them. When you are ready, return here to continue.)

Conversation

What feelings are rising in me
as I pray and reflect on God's Word?
I imagine Jesus himself sitting or standing beside me,
and open my heart to him.

Conclusion

Glory be to the Father, and to the Son, and to the Holy Spirit,
As it was in the beginning, is now, and ever shall be,
World without end. Amen

Sunday 7th August,
Nineteenth Sunday in Ordinary Time Matthew 14:28–33

Peter answered Jesus, "Lord, if it is you, command me to come to you on the water." He said, "Come." So Peter got out of the boat, started walking on the water, and came towards Jesus. But when he noticed the strong wind, he became frightened, and beginning to sink, he cried out, "Lord, save me!" Jesus immediately reached out his hand and caught him, saying to him, "You of little faith, why did you doubt?" When they got into the boat, the wind ceased. And those in the boat worshipped him, saying, "Truly you are the Son of God."

- The hand of God is a human hand. Jesus reaches out to guide us, steady us, support us—all the things a touch of the hand can do. Peter found that also in Jesus; when he took his eyes off the Lord on the water, he began to sink. The Lord then held him close.
- Like Peter, we are always walking on water, putting our trust in Jesus, especially in the most frightening times of life.
- At times we can do nothing for those we love except place them in the hand of God, knowing that God loves them even more than we do.

Monday 8th August,
St. Mary MacKillop Matthew 17:22–23

As they were gathering in Galilee, Jesus said to the disciples, "The Son of Man is going to be betrayed into human hands, and they will kill him, and on the third day he will be raised." And they were greatly distressed.

- This is plain language from Jesus, and distressing for the twelve; they now knew what was coming—for Jesus, and for them. Yet still they went on.

- How do I respond to this? Let me share my fears with the Lord who stands alongside me.

Tuesday 9th August **Matthew 18:1–5, 10, 12–14**

At that time the disciples came to Jesus and asked, "Who is the greatest in the kingdom of heaven?" He called a child, whom he put among them, and said, "Truly I tell you, unless you change and become like children, you will never enter the kingdom of heaven. Whoever becomes humble like this child is the greatest in the kingdom of heaven. Whoever welcomes one such child in my name welcomes me. Take care that you do not despise one of these little ones; for, I tell you, in heaven their angels continually see the face of my Father in heaven. What do you think? If a shepherd has a hundred sheep, and one of them has gone astray, does he not leave the ninety-nine on the mountains and go in search of the one that went astray? And if he finds it, truly I tell you, he rejoices over it more than over the ninety-nine that never went astray. So it is not the will of your Father in heaven that one of these little ones should be lost."

- Jesus valued the lost and the little—the child was not valued much in his culture; and who would want to search for one lost sheep and risk losing the ninety-nine?
- A constant theme of Jesus' preaching and of his life was the importance of the little one and the lost one. That's why he looks for you and me!

Wednesday 10th August,
St. Lawrence **John 12:24–26**

Very truly, I tell you, unless a grain of wheat falls into the earth and dies, it remains just a single grain; but if it dies, it bears much fruit. Those who love their life lose it, and those who hate their life in this world will keep it for eternal life. Whoever serves me must follow me, and where I am, there will my servant be also. Whoever serves me, the Father will honor.

- Serving Jesus involves a certain losing of our ambitions and wishes. Saints converted much ordinary ambition for success, love, and health into ambition for proclaiming and living out the values of the gospel and of the kingdom of God.
- When anything in us dies in the service of God, something better is born.

Thursday 11th August **Matthew 18:21–22**

Then Peter came and said to him, "Lord, if another member of the church sins against me, how often should I forgive? As many as seven times?" Jesus said to him, "Not seven times, but, I tell you, seventy-seven times."

- The Lord is like that with us: totally forgiving, and not remembering our sins. He does expect that we try to forgive.
- Forgiveness comes slowly—one beginning is to pray for someone who hurt us badly. That is a gift for the person. "Forgive us our sins, as we (try to) forgive those who sin against us."

Friday 12th August **Matthew 19:3–11**

Some Pharisees came to him, and to test him they asked, "Is it lawful for a man to divorce his wife for any cause?" He answered, "Have you not read that the one who made them at the beginning 'made them male and female,' and said, 'For this reason a man shall leave his father and mother and be joined to his wife, and the two shall become one flesh'? So they are no longer two, but one flesh. Therefore what God has joined together, let no one separate." They said to him, "Why then did Moses command us to give a certificate of dismissal and to divorce her?" He said to them, "It was because you were so hard-hearted that

Moses allowed you to divorce your wives, but at the beginning it was not so. And I say to you, whoever divorces his wife, except for unchastity, and marries another commits adultery." His disciples said to him, "If such is the case of a man with his wife, it is better not to marry." But he said to them, "Not everyone can accept this teaching, but only those to whom it is given."

- God's desire is for man and woman to come together in body, mind, and soul. In marriage, the two are deeply united.
- Jesus doesn't seem to give a last word on marriage and unfaithfulness here. He looks with compassion. His heart reaches out to all who are in any way connected with marital difficulties and break-up. His call is for us to reach out also, in personal relations and in the teachings and proposals of the Church.

Saturday 13th August **Matthew 19:13–15**

Then little children were being brought to Jesus in order that he might lay his hands on them and pray. The disciples spoke sternly to those who brought them; but Jesus said, "Let the little children come to me, and do not stop them; for it is to such as these that the kingdom of heaven belongs." And he laid his hands on them and went on his way.

- By insisting that children had a central place in the community, Jesus was confronting his followers and the onlookers. He sealed his words with his blessing.
- We have much to learn from children about the true nature of the kingdom.

august 14–20

Something to think and pray about each day this week:

Stepping Up

The Canaanite woman in Matthew 15:21 is an unexpected model of prayer: she argues and she persists. She is not the first biblical figure to argue with the Lord: Genesis and Exodus describe Abraham and Moses debating with God. The Canaanite woman is different from the scribes who tried to trap Jesus with arguments. She is begging for her daughter. At first Jesus does not answer her at all. It would have been easy for her to give up in bitterness. She is thrice handicapped: a woman alone in a man's world; a Gentile and therefore unclean; a parent with an afflicted daughter. But in spite of Jesus' silence she trusts him, keeps at him, and bests him in debate. There is something teasing and humorous about Jesus' reply to her. He enjoys that Semitic style of thrust and counter. His first response is what we often experience in prayer: nothing. But a mother seeking health for her child is not easily deterred, and Jesus rewards her persistence. We can imagine him smiling as he blesses her.

Lord, I need to remember this. When I want something badly, I will keep after you. May I never be discouraged by your silence.

The Presence of God

As I sit here, God is present,
breathing life into me and into everything around me.
For a few moments, I sit silently,
and become aware of God's loving presence.

Freedom

If God were trying to tell me something, would I know?
If God were reassuring me or challenging me, would I notice?
I ask for the grace to be free of my own preoccupations
and open to what God may be saying to me.

Consciousness

How am I really feeling? Light-hearted? Heavy-hearted?
I may be very much at peace, happy to be here.
Equally, I may be frustrated, worried, or angry.
I acknowledge how I really am. It is the real me that the Lord loves.

The Word

I take my time to read the Word of God, slowly, a few times, allowing myself to dwell on anything that strikes me. (Please turn to your scripture on the following pages. Inspiration points are there should you need them. When you are ready, return here to continue.)

Conversation

What is stirring in me as I pray?
Am I consoled, troubled, left cold?
I imagine Jesus himself standing or sitting at my side,
and share my feelings with him.

Conclusion

Glory be to the Father, and to the Son, and to the Holy Spirit,
As it was in the beginning, is now, and ever shall be,
World without end. Amen

Sunday 14th August,
Twentieth Sunday in Ordinary Time **Matthew 15:21–28**

Jesus left that place and went away to the district of Tyre and Sidon. Just then a Canaanite woman from that region came out and started shouting, "Have mercy on me, Lord, Son of David; my daughter is tormented by a demon." But he did not answer her at all. And his disciples came and urged him, saying, "Send her away, for she keeps shouting after us." He answered, "I was sent only to the lost sheep of the house of Israel." But she came and knelt before him, saying, "Lord, help me." He answered, "It is not fair to take the children's food and throw it to the dogs." She said, "Yes, Lord, yet even the dogs eat the crumbs that fall from their masters' table." Then Jesus answered her, "Woman, great is your faith! Let it be done for you as you wish." And her daughter was healed instantly.

- We admire the parent who really fights for their child. They won't take no for an answer. The woman in the gospel is like that. She has a sick child and desperately wants healing.
- Who would not want the same? She almost forces Jesus into curing her little daughter. Her persistence is an effect of her faith, and because of her faith Jesus cures her child.

Monday 15th August,
Assumption of the Virgin Mary **Luke 1:46–55**

Mary said, "My soul magnifies the Lord, and my spirit rejoices in God my Savior, for he has looked with favor on the lowliness of his servant. Surely, from now on all generations will call me blessed; for the Mighty One has done great things for me, and holy is his name. His mercy is for those who fear him from generation to generation. He has shown strength with his arm; he has scattered the proud in the thoughts of their hearts.

He has brought down the powerful from their thrones, and lifted up the lowly; he has filled the hungry with good things, and sent the rich away empty. He has helped his servant Israel, in remembrance of his mercy, according to the promise he made to our ancestors, to Abraham and to his descendants for ever."

- Try today to walk around or imagine a place of beauty. Look and listen, smell and touch the beauty of nature.
- As you walk, pray the first lines of Mary's poem, "My soul glorifies the Lord." Be filled for this time with thanks for all you see, hear, touch, and feel of the creation of God.

Tuesday 16th August **Matthew 19:23–26**

Jesus said to his disciples, "Truly I tell you, it will be hard for a rich person to enter the kingdom of heaven. Again I tell you, it is easier for a camel to go through the eye of a needle than for someone who is rich to enter the kingdom of God." When the disciples heard this, they were greatly astounded and said, "Then who can be saved?" But Jesus looked at them and said, "For mortals it is impossible, but for God all things are possible."

- The Eye of the Needle is a doorway in the old wall of Jerusalem. It was constructed to keep camels out and treasures in. The people would have enjoyed Jesus' word play on the place name.
- Possessions can keep us from God. What is the baggage that keeps me from entering the freedom of the children of God—love of wealth and comfort, holding onto hurt in the past, or just the pride of wanting to be in charge of my own world?

Wednesday 17th August **Matthew 20:1–16**

Jesus said to his disciples, "For the kingdom of heaven is like a landowner who went out early in the morning to hire laborers for his vineyard. After agreeing with the laborers for the usual daily wage, he sent them into his vineyard. When he went out about nine o'clock, he saw others standing idle in the market-place; and he said to them, 'You also go into the vineyard, and I will pay you whatever is right.' So they went. When he went out again about noon and about three o'clock, he did the same. And about five o'clock he went out and found others standing around; and he said to them, 'Why are you standing here idle all day?' They said to him, 'Because no one has hired us.' He said to them, 'You also go into the vineyard.' When evening came, the owner of the vineyard said to his manager, 'Call the laborers and give them their pay, beginning with the last and then going to the first.' When those hired about five o'clock came, each of them received the usual daily wage. Now when the first came, they thought they would receive more; but each of them also received the usual daily wage. And when they received it, they grumbled against the landowner, saying, 'These last worked only one hour, and you have made them equal to us who have borne the burden of the day and the scorching heat.' But he replied to one of them, 'Friend, I am doing you no wrong; did you not agree with me for the usual daily wage? Take what belongs to you and go; I choose to give to this last the same as I give to you. Am I not allowed to do what I choose with what belongs to me? Or are you envious because I am generous?' So the last will be first, and the first will be last."

- This is a strange story—those who work little will get paid as much as those who worked all day in the heat of the sun.

- One good lesson from it is to allow God to be God: what God gives to others is between God and them. From God we all receive gifts. We can rejoice in the good graces and fortune of others.

Thursday 18th August **Matthew 22:1–2, 8–14**

Once more Jesus spoke to them in parables, saying: "The kingdom of heaven may be compared to a king who gave a wedding banquet for his son. Then he said to his slaves, 'The wedding is ready. Go therefore into the main streets, and invite everyone you find to the wedding banquet.' Those slaves went out into the streets and gathered all whom they found, both good and bad; so the wedding hall was filled with guests. But when the king came in to see the guests, he noticed a man there who was not wearing a wedding robe, and he said to him, 'Friend, how did you get in here without a wedding robe?' And he was speechless. Then the king said to the attendants, 'Bind him hand and foot, and throw him into the outer darkness, where there will be weeping and gnashing of teeth.' For many are called, but few are chosen."

- It seems harsh that someone who was dragged in from the street to a wedding is condemned for not being dressed properly! One meaning is that wedding garb was offered to everyone at the door of the reception. This man has no excuse. He has refused the gift of the king.
- We are offered much by God—in prayer we open our hearts to what he gives us each day.

Friday 19th August **Matthew 22:34–40**

When the Pharisees heard that Jesus had silenced the Sadducees, they gathered together, and one of them, a lawyer, asked him a question to test him. "Teacher, which commandment in the law is the greatest?" He said to him, "'You shall love the Lord your God with all your heart, and with all your soul, and with all your mind.' This is the greatest and first commandment. And a second is like it: 'You shall love your neighbor as yourself.' On these two commandments hang all the law and the prophets."

- Jesus' religious education stressed love of the neighbour. He brought it to its farthest point—love to death. The life and death of Jesus is a self-sacrificing love.
- Prayer is our moment of being open to the total love of Jesus for all. We welcome this love, to better understand our faith.

Saturday 20th August **Matthew 23:8–12**

Then Jesus said to the crowds and to his disciples, "You are not to be called rabbi, for you have one teacher, and you are all students. And call no one your father on earth, for you have one Father—the one in heaven. Nor are you to be called instructors, for you have one instructor, the Messiah. The greatest among you will be your servant. All who exalt themselves will be humbled, and all who humble themselves will be exalted."

- Greatness in the company of Jesus has its source in service and humility. The pomposity of religious leaders comes in for colourful condemnation.
- Jesus has a conviction about the right use of religion—to care for the things of God and for the poor. The greatest among us could be the simplest person and of any age, caring for another.

august 21–27

Something to think and pray about each day this week:

Knowing Jesus

Those who lived with Jesus in Nazareth thought that they knew him. He fixed their tables and chairs. They recognized him as the carpenter, Mary's son (Mark 6:3). They ate and drank with his extended family. When he opened Isaiah in the synagogue, and interpreted it with authority, he was stepping outside the role they had fixed for him. So they put him down as just a workman. François Mauriac marveled at this: "It is baffling to record that, for a period of thirty years, the Son of Man did not appear to be anything other than a man." Jesus is a prophet in his own country, undervalued, talked down. Am I guilty of this sort of undervaluing?

Lord, there are depths in each of us, even those we think we know well, that only you can glimpse. A put-down tells more about the speaker than about the victim. Save me, Lord, from such folly. The fact that I know someone's family and history can blind me to the depths and dreams that make them precious to others.

The Presence of God
As I sit here with my book, God is here.
Around me, in my sensations, in my thoughts and deep within me.
I pause for a moment, and become aware
of God's life-giving presence.

Freedom
I need to close out the noise, to rise above the noise;
The noise that interrupts, that separates,
The noise that isolates.
I need to listen to God again.

Consciousness
Knowing that God loves me unconditionally,
I can afford to be honest about how I am.
How has the last day been, and how do I feel now?
I share my feelings openly with the Lord.

The Word
God speaks to each one of us individually. I need to listen to what he is saying to me. (Please turn to your scripture on the following pages. Inspiration points are there should you need them. When you are ready, return here to continue.)

Conversation
Do I notice myself reacting as I pray with the Word of God?
Do I feel challenged, comforted, angry?
Imagining Jesus sitting or standing by me,
I speak out my feelings, as one trusted friend to another.

Conclusion
Glory be to the Father, and to the Son, and to the Holy Spirit,
As it was in the beginning, is now, and ever shall be,
World without end. Amen

Sunday 21st August,
Twenty-first Sunday in Ordinary Time Matthew 16:13–20

Now when Jesus came into the district of Caesarea Philippi, he asked his disciples, "Who do people say that the Son of Man is?" And they said, "Some say John the Baptist, but others Elijah, and still others Jeremiah or one of the prophets." He said to them, "But who do you say that I am?" Simon Peter answered, "You are the Messiah, the Son of the living God." And Jesus answered him, "Blessed are you, Simon son of Jonah! For flesh and blood has not revealed this to you, but my Father in heaven. And I tell you, you are Peter, and on this rock I will build my church, and the gates of Hades will not prevail against it. I will give you the keys of the kingdom of heaven, and whatever you bind on earth will be bound in heaven, and whatever you loose on earth will be loosed in heaven." Then he sternly ordered the disciples not to tell anyone that he was the Messiah.

- Peter's faith, like ours, is a gift. Faith in God is the rock on which the rest of Jesus' community will stand, and this rock is what our faith stands on.
- During our lives, our faith can grow, develop, or get stuck. Many people seem to try to live from a faith that has not grown since their schooldays.
- Faith is a gift that needs nourishing. The God of Jesus Christ is the living God and the God who loves all that lives.

Monday 22nd August 1 Thessalonians 1:2–5, 8

We always give thanks to God for all of you and mention you in our prayers, constantly remembering before our God and Father your work of faith and labor of love and steadfastness of hope in our Lord Jesus Christ. For we know, brothers and sisters beloved by God, that he has chosen you, because our message of the gospel came to you not in word only, but also in power and in the Holy Spirit and with full conviction; just as you know what kind of people we proved to be among you for your sake. For the word of the Lord has sounded forth from you not only in Macedonia and Achaia, but in every place where your faith in God has become known, so that we have no need to speak about it.

- If the scholars are correct, this may be some of the earliest Christian writing we have. It begins with words of prayerful thanks for the faith that has flowered in the community.
- How do these words apply to my actions, to my convictions, to the expression of my faith? Do I know the Spirit in my life?

Tuesday 23rd August **Matthew 23:23–26**

Jesus said, "Woe to you, scribes and Pharisees, hypocrites! For you tithe mint, dill, and cummin, and have neglected the weightier matters of the law: justice and mercy and faith. It is these you ought to have practiced without neglecting the others. You blind guides! You strain out a gnat but swallow a camel! Woe to you, scribes and Pharisees, hypocrites! For you clean the outside of the cup and of the plate, but inside they are full of greed and self-indulgence. You blind Pharisee! First clean the inside of the cup, so that the outside also may become clean."

- Without mercy, religion is empty. Without mercy, the law is stronger than the love at its source.
- With mercy God is near, always offering a new chance to live the gospel of love.

Wednesday 24th August,
St. Bartholomew, Apostle **John 1:45–51**

Philip found Nathanael and said to him, "We have found him about whom Moses in the law and also the prophets wrote, Jesus son of Joseph from Nazareth." Nathanael said to him, "Can anything good come out of Nazareth?" Philip said to him, "Come and see." When Jesus saw Nathanael coming towards him, he said of him, "Here is truly an Israelite in whom there is no deceit!" Nathanael asked him, "Where did you come to know me?" Jesus answered, "I saw you under the fig tree before Philip called you." Nathanael replied, "Rabbi, you are the Son of God! You are the King of Israel!" Jesus answered, "Do you believe because I told you that I saw you under the fig tree? You will see greater things than these." And he said to him, "Very truly, I tell you, you will see heaven opened and the angels of God ascending and descending upon the Son of Man."

- The apostles knew who they were looking for, and Jesus fitted the bill. He was no stranger to them because they had read their scriptures and worshipped in the synagogue. They were open to the "more" of Jesus—the "more" that he is, and the "more" which he asks of us.
- Our prayer opens us to the mind of Jesus so that we recognize him in his people and in the breaking of the bread.

Thursday 25th August **Matthew 24:42–46**

Jesus said to his disciples, "Keep awake therefore, for you do not know on what day your Lord is coming. But understand this: if the owner of the house had known in what part of the night the thief was coming, he would have stayed awake and would not have let his house be broken into. Therefore you also must be ready, for the Son of Man is coming at an unexpected hour. Who then is the faithful and wise slave, whom his master has put in charge of his household, to give the other slaves their allowance of food at the proper time? Blessed is that slave whom his master will find at work when he arrives."

- The grace and presence of God can hit us at any time. A moment in the countryside, a prayer at Mass, a hug with a loved one—all and much more can be doors opening to God.
- Recall the moments when the Lord came your way. How did you respond?

Friday 26th August **Matthew 25:1–13**

Jesus said to his disciples, "Then the kingdom of heaven will be like this. Ten bridesmaids took their lamps and went to meet the bridegroom. Five of them were foolish, and five were wise. When the foolish took their lamps, they took no oil with them; but the wise took flasks of oil with their lamps. As the bridegroom was delayed, all of them became drowsy and slept. But at midnight there was a shout, 'Look! Here is the bridegroom! Come out to meet him.' Then all those bridesmaids got up and trimmed their lamps. The foolish said to the wise, 'Give us some of your oil, for our lamps are going out.' But the wise replied, 'No! there will not be enough for you and for us; you had better go to the dealers and buy some for yourselves.' And while they went to buy it, the bridegroom came, and those who were ready went with him into the wedding banquet; and the door was shut. Later the other bridesmaids came also, saying, 'Lord, lord, open to us.' But he replied, 'Truly I tell you, I do not know you.' Keep awake therefore, for you know neither the day nor the hour."

- The lamp is given us by God and our time given to God is the oil. All of God's action in our lives is his gift, but it needs our openness and welcome.

- Prayer builds up our "supply of oil," which can give light and fragrance to the rest of our lives.

Saturday 27th August **Matthew 25:14–30**

Jesus told his disciples this parable, "For it is as if a man, going on a journey, summoned his slaves and entrusted his property to them; to one he gave five talents, to another two, to another one, to each according to his ability. Then he went away. The one who had received the five talents went off at once and traded with them, and made five more talents. In the same way, the one who had the two talents made two more talents. But the one who had received the one talent went off and dug a hole in the ground and hid his master's money. After a long time the master of those slaves came and settled accounts with them. Then the one who had received the five talents came forward, bringing five more talents, saying, 'Master, you handed over to me five talents; see, I have made five more talents.' His master said to him, 'Well done, good and trustworthy slave; you have been trustworthy in a few things, I will put you in charge of many things; enter into the joy of your master.' And the one with the two talents also came forward, saying, 'Master, you handed over to me two talents; see, I have made two more talents.' His master said to him, 'Well done, good and trustworthy slave; you have been trustworthy in a few things, I will put you in charge of many things; enter into the joy of your master.' Then the one who had received the one talent also came forward, saying, 'Master, I knew that you were a harsh man, reaping where you did not sow, and gathering where you did not scatter seed; so I was afraid, and I went and hid your talent in the ground. Here you have what is yours.' But his master replied, 'You wicked and lazy slave! You knew, did you, that I reap where I did not sow, and gather where I did not scatter? Then you ought to have invested my money with the bankers, and on my return I would have received what was my own with interest. So take the talent from him, and give it to the one with the ten talents. For to all those who have, more will be given, and they will have an abundance; but from those who have nothing, even what they have will be taken away. As for this worthless slave, throw him into the outer darkness, where there will be weeping and gnashing of teeth.'"

- A central point of this parable is that the man entrusted his property to servants. God entrusts the world to us, to create a world of justice, peace, beauty, and love with him. God entrusts the environment to us.
- Jesus has entrusted to us the future of his community, the Church. Let us welcome this responsibility and do our best in all we do and say "to do the world a world of good."

august 28–september 3

Something to think and pray about each day this week:

Dying in Small Ways

"Unless a grain of wheat falls into the earth and dies, it remains just a single grain; but if it dies, it bears much fruit. Those who love their life lose it, and those who hate their life in this world will keep it for eternal life" (John 12:24). Jesus' image of the wheat grain symbolizes not just our mortal life, but the many times we die a little before our death: with every parting, moving of house or job, loss of a friend or dear one, with any loss of property. To cling to what we have lost is to bury our life in the past. Even the most painful loss can be a new beginning.

Lord, you sometimes ask us to face the death to our own desires and ego in the daily contradictions and rebuffs of our long lifetimes. There too the sacrifice of the ego enables us to bear much fruit.

The Presence of God
I pause for a moment, aware that God is here.
I think of how everything around me,
the air I breathe, my whole body,
is tingling with the presence of God.

Freedom
I will ask God's help,
to be free from my own preoccupations,
to be open to God in this time of prayer,
to come to love and serve him more.

Consciousness
In the presence of my loving Creator,
I look honestly at my feelings over the last day,
the highs, the lows, and the level ground.
Can I see where the Lord has been present?

The Word
I read the Word of God slowly, a few times over, and I listen to what God is saying to me. (Please turn to your scripture on the following pages. Inspiration points are there should you need them. When you are ready, return here to continue.)

Conversation
Remembering that I am still in God's presence,
I imagine Jesus himself standing or sitting beside me,
and say whatever is on my mind, whatever is in my heart,
speaking as one friend to another.

Conclusion
Glory be to the Father, and to the Son, and to the Holy Spirit,
As it was in the beginning, is now, and ever shall be,
World without end. Amen

Sunday 28th August,
Twenty-second Sunday in Ordinary Time Matthew 16:21–27

From that time on, Jesus began to show his disciples that he must go to Jerusalem and undergo great suffering at the hands of the elders and chief priests and scribes, and be killed, and on the third day be raised. And Peter took him aside and began to rebuke him, saying, "God forbid it, Lord! This must never happen to you." But he turned and said to Peter, "Get behind me, Satan! You are a stumbling block to me; for you are setting your mind not on divine things but on human things." Then Jesus told his disciples, "If any want to become my followers, let them deny themselves and take up their cross and follow me. For those who want to save their life will lose it, and those who lose their life for my sake will find it. For what will it profit them if they gain the whole world but forfeit their life? Or what will they give in return for their life? For the Son of Man is to come with his angels in the glory of his Father, and then he will repay everyone for what has been done."

- Taking up one's cross is a central thought in the gospels. In life, it takes many forms, but it is always painful. Sometimes it never ends; Jesus bore a cross to the end of his life.
- On the way to Calvary, Jesus was helped by one man, Simon from Africa. Help can come from expected or unexpected quarters: from family, friends, or even foes, but help there must be if we are to bear our crosses in life.
- Can I help and support someone near me to carry the burdens of their lives? It might start with a smile, with a word, with a hand outstretched.

Monday 29th August **Luke 4:16–22**

When he came to Nazareth, where he had been brought up, he went to the synagogue on the sabbath day, as was his custom. He stood up to read, and the scroll of the prophet Isaiah was given to him. He unrolled the scroll and found the place where it was written: "The Spirit of the Lord is upon me, because he has anointed me to bring good news to the poor. He has sent me to proclaim release to the captives and recovery of sight to the blind, to let the oppressed go free, to proclaim the year of the Lord's favor." And he rolled up the scroll, gave it back to the attendant, and sat down. The eyes of all in the synagogue were fixed on him. Then he began to say to them, "Today this scripture has been fulfilled in your hearing." All spoke well of him and were amazed at the gracious words that came from his mouth.

- From the beginning of his public life Jesus looked outwards to the poor, the oppressed, and those in his society who needed help. He saw himself as sent especially by God for them.
- For Jesus, God his Father was the one in whom he lived; in Jesus, God becomes totally one with the people of God.

Tuesday 30th August **Luke 4:31–37**

He went down to Capernaum, a city in Galilee, and was teaching them on the sabbath. They were astounded at his teaching, because he spoke with authority. In the synagogue there was a man who had the spirit of an unclean demon, and he cried out with a loud voice, "Let us alone! What have you to do with us, Jesus of Nazareth? Have you come to destroy us? I know who you are, the Holy One of God." But Jesus rebuked him, saying, "Be silent, and come out of him!" When the demon had thrown him down before them, he came out of him without having done him any harm. They were all amazed and kept saying to one another, "What kind of utterance is this? For with authority and power he commands the unclean spirits, and out they come!" And a report about him began to reach every place in the region.

- The healing and quieting of the tormented people gave Jesus a huge reputation in his ministry. What we might today put down to mental or psychological imbalance was seen then as a sign of demons and unclean spirits.
- Whatever our understanding, the same Jesus today can heal the fears, anxieties, and worries of every day.

Wednesday 31st August **Luke 4:40–44**

As the sun was setting, all those who had any who were sick with various kinds of diseases brought them to Jesus; and he laid his hands on each of them and cured them. Demons also came out of many, shouting, "You are the Son of God!" But he rebuked them and would not allow them to speak, because they knew that he was the Messiah. At daybreak he departed and went into a deserted place. And the crowds were looking for him; and when they reached him, they wanted to prevent him from leaving them. But he said to them, "I must proclaim the good news of the kingdom of God to the other cities also; for I was sent for this purpose." So he continued proclaiming the message in the synagogues of Judea.

- Jesus' mission will bring him from town to town. He seems never satisfied with staying in one place, and seems to think of his future as he moves from place to place.
- Our call is similar: we are not necessarily asked to move from place to place but are always concerned with building the kingdom of God in our own way and in our own place.

Thursday 1st September **Luke 5:4–11**

When Jesus had finished speaking, he said to Simon, "Put out into the deep water and let down your nets for a catch." Simon answered, "Master, we have worked all night long but have caught nothing. Yet if you say so, I will let down the nets." When they had done this, they caught so many fish that their nets were beginning to break. So they signaled their partners in the other boat to come and help them. And they came and filled both boats, so that they began to sink. But when Simon Peter saw it, he fell down at Jesus' knees, saying, "Go away from me, Lord, for I am a sinful man!" For he and all who were with him were amazed at the catch of fish that they had taken; and so also were James and John, sons of Zebedee, who were partners with Simon. Then Jesus said to Simon, "Do not be afraid; from now on you will be catching people." When they had brought their boats to shore, they left everything and followed him.

- Did Peter really like Jesus assuming control of his boat, his most valuable asset? It probably smelt strongly and was not likely to be the best boat on Lake Gennesaret.
- We take this as Jesus asking Peter to allow him into his life; just as his boat would be at Jesus' disposal today, very soon Peter's whole life would be for Jesus.

Friday 2nd September **Luke 5:33–38**

Then the Pharisees and the scribes said to Jesus, "John's disciples, like the disciples of the Pharisees, frequently fast and pray, but your disciples eat and drink." Jesus said to them, "You cannot make wedding guests fast while the bridegroom is with them, can you? The days will come when the bridegroom will be taken away from them, and then they will fast in those days." He also told them a parable: "No one tears a piece from a new garment and sews it on an old garment; otherwise the new will be torn, and the piece from the new will not match the old. And no one puts new wine into old wineskins; otherwise the new wine will burst the skins and will be spilled, and the skins will be destroyed. But new wine must be put into fresh wineskins.'"

- "Live in the present" seems to be the message of Jesus here. Celebrate the presence of the Lord—one day we will mark his absence. He seems to be against the gloomy face of religion.
- Our faith gives us so much to be grateful for. As we pray, we might mention some of the gifts our faith gives us.
- We fast only to appreciate these gifts more. Even our fasting is to be cheerful.

Saturday 3rd September **Luke 6:1–5**

One sabbath while Jesus was going through the grainfields, his disciples plucked some heads of grain, rubbed them in their hands, and ate them. But some of the Pharisees said, "Why are you doing what is not lawful on the sabbath?" Jesus answered, "Have you not read what David did when he and his companions were hungry? He entered the house of God and took and ate the bread of the Presence, which it is not lawful for any but the priests to eat, and gave some to his companions?" Then he said to them, "The Son of Man is lord of the sabbath."

- While Jesus valued rituals, he did not see them as the source and summit of religion. Ritual is empty if it is not sourced in relationship. Ritual is alive and relevant when begun in personal and communal prayer.
- What we gather from God in the time of prayer brings life, joy, and relevance to the rituals and the customs of religion. No ritual is to lord it over us.

september 4–10

Something to think and pray about each day this week:

Learning with God

Jesus once quoted a strong phrase from the prophet Isaiah, "And they shall all be taught by God" (John 6:45).

How does God teach us? Usually without words, touching us by the encounters, pleasures, and pains of everyday living. Lord, as I pray, show me, in the movements of my heart, what you want me to learn from you. You are beyond all human imagining or language, and you teach me not so much in words as in the crises that stir my heart. Help me to read you in them.

The Presence of God

For a few moments, I think of God's veiled presence in things:
in the elements, giving them existence;
in plants, giving them life; in animals, giving them sensation;
and finally, in me, giving me all this and more,
making me a temple, a dwelling-place of the Spirit.

Freedom

God is not foreign to my freedom.
Instead the Spirit breathes life into my most intimate desires,
gently nudging me towards all that is good.
I ask for the grace to let myself be enfolded by the Spirit.

Consciousness

Knowing that God loves me unconditionally,
I look honestly over the last day, its events and my feelings.
Do I have something to be grateful for? Then I give thanks.
Is there something I am sorry for? Then I ask forgiveness.

The Word

I take my time to read the Word of God, slowly, a few times, allowing myself to dwell on anything that strikes me. (Please turn to your scripture on the following pages. Inspiration points are there should you need them. When you are ready, return here to continue.)

Conversation

How has God's Word moved me? Has it left me cold?
Has it consoled me or moved me to act in a new way?
I imagine Jesus standing or sitting beside me,
I turn and share my feelings with him.

Conclusion

Glory be to the Father, and to the Son, and to the Holy Spirit,
As it was in the beginning, is now, and ever shall be,
World without end. Amen

Sunday 4th September,
Twenty-third Sunday in Ordinary Time Matthew 18:15–17

Jesus said, "If another member of the church sins against you, go and point out the fault when the two of you are alone. If the member listens to you, you have regained that one. But if you are not listened to, take one or two others along with you, so that every word may be confirmed by the evidence of two or three witnesses. If the member refuses to listen to them, tell it to the church; and if the offender refuses to listen even to the church, let such a one be to you as a Gentile and a tax collector."

- Jesus is pointing out that we have social responsibility in family, in community, and in neighbourhood. We have a responsibility for each other, for the common good.
- When there are issues that we cannot walk away from, we pray to God for help, and we do this with others. That's where God is—two or three gathered is the community of God.
- We can help each other to goodness, we can support each other, correct each other, and help each other on our way to God.

Monday 5th September Luke 6:6–11

On another sabbath he entered the synagogue and taught, and there was a man there whose right hand was withered. The scribes and the Pharisees watched him to see whether he would cure on the sabbath, so that they might find an accusation against him. Even though he knew what they were thinking, he said to the man who had the withered hand, "Come and stand here." He got up and stood there. Then Jesus said to them, "I ask you, is it lawful to do good or to do harm on the sabbath, to save life or to destroy it?" After looking around at all of them, he said to him, "Stretch out your hand." He did so, and his hand was restored. But they were filled with fury and discussed with one another what they might do to Jesus.

- The man with the withered hand was ashamed not only of his ugly hand, but of himself.
- In Jesus' time illness like this was seen as sinfulness. When Jesus was saving life on the sabbath, he was doing more than healing the man's hand. He was healing the whole man.
- In prayer we bring before God the shame that may often be part of us and pray for the healing grace of his love.

Tuesday 6th September **Luke 6:12–16**

Now during those days he went out to the mountain to pray; and he spent the night in prayer to God. And when day came, he called his disciples and chose twelve of them, whom he also named apostles: Simon, whom he named Peter, and his brother Andrew, and James, and John, and Philip, and Bartholomew, and Matthew, and Thomas, and James son of Alphaeus, and Simon, who was called the Zealot, and Judas son of James, and Judas Iscariot, who became a traitor.

- This is an important moment, a solemn choice, an extension of the mission given to Jesus by his Father. Jesus spends the night in prayer.
- In prayer we can know reality in a totally different way. True prayer stops promoting its own agenda, it lets go of opposing attitudes or fears; it waits for, expects, and receives guidance.

Wednesday 7th September **Luke 6:20–23**

Then Jesus looked up at his disciples and said: "Blessed are you who are poor, for yours is the kingdom of God. Blessed are you who are hungry now, for you will be filled. Blessed are you who weep now, for you will laugh. Blessed are you when people hate you, and when they exclude you, revile you, and defame you on account of the Son of Man. Rejoice in that day and leap for joy, for surely your reward is great in heaven; for that is what their ancestors did to the prophets."

- In this Sermon on the Plain, Jesus' words are tough and strange—"leap for joy" when you are poor, hungry, and all else he names.
- We ask in prayer to be like him or to find a blessing in all of our lives, good times and bad. He found this himself, and knew that the love of his Father was never far from him.

Thursday 8th September,
Birth of the Blessed Virgin Mary **Matthew 1:18–23**

Now the birth of Jesus the Messiah took place in this way. When his mother Mary had been engaged to Joseph, but before they lived together, she was found to be with child from the Holy Spirit. Her husband Joseph, being a righteous man and unwilling to expose her to public disgrace, planned to dismiss her quietly. But just when he had resolved to do this, an angel of the Lord appeared to him in a dream and said, "Joseph, son of David, do not be afraid to take Mary as your wife, for the child conceived in her is from the Holy Spirit. She will bear a son, and you are to name him Jesus, for he will save his people from their sins." All this took place to fulfill what had been spoken by the Lord through the prophet: "Look, the virgin shall conceive and bear a son, and they shall name him Emmanuel," which means, "God is with us."

- The feast of the birth of Mary is focused on the birth of Jesus. Her life was given in care and love for her Son and his mission. She knew when to be around and when to let him go for the sake of the kingdom of God.

- Mary let him go with love to his death and then took her new place and relationship with him after the Resurrection.

Friday 9th September **Luke 6:39–42**

He also told them a parable: "Can a blind person guide a blind person? Will not both fall into a pit? A disciple is not above the teacher, but everyone who is fully qualified will be like the teacher. Why do you see the speck in your neighbor's eye, but do not notice the log in your own eye? Or how can you say to your neighbor, 'Friend, let me take out the speck in your eye,' when you yourself do not see the log in your own eye? You hypocrite, first take the log out of your own eye, and then you will see clearly to take the speck out of your neighbor's eye."

- Perhaps Jesus looked at somebody trying to take the speck from the eye; everyday experiences in normal life reminded him of ways to speak his message.
- He looked around and saw reminders of God everywhere, of life to the full. He spoke from the ordinary. Watch today for the love of God and the call of God in ordinary events and interchanges.

Saturday 10th September **Luke 6:43–49**

Jesus said to the people, "No good tree bears bad fruit, nor again does a bad tree bear good fruit; for each tree is known by its own fruit. Figs are not gathered from thorns, nor are grapes picked from a bramble bush. The good person out of the good treasure of the heart produces good, and the evil person out of evil treasure produces evil; for it is out of the abundance of the heart that the mouth speaks. Why do you call me 'Lord, Lord,' and do not do what I tell you? I will show you what someone is like who comes to me, hears my words, and acts on them. That one is like a man building a house, who dug deeply and laid the foundation on rock; when a flood arose, the river burst against that house but could not shake it, because it had been well built. But the one who hears and does not act is like a man who built a house on the ground without a foundation. When the river burst against it, immediately it fell, and great was the ruin of that house."

- There are some practical and homely sayings from Jesus in today's gospel reading. He stresses that what is on the inside of a person is the source of actions for good or bad.
- Prayer—even sitting silently before God—is one way of bringing light and sincerity to the motivations of our lives. Nobody can be aware of God's presence, silently or with words, and not change for the better!

september 11–17

Something to think and pray about each day this week:

Shaped by God

As Alzheimer's took over my cousin Moira, she became quite unable to manage herself. She needed constant care and nursing. When you visited her, you might get a smile, a flicker of recognition. At no one stage could you say "Goodbye." It was a slow parting. When she died, she who loved people was quite out of touch with humankind. I wondered, what was God up to?

I used to imagine it was our job to make ourselves holy. I've slowly realized that we often seek for ourselves our own satisfactions and complacency—even in the most apparently unselfish efforts. God shapes us, not we ourselves. Through life, in ways we would never have planned, God strips us of our ego, prepares us for Godself. For an active person, the hardest penance is to be unable to act. For Jesus at the height of his powers and vigor, the cross meant being passive, nailed down, speechless, helpless. We could not and would not plan these experiences for ourselves. Jesus begged for the chalice to pass from him.

Who would ask for Alzheimer's as a way to go? But if we believe in God's Providence—and that is not easy—that must be what he was doing to Moira, who had given him an enthusiastic life. The real achievement of that life was not in her creative efforts or sleepless nights at the service of others, but in her recognition of God's hand in the suffering which accompanied her to the grave.

The Presence of God
Jesus waits silent and unseen to come into my heart.
I will respond to his call.
He comes with his infinite power and love
May I be filled with joy in his presence.

Freedom
Everything has the potential to draw forth from me a fuller love and life.
Yet my desires are often fixed, caught, on illusions of fulfillment.
I ask that God, through my freedom, may orchestrate
my desires in a vibrant loving melody rich in harmony.

Consciousness
How do I find myself today?
Where am I with God? With others?
Do I have something to be grateful for? Then I give thanks.
Is there something I am sorry for? Then I ask forgiveness.

The Word
God speaks to each one of us individually. I need to listen to what he is saying to me. (Please turn to your scripture on the following pages. Inspiration points are there should you need them. When you are ready, return here to continue.)

Conversation
What feelings are rising in me
as I pray and reflect on God's Word?
I imagine Jesus himself sitting or standing beside me,
and open my heart to him.

Conclusion
Glory be to the Father, and to the Son, and to the Holy Spirit,
As it was in the beginning, is now, and ever shall be,
World without end. Amen

Sunday 11th September,
Twenty-fourth Sunday in Ordinary Time Romans 14:7–9

We do not live to ourselves, and we do not die to ourselves. If we live, we live to the Lord, and if we die, we die to the Lord; so then, whether we live or whether we die, we are the Lord's. For to this end Christ died and lived again, so that he might be Lord of both the dead and the living.

- In baptism we accept Jesus as the only Lord. All that we do, all that we are in life and even in death, belongs to the Lord.
- So we are completely bound up with him who is "Lord of both the dead and the living." Take some time to pray about this.

Monday 12th September 1 Timothy 2:1–7

First of all, then, I urge that supplications, prayers, intercessions, and thanksgivings should be made for everyone, for kings and all who are in high positions, so that we may lead a quiet and peaceable life in all godliness and dignity. This is right and is acceptable in the sight of God our Savior, who desires everyone to be saved and to come to the knowledge of the truth. For there is one God; there is also one mediator between God and humankind, Christ Jesus, himself human, who gave himself a ransom for all—this was attested at the right time. For this I was appointed a herald and an apostle (I am telling the truth, I am not lying), a teacher of the Gentiles in faith and truth.

- The unity of prayer does not come from its form or from those who pray; it comes from the one God, and the mediator through whom we pray, Jesus Christ.
- Let me pray today, with praise and petition, for people of other faiths, or of no faith at all. Each of us is loved by the one God.

Tuesday 13th September **Luke 7:11–17**

Soon afterwards he went to a town called Nain, and his disciples and a large crowd went with him. As he approached the gate of the town, a man who had died was being carried out. He was his mother's only son, and she was a widow; and with her was a large crowd from the town. When the Lord saw her, he had compassion for her and said to her, "Do not weep." Then he came forward and touched the bier, and the bearers stood still. And he said, "Young man, I say to you, rise!" The dead man sat up and began to speak, and Jesus gave him to his mother. Fear seized all of them; and they glorified God, saying, "A great prophet has risen among us!" and "God has looked favorably on his people!" This word about him spread throughout Judea and all the surrounding country.

- The raising of someone from death was a highly unusual event in Jesus' life. It is a direct compassionate response to the situation of a family who has lost a loved one, as it was with Lazarus.
- It is also the promise of Jesus to us all—that our death is our rising to new life.

Wednesday 14th September,
Triumph of the Holy Cross **John 3:14–17**

Jesus said, "And just as Moses lifted up the serpent in the wilderness, so must the Son of Man be lifted up, that whoever believes in him may have eternal life. For God so loved the world that he gave his only Son, so that everyone who believes in him may not perish but may have eternal life. Indeed, God did not send the Son into the world to condemn the world, but in order that the world might be saved through him."

- For people in Jesus' time a cross was the ultimate sign of humiliation; thousands ended their lives by dying on crosses. Thousands of Jesus' own countrymen were crucified. For all who knew them it was torture and humiliation.
- For us now, because of Jesus' love and resurrection, it is the great sign of eternal life and love.

Thursday 15th September **Luke 7:36–50**

One of the Pharisees asked Jesus to eat with him, and he went into the Pharisee's house and took his place at the table. And a woman in the city, who was a sinner, having learned that he was eating in the Pharisee's house, brought an alabaster jar of ointment. She stood behind him at his feet, weeping, and began to bathe his feet with her tears and to dry them with her hair. Then she continued kissing his feet and anointing them with the ointment. Now when the Pharisee who had invited him saw it, he said to himself, "If this man were a prophet, he would have known who and what kind of woman this is who is touching him—that she is a sinner." Jesus spoke up and said to him, "Simon, I have something to say to you." "Teacher," he replied, "speak." "A certain creditor had two debtors; one owed five hundred denarii; and the other fifty. When they could not pay, he cancelled the debts for both of them. Now which of them will love him more?" Simon answered, "I suppose the one for whom he cancelled the greater debt." And Jesus said to him, "You have judged rightly." Then turning towards the woman, he said to Simon, "Do you see this woman? I entered your house; you gave me no water for my feet, but she has bathed my feet with her tears and dried them with her hair. You gave me no kiss, but from the time I came in she has not stopped kissing my feet. You did not anoint my head with oil, but she has anointed my feet with ointment. Therefore, I tell you, her sins, which were many, have been forgiven; hence she has shown great love. But the one to whom little is forgiven, loves little." Then he said to her, "Your sins are forgiven." But those who were at the table with him began to say among themselves, "Who is this who even forgives sins?" And he said to the woman, "Your faith has saved you; go in peace."

- The jar of ointment was expensive, and highlights the generosity of the unnamed woman, the sinner. Somehow the compassion and forgiveness of Jesus hit her so deeply that she poured out love for him as a response to his relationship with her.
- In prayer we can sometimes think of God's care, protection, and forgiveness in our lives, and be grateful, with words or in silence.

Friday 16th September **Luke 8:1–3**

Soon afterwards he went on through cities and villages, proclaiming and bringing the good news of the kingdom of God. The twelve were with him, as well as some women who had been cured of evil spirits and infirmities: Mary, called Magdalene, from whom seven demons had gone out, and Joanna, the wife of Herod's steward Chuza, and Susanna, and many others, who provided for them out of their resources.

- Jesus traveled with a motley group of followers, men and women inspired by his way of life and his teachings. Our picture is of him leading a group into his way of life.
- It's good to imagine ourselves becoming part of that group; each of us walks with his followers as we bind our lives with his.

Saturday 17th September **Luke 8:4–10**

When a great crowd gathered and people from town after town came to Jesus, he said in a parable: "A sower went out to sow his seed; and as he sowed, some fell on the path and was trampled on, and the birds of the air ate it up. Some fell on the rock; and as it grew up, it withered for lack of moisture. Some fell among thorns, and the thorns grew with it and choked it. Some fell into good soil, and when it grew, it produced a hundredfold." As he said this, he called out, "Let anyone with ears to hear listen!" Then his disciples asked him what this parable meant. He said, "To you it has been given to know the secrets of the kingdom of God; but to others I speak in parables, so that 'looking they may not perceive, and listening they may not understand.'"

- It's interesting how much Jesus was an out-of-doors person. He gave a lot of his sermons outside rather than in the synagogue or temple; and his images were so often of seeds and growth, trees and fields. He met his people in their ordinary situations.
- This story draws in all Jesus' sensitivity to the growth of faith, spoken in words and images, in ordinary places, that everyone could understand. He meets us in the ordinariness of our lives.

september 18–24

Something to think and pray about each day this week:

Growing Older with God

The Jesus of the gospels was a man whose health, strength, energy, and vitality roused admiration and love, as from the woman who cried, "Blessed is the womb that bore you, the breasts you sucked!" (Luke 11:27). But he was never seventy. He never suffered the infirmities of age, stiff limbs, slow apprehension, failing memory, blunting of senses, tottering balance. You sometimes feel, as you get older, that the old Victorian adage about children is reversed. "Old people should be seen but not heard." But God has plans for us too, and works on us in other ways. You may know of the prayer they discovered at an old nun's kneeler:

"Lord, you know better than I that I am growing old, and will some day be old. Keep me from getting talkative and particularly from the fatal habit of thinking I must say something on every subject on every occasion. With my vast store of wisdom it seems a pity not to use it all.

"Make me thoughtful but not moody, helpful but not bossy. Teach me the glorious lesson that, occasionally, it is possible that I may be mistaken! Keep me reasonably sweet. Release me from the craving to try to straighten out everybody's affairs. Keep my mind free from the recital of endless details—give me wings to get to the point. I ask for grace enough to listen to the tales of others' pains. Help me to endure them with patience."

The Presence of God

"I stand at the door and knock," says the Lord.
What a wonderful privilege
that the Lord of all creation desires to come to me.
I welcome his presence.

Freedom

Lord, grant me the grace to be free from the excesses of this life.
Let me not get caught up with the desire for wealth.
Keep my heart and mind free to love and serve you.

Consciousness

"There is a time and place for everything," as the saying goes.
Lord, grant that I may always desire
to spend time in your presence. To hear your call.

The Word

God speaks to each one of us individually. I need to listen to what he is saying to me. (Please turn to your scripture on the following pages. Inspiration points are there should you need them. When you are ready, return here to continue.)

Conversation

The gift of speech is a wonderful gift.
May I use this gift with kindness.
May I be slow to utter harsh words,
hurtful words, and words spoken in anger.

Conclusion

Glory be to the Father, and to the Son, and to the Holy Spirit,
As it was in the beginning, is now, and ever shall be,
World without end. Amen

Sunday 18th September,
Twenty-fifth Sunday in Ordinary Time Matthew 20:1–16

And Jesus said, "For the kingdom of heaven is like a landowner who went out early in the morning to hire laborers for his vineyard. After agreeing with the laborers for the usual daily wage, he sent them into his vineyard. When he went out about nine o'clock, he saw others standing idle in the marketplace; and he said to them, 'You also go into the vineyard, and I will pay you whatever is right.' So they went. When he went out again about noon and about three o'clock, he did the same. And about five o'clock he went out and found others standing around; and he said to them, 'Why are you standing here idle all day?' They said to him, 'Because no one has hired us.' He said to them, 'You also go into the vineyard.' When evening came, the owner of the vineyard said to his manager, 'Call the laborers and give them their pay, beginning with the last and then going to the first.' When those hired about five o'clock came, each of them received the usual daily wage. Now when the first came, they thought they would receive more; but each of them also received the usual daily wage. And when they received it, they grumbled against the landowner, saying, 'These last worked only one hour, and you have made them equal to us who have borne the burden of the day and the scorching heat.' But he replied to one of them, 'Friend, I am doing you no wrong; did you not agree with me for the usual daily wage? Take what belongs to you and go; I choose to give to this last the same as I give to you. Am I not allowed to do what I choose with what belongs to me? Or are you envious because I am generous?' So the last will be first, and the first will be last."

- The "kingdom of heaven," which this parable tries to explain, is not a reward ceremony at which comparisons are made about work done and time given to God. Those who labour long in the field of virtue do so not to win any reward, but to reveal the goodness they experience through their relationship with God.
- Whatever goodness we have is a gift to us from God through others. God will surprise us all the time with generosity.

Monday 19th September **Luke 8:16–18**

Jesus said to his disciples, "No one after lighting a lamp hides it under a jar, or puts it under a bed, but puts it on a lampstand, so that those who enter may see the light. For nothing is hidden that will not be disclosed, nor is anything secret that will not become known and come to light. Then pay attention to how you listen; for to those who have, more will be given; and from those who do not have, even what they seem to have will be taken away."

- We must take care of the way we receive, nurture, and share the word we receive. It is like light—precious, refreshing, calming, energizing, reassuring.
- How do I share this precious word with others? Can I do more?

Tuesday 20th September **Luke 8:19–21**

Then his mother and his brothers came to him, but they could not reach him because of the crowd. And he was told, "Your mother and your brothers are standing outside, wanting to see you." But he said to them, "My mother and my brothers are those who hear the word of God and do it."

- Even the deepest of human family relationships—with mother and siblings—are not as full as the relationship we have with God in Jesus.

- Mary would have understood this; her deepest bond with her Son was not just physical birth, but in hearing and doing the Word of God which became flesh in her.
- Our time of prayer is our daily time of hearing this word.

Wednesday 21st September,
St. Matthew, Apostle and Evangelist **Matthew 9:9–13**

As Jesus was walking along, he saw a man called Matthew sitting at the tax booth; and he said to him, "Follow me." And he got up and followed him. And as he sat at dinner in the house, many tax collectors and sinners came and were sitting with him and his disciples. When the Pharisees saw this, they said to his disciples, "Why does your teacher eat with tax collectors and sinners?" But when he heard this, he said, "Those who are well have no need of a physician, but those who are sick. Go and learn what this means, 'I desire mercy, not sacrifice.' For I have come to call not the righteous but sinners."

- Jesus' choice of the unpopular Matthew would have embarrassed his other followers who were then, as now, an ordinary group of generous men and women who wanted to follow him, even if they did not always like each other.
- So it may be today. Jesus' followers may have had shady and sinful pasts. Neither would they always live up to their calling. Same today. They were willing to change their lives, repent, and be converted to the way of Jesus Christ. So must we.

Thursday 22nd September **Luke 9:7–9**

Now Herod the ruler heard about all that had taken place, and he was perplexed, because it was said by some that John had been raised from the dead, by some that Elijah had appeared, and by others that one of the ancient prophets had arisen.

Herod said, "John I beheaded; but who is this about whom I hear such things?" And he tried to see him.

- For good or bad reasons, people are interested in Jesus. Herod wondered about him and eventually did see him, at the time of his passion. But his lifestyle made any meeting with Jesus a mockery. Jesus knew this and was genuinely scared when he knew Herod was around.
- The one who beheaded John would help send Jesus to his death.

Friday 23rd September **Luke 9:18–22**

Once when Jesus was praying alone, with only the disciples near him, he asked them, "Who do the crowds say that I am?" They answered, "John the Baptist; but others, Elijah; and still others, that one of the ancient prophets has arisen." He said to them, "But who do you say that I am?" Peter answered, "The Messiah of God." He sternly ordered and commanded them not to tell anyone, saying, "The Son of Man must undergo great suffering, and be rejected by the elders, chief priests, and scribes, and be killed, and on the third day be raised."

- When we believe in Jesus we believe in death and resurrection. We believe that bad things can happen in life.
- We believe also that nothing bad is ever final, but that the love and power of the risen Lord are with us. Every day can be a "third day."

Saturday 24th September **Luke 9:43–45**

And all were astounded at the greatness of God. While everyone was amazed at all that he was doing, he said to his disciples, "Let these words sink into your ears: The Son of Man is going to be betrayed into human hands." But they did not understand this saying; its meaning was concealed from them, so that they could not perceive it. And they were afraid to ask him about this saying.

- When we look at Jesus in prayer, we are looking at the one who will soon be betrayed into the hands of his brothers and sisters, for all are brothers and sisters to him. He would be betrayed by those who shared his background of faith.
- When we look at Jesus in prayer, we look on the one who would go to death for us, betrayed by one like us.

september 25–october 1

Something to think and pray about each day this week:

Resting Awhile

We need to recognize exhaustion, in ourselves and in others. When Jesus saw it in his disciples, exhausted by all the unscripted coming and going of the crowds (Mark 6:30), he said, "Come away by yourselves to a lonely place, and rest awhile." This is the origin of the Christian practice of making a retreat: a lonely place, where we can drop our public mask, reflect on our life, and rest. I do it in a small way whenever I open up *Sacred Space* and devote some time to just God and me.

As you read *Sacred Space*, you are answering Jesus' invitation to come away to a deserted place and rest a while. Do not be afraid of being alone. Fear rather the opposite: as the philosopher Blaise Pascal wrote, "The sole cause of man's unhappiness is that he does not know how to stay quietly in his room." Jesus allowed the crowds to surround him and draw comfort from him; but to refresh his own strength he retreated alone into communion with his heavenly Father.

Lord, there are times when I want to get away from the crowds, when I feel oppressed by company. If I can reach you in prayer, and know that you are more central to me than my own thoughts, I feel at peace, as the apostles must have felt.

The Presence of God
I remind myself that, as I sit here now,
God is gazing on me with love and holding me in being.
I pause for a moment and think of this.

Freedom
Lord, grant me the grace to be free from the excesses of this life.
Let me not get caught up with the desire for wealth.
Keep my heart and mind free to love and serve you.

Consciousness
How am I really feeling? Light-hearted? Heavy-hearted?
I may be very much at peace, happy to be here.
Equally, I may be frustrated, worried, or angry.
I acknowledge how I really am. It is the real me that the Lord loves.

The Word
I take my time to read the Word of God, slowly, a few times, allowing myself to dwell on anything that strikes me. (Please turn to your scripture on the following pages. Inspiration points are there should you need them. When you are ready, return here to continue.)

Conversation
Do I notice myself reacting as I pray with the Word of God?
Do I feel challenged, comforted, angry?
Imagining Jesus sitting or standing by me,
I speak out my feelings, as one trusted friend to another.

Conclusion
Glory be to the Father, and to the Son, and to the Holy Spirit,
As it was in the beginning, is now, and ever shall be,
World without end. Amen

Sunday 25th September,
Twenty-sixth Sunday in Ordinary Time Matthew 21:28–32

Jesus said, "What do you think? A man had two sons; he went to the first and said, 'Son, go and work in the vineyard today.' He answered, 'I will not'; but later he changed his mind and went. The father went to the second and said the same; and he answered, 'I go, sir'; but he did not go. Which of the two did the will of his father?" They said, "The first." Jesus said to them, "Truly I tell you, the tax collectors and the prostitutes are going into the kingdom of God ahead of you. For John came to you in the way of righteousness and you did not believe him, but the tax collectors and the prostitutes believed him; and even after you saw it, you did not change your minds and believe him."

- We all want more than talk. We look for integrity in our lives and in the lives of others. We find it hard to live with hypocrisy. Jesus seems to accept that we will not always do good willingly. This is spiritual and human realism.
- Christian commitment is walking with Jesus. It is being in the world like Jesus, bringing his attitudes of compassion and justice with us. It is trying to affect the world as he did.

Monday 26th September Luke 9:46–48

An argument arose among them as to which one of them was the greatest. But Jesus, aware of their inner thoughts, took a little child and put it by his side, and said to them, "Whoever welcomes this child in my name welcomes me, and whoever welcomes me welcomes the one who sent me; for the least among all of you is the greatest."

- In acknowledging children in the group and giving them time, Jesus was going against his culture and religion. Children, while loved, would not find time with a religious teacher.

- Jesus is the one for all, and the surest way of showing this was to give time to the children, against the advice of his disciples.

Tuesday 27th September **Luke 9:51–56**

When the days drew near for him to be taken up, Jesus set his face to go to Jerusalem. And he sent messengers ahead of him. On their way they entered a village of the Samaritans to make ready for him; but they did not receive him, because his face was set toward Jerusalem. When his disciples James and John saw it, they said, "Lord, do you want us to command fire to come down from heaven and consume them?" But he turned and rebuked them. Then they went on to another village.

- Jesus is a picture of determination, taking the direct route to Jerusalem, even if it meant potential trouble with Samaritans. He had "set his face" and would not deviate nor respond to rejection.
- Can I echo this resolve in my own life, holding firm despite people or events that may tend to lead me away from Jesus?

Wednesday 28th September **Luke 9:57–62**

As they were going along the road, someone said to him, "I will follow you wherever you go." And Jesus said to him, "Foxes have holes, and birds of the air have nests; but the Son of Man has nowhere to lay his head." To another he said, "Follow me." But he said, "Lord, first let me go and bury my father." But Jesus said to him, "Let the dead bury their own dead; but as for you, go and proclaim the kingdom of God." Another said, "I will follow you, Lord; but let me first say farewell to those at my home." Jesus said to him, "No one who puts a hand to the plow and looks back is fit for the kingdom of God."

- We can look back on this month and give thanks for the graces of prayer and other times.

- We can look forward as Jesus recommends today—to move into full-hearted service and love of him, knowing that his call involves us in all of our lives—prayer and action, love and friendship, justice and reconciliation.

Thursday 29th September,
Sts. Michael, Gabriel, and Raphael **John 1:47–51**

When Jesus saw Nathanael coming toward him, he said of him, "Here is truly an Israelite in whom there is no deceit!" Nathanael asked him, "Where did you get to know me?" Jesus answered, "I saw you under the fig tree before Philip called you." Nathanael replied, "Rabbi, you are the Son of God! You are the King of Israel!" Jesus answered, "Do you believe because I told you that I saw you under the fig tree? You will see greater things than these." And he said to him, "Very truly, I tell you, you will see heaven opened and the angels of God ascending and descending upon the Son of Man."

- Jesus is never finished with doing good! Nathanael was promised more of the good things of God, at a time when he was in the fullness of consolation. With Jesus the best is always yet to come.
- Our time with the Lord means opening ourselves in words and in silence to the best of God's love.

Friday 30th September **Luke 10:13–16**

Woe to you, Chorazin! Woe to you, Bethsaida! For if the deeds of power done in you had been done in Tyre and Sidon, they would have repented long ago, sitting in sackcloth and ashes. But at the judgment it will be more tolerable for Tyre and Sidon than for you. And you, Capernaum, will you be exalted to heaven? No, you will be brought down to Hades. Whoever listens to you listens to me, and whoever rejects you rejects me, and whoever rejects me rejects the one who sent me."

- Jesus berates the people for not recognizing him and listening to him. They had rejected him and his message. They had turned their faces away from him.
- We need a discerning heart to repent, to hear our personal invitation and turn back towards God. Jesus still "speaks" to us in many ways—in the ordinary loves and events of the day.

Saturday 1st October **Luke 10:21–24**

At that same hour Jesus rejoiced in the Holy Spirit and said, "I thank you, Father, Lord of heaven and earth, because you have hidden these things from the wise and the intelligent and have revealed them to infants; yes, Father, for such was your gracious will. All things have been handed over to me by my Father; and no one knows who the Son is except the Father, or who the Father is except the Son and anyone to whom the Son chooses to reveal him." Then turning to the disciples, Jesus said to them privately, "Blessed are the eyes that see what you see! For I tell you that many prophets and kings desired to see what you see, but did not see it, and to hear what you hear, but did not hear it."

- Sometimes people like to know that their names are on a park or church bench, or on the wall where they worked; they know then they might be remembered.
- Our names are carved on the hand of God and are written in heaven; all ways of saying we are known by God and are important to him. What better place than heaven for our names to be written. We know then that we are expected!

october 2–8

Something to think and pray about each day this week:

The Innocent Lamb

John the Baptist called Jesus "the Lamb of God" (John 1:29). The title had biblical overtones of the Passover lamb and of the Suffering Servant in Isaiah, led like a lamb to the slaughter, an innocent victim who would endure his sufferings to redeem his people.

Lord, whenever I hear of some atrocious barbarisms by one of our race, and of the injustice and pain which people suffer through others' wickedness, I remember that this is the world you entered, the burden you took on yourself. You had a strong back to carry the evil that is in the world. Jesus, Lamb of God, we will never exhaust our knowledge of you with titles. Let me grow steadily in that knowledge, making my picture of you ever richer.

The Presence of God
In the silence of my innermost being,
in the fragments of my yearned-for wholeness,
can I hear the whispers of God's presence?
Can I remember when I felt God's nearness?
When we walked together and I let myself be embraced by God's love.

Freedom
I ask for the grace
to let go of my own concerns
and be open to what God is asking of me,
to let myself be guided and formed by my loving Creator.

Consciousness
I exist in a web of relationships—links to nature, people, God.
I trace out these links, giving thanks for the life that flows through them.
Some links are twisted or broken: I may feel regret, anger, disappointment.
I pray for the gift of acceptance and forgiveness.

The Word
The Word of God comes down to us through the scriptures. May the Holy Spirit enlighten my mind and my heart to respond to the gospel teachings. (Please turn to your scripture on the following pages. Inspiration points are there should you need them. When you are ready, return here to continue.)

Conversation
Remembering that I am still in God's presence,
I imagine Jesus himself standing or sitting beside me,
and say whatever is on my mind, whatever is in my heart,
speaking as one friend to another.

Conclusion

Glory be to the Father, and to the Son, and to the Holy Spirit,
As it was in the beginning, is now, and ever shall be,
World without end. Amen

Sunday 2nd October, Twenty-seventh Sunday in Ordinary Time **Matthew 21:42–43**

Jesus said to them, "Have you never read in the scriptures: 'The stone that the builders rejected has become the cornerstone; this was the Lord's doing, and it is amazing in our eyes'? Therefore I tell you, the kingdom of God will be taken away from you and given to a people that produces the fruits of the kingdom."

- The stone at the top of the arch holds the arch together. Without its strength and correct positioning, the arch falls. Jesus is the rejected one who has become the centre of our faith and our lives.
- When Jesus is rejected, it only strengthens his relationship with his Father, who makes him the keystone and the centre of gospel-faith. He knows our weakness and the pain of rejection; is this what makes us want to be close to him and to follow him closely?

Monday 3rd October **Luke 10:25–37**

Just then a lawyer stood up to test Jesus. "Teacher," he said, "what must I do to inherit eternal life?" He said to him, "What is written in the law? What do you read there?" He answered, "You shall love the Lord your God with all your heart, and with all your soul, and with all your strength, and with all your mind; and your neighbor as yourself." And he said to him, "You have given the right answer; do this, and you will live." But wanting to justify himself, he asked Jesus, "And who is my neighbor?" Jesus replied, "A man was going down from Jerusalem to Jericho, and fell into the hands of robbers, who stripped him, beat him, and went away, leaving him half dead. Now by chance a priest was going down that road; and when he saw him, he passed by on the other side. So likewise a Levite, when he came to the place and saw him, passed by on the other side. But a Samaritan while traveling came near him; and when he saw him, he was moved with pity. He went to him and bandaged his wounds, having poured oil and wine on them. Then he put him on his own animal, brought him to an inn, and took care of him. The next day he took out two denarii, gave them to the innkeeper, and said, 'Take care of him; and when I come back, I will repay you whatever more you spend.' Which of these three, do you think, was a neighbor to the man who fell into the hands of the robbers?" He said, "The one who showed him mercy." Jesus said to him, "Go and do likewise."

- Some say this is the best story and best-remembered story ever told.
- Let it hit you anew in prayer. Ask yourself: What makes me go to the other side? What makes me avoid some type of people in need? Who might they be?

Tuesday 4th October,
St. Francis of Assisi **Matthew 11:25–27**

Jesus said, "I thank you, Father, Lord of heaven and earth, because you have hidden these things from the wise and the intelligent and have revealed them to infants; yes, Father, for such was your gracious will. All things have been handed over to me by my Father; and no one knows the Son except the Father, and no one knows the Father except the Son and anyone to whom the Son chooses to reveal him."

- There are famous stories about Francis—meeting and kissing a leper, taming a wolf, and many others. Each of them can teach us.
- It is on the inside that the leper and wolf are encountered. Have we made friends with our "leper" or "wolf" yet? What do we fear in them? Can I ask the Lord for the courage to accept them?

Wednesday 5th October **Luke 11:1–4**

Jesus was praying in a certain place, and after he had finished, one of his disciples said to him, "Lord, teach us to pray, as John taught his disciples." He said to them, "When you pray, say: Father, hallowed be your name. Your kingdom come. Give us each day our daily bread. And forgive us our sins, for we ourselves forgive everyone indebted to us. And do not bring us to the time of trial."

- It is difficult to forgive even small hurts, let alone injustice, abuse, or neglect. Jesus encourages us to think of these in prayer.
- One step towards forgiveness is to pray for someone. Even when we can't talk to a person, or think kindly of them, maybe we can pray for them.

Thursday 6th October **Luke 11:5–10**

And Jesus said to them, "Suppose one of you has a friend, and you go to him at midnight and say to him, 'Friend, lend me three loaves of bread; for a friend of mine has arrived, and I have nothing to set before him.' And he answers from within, 'Do not bother me; the door has already been locked, and my children are with me in bed; I cannot get up and give you anything.' I tell you, even though he will not get up and give him anything because he is his friend, at least because of his persistence he will get up and give him whatever he needs. So I say to you, Ask, and it will be given you; search, and you will find; knock, and the door will be opened for you. For everyone who asks receives, and everyone who searches finds, and for everyone who knocks, the door will be opened."

- We may feel we have been knocking at the door of God for years in prayer for ourselves or for someone else; we may feel tired of asking. What does it mean that we always receive?
- Prayer is always heard by God, but not always answered as we might wish. We can ask ourselves what we receive by knocking at the door of God. We receive something of God's love and Holy Spirit every time we pray.

Friday 7th October **Luke 11:15–20**

Some of the crowd said of Jesus, "He casts out demons by Beelzebul, the ruler of the demons." Others, to test him, kept demanding from him a sign from heaven. But he knew what they were thinking and said to them, "Every kingdom divided against itself becomes a desert, and house falls on house. If Satan also is divided against himself, how will his kingdom stand?—for you say that I cast out the demons by Beelzebul. Now if I cast out the demons by Beelzebul, by whom do your exorcists cast them out? Therefore they will be your judges. But if it is by the finger of God that I cast out the demons, then the kingdom of God has come to you."

- Temptations to stray off the path of Jesus are always part of life. We find ourselves challenged in all sorts of areas of life like wealth, success, sexuality, comfort, justice.
- The humble person knows that we can fall often, but that the real follower of Jesus is the one who can rise from a fall and do better in the future.

Saturday 8th October **Luke 11:27–28**

While Jesus was speaking, a woman in the crowd raised her voice and said to him, "Blessed is the womb that bore you and the breasts that nursed you!" But he said, "Blessed rather are those who hear the word of God and obey it!"

- People often broke out in spontaneous praise of Jesus, like when he spoke well or healed people. The woman in question here got so excited that she praised Jesus' mother.
- Jesus' reply says what most praises him and God: the person who lives by the Word of God and puts this word into action. In this way the word becomes flesh every day among us.

october 9–15

Something to think and pray about each day this week:

Come and See

In the first encounter of the Baptist's disciples with Jesus (John 1:35), there is a lovely moment that the two disciples remembered with a dart of pleasure. They were watching Jesus with curiosity, following him from a distance. But we cannot be merely spectators with Jesus. He involves us. I could not begin to look for God unless God had already found me. Jesus turns and asks the two men a searching question: "What are you looking for?" Many would say, "I'm not looking for anything. I am just trying to survive." But in sober moments we realize that we would like our lives to amount to more than just getting and spending, eating and sleeping.

This is a scene to imagine my way into. I ask you, Lord, "Where are you staying?" And when you say, "Come and see," I explore. What do I find? The gospel gives no hint of the style of the dwelling, maybe a rented room. But the two disciples remained there for the rest of the day. It was your company that held them. In that company they felt hope, and saw the good in people around them. They were excited, and told their family and friends about this man.

The Presence of God
God is with me, but more,
God is within me, giving me existence.
Let me dwell for a moment on God's life-giving presence
in my body, my mind, my heart
and in the whole of my life.

Freedom
I ask for the grace to believe
in what I could be and do
if I only allowed God, my loving Creator,
to continue to create me, guide me and shape me.

Consciousness
Knowing that God loves me unconditionally,
I can afford to be honest about how I am.
How has the last day been, and how do I feel now?
I share my feelings openly with the Lord.

The Word
I read the Word of God slowly, a few times over, and I listen to what God is saying to me. (Please turn to your scripture on the following pages. Inspiration points are there should you need them. When you are ready, return here to continue.)

Conversation
How has God's Word moved me? Has it left me cold?
Has it consoled me or moved me to act in a new way?
I imagine Jesus standing or sitting beside me,
I turn and share my feelings with him.

Conclusion
Glory be to the Father, and to the Son, and to the Holy Spirit,
As it was in the beginning, is now, and ever shall be,
World without end. Amen

Sunday 9th October,
Twenty-eighth Sunday in Ordinary Time Matthew 22:1–14

Once more Jesus spoke to them in parables, saying: "The kingdom of heaven may be compared to a king who gave a wedding banquet for his son. He sent his slaves to call those who had been invited to the wedding banquet, but they would not come. Again he sent other slaves, saying, 'Tell those who have been invited: Look, I have prepared my dinner, my oxen and my fat calves have been slaughtered, and everything is ready; come to the wedding banquet.' But they made light of it and went away, one to his farm, another to his business, while the rest seized his slaves, mistreated them, and killed them. The king was enraged. He sent his troops, destroyed those murderers, and burned their city. Then he said to his slaves, 'The wedding is ready, but those invited were not worthy. Go therefore into the main streets, and invite everyone you find to the wedding banquet.' Those slaves went out into the streets and gathered all whom they found, both good and bad; so the wedding hall was filled with guests. But when the king came in to see the guests, he noticed a man there who was not wearing a wedding robe, and he said to him, 'Friend, how did you get in here without a wedding robe?' And he was speechless. Then the king said to the attendants, 'Bind him hand and foot, and throw him into the outer darkness, where there will be weeping and gnashing of teeth.' For many are called, but few are chosen."

- Can you imagine throwing a party that nobody comes to? Or the few who turn up staying just a short time and then going away? It's something like that in the gospel story today.

- What does God do? God really goes after us. God wants us there and wants a full table. The table of God is for everyone. He goes right into the middle of life to look for all sorts of people—not just one type of person. God wants our Yes.

Monday 10th October **Luke 11:29–32**

When the crowds were increasing, Jesus began to say, "This generation is an evil generation; it asks for a sign, but no sign will be given to it except the sign of Jonah. For just as Jonah became a sign to the people of Nineveh, so the Son of Man will be to this generation. The queen of the South will rise at the judgment with the people of this generation and condemn them, because she came from the ends of the earth to listen to the wisdom of Solomon, and see, something greater than Solomon is here! The people of Nineveh will rise up at the judgment with this generation and condemn it, because they repented at the proclamation of Jonah, and see, something greater than Jonah is here!"

- Crowds followed Jesus, but he was not "into the numbers game." He reminded people that not everyone who follows a religious leader leads a religious life.
- Prayer is a time to leave the crowd and follow the Lord who speaks to the heart of each of us. Spend time in prayer looking in, rather than out, listening rather than speaking.

Tuesday 11th October **Luke 11:37–41**

While Jesus was speaking, a Pharisee invited him to dine with him; so he went in and took his place at the table. The Pharisee was amazed to see that he did not first wash before dinner. Then the Lord said to him, "Now you Pharisees clean the outside of the cup and of the dish, but inside you are full of greed and wickedness. You fools! Did not the one who made the outside make the inside also? So give for alms those things that are within; and see, everything will be clean for you."

- It's one thing to speak a lot about God and holy things; it's another to live out what we hear and believe.
- Take time to deepen what is most relevant about our faith and life, time to allow the Word to seep into our hearts and minds.

Wednesday 12th October **Luke 11:42–46**

But woe to you Pharisees! For you tithe mint and rue and herbs of all kinds, and neglect justice and the love of God; it is these you ought to have practiced, without neglecting the others. Woe to you Pharisees! For you love to have the seat of honor in the synagogues and to be greeted with respect in the market places. Woe to you! For you are like unmarked graves, and people walk over them without realizing it." One of the lawyers answered him, "Teacher, when you say these things, you insult us too." And he said, "Woe also to you lawyers! For you load people with burdens hard to bear, and you yourselves do not lift a finger to ease them."

- God may be the God of small things, but not of the small mind or small heart. Jesus rebukes people who get uptight and upset over the small things of religion or for those who want to be honoured for religious ceremony.
- The religion God looks for is the faith of the heart, and the love that is born of faith and itself gives birth to deeper faith.

Thursday 13th October **Luke 11:47–54**

Jesus said to the lawyers, "Woe to you! For you build the tombs of the prophets whom your ancestors killed. So you are witnesses and approve of the deeds of your ancestors; for they killed them, and you build their tombs. Therefore also the Wisdom of God said, 'I will send them prophets and apostles, some of whom they will kill and persecute,' so that this generation may be charged with the blood of all the prophets shed since the foundation of the world, from the blood of Abel to the blood of Zechariah, who perished between the altar and the sanctuary. Yes, I tell you, it will be charged against this generation. Woe to you lawyers! For you have taken away the key of knowledge; you did not enter yourselves, and you hindered those who were entering." When he went outside, the scribes and the Pharisees began to be very hostile towards him and to cross-examine him about many things, lying in wait for him, to catch him in something he might say.

- Jesus is challenging the strong religious beliefs and practices of many of the people; and he challenges us in the same way.
- True prayer brings us in touch with our bigness and smallness of mind and heart. God's love touches the heart to widen its love for all sorts of people.

Friday 14th October **Luke 12:1–7**

Meanwhile, when the crowd gathered by the thousands, so that they trampled on one another, Jesus began to speak first to his disciples, "Beware of the yeast of the Pharisees, that is, their hypocrisy. Nothing is covered up that will not be uncovered, and nothing secret that will not become known. Therefore whatever you have said in the dark will be heard in the light, and what you have whispered behind closed doors will be proclaimed from the housetops. I tell you, my friends, do not fear those who kill the body, and after that can do nothing more. But I will warn you whom to fear: fear him who, after he has killed, has authority to cast into hell. Yes, I tell you, fear him! Are not five sparrows sold for two pennies? Yet not one of them is forgotten in God's sight. But even the hairs of your head are all counted. Do not be afraid; you are of more value than many sparrows."

- Jesus points out that people may try to lead others astray. The world can be a sort of battlefield between good and evil; communities and individuals need to take care not to be misled.
- God is the carer, the one who values each of us fully. Can we do the same, and treat others as God treats us—each of us being of infinite value?

Saturday 15th October,
St. Teresa of Avila **John 15:4–5**

Jesus said to his apostles, "Abide in me as I abide in you. Just as the branch cannot bear fruit by itself unless it abides in the vine, neither can you unless you abide in me. I am the vine, you are the branches. Those who abide in me and I in them bear much fruit, because apart from me you can do nothing."

- There is a wonderful intimacy in these words—"abide in me as I abide in you." It is already happening.
- Jesus is with us, God is with us; bound together, this is how we communicate new life to others.

october 16–22

Something to think and pray about each day this week:

The Image of God

One way into prayer is through the imagination. Take a Gospel scene such as the question put to Jesus (Matthew 22:15): "Is it lawful to pay tribute to Caesar?" Read the text slowly; then read it again. Place yourself in the scene, standing beside Jesus, watching him as the Pharisees lay a trap with their question. If you can, see the place, the people, the coin of tribute. Imagine the tension provoked by their words. Be present with Jesus as he asks for the denarius. Hear his voice as he exposes the hypocrisy of their flattery, but takes their question seriously and gives an answer that has echoed down the centuries: "Give therefore to the emperor the things that are the emperor's, and to God the things that are God's." Savor its implications.

The Presence of God
To be present is to arrive as one is and open up to the other.
At this instant, as I arrive here, God is present waiting for me.
God always arrives before me, desiring to connect with me
even more than my most intimate friend.
I take a moment and greet my loving God.

Freedom
In these days, God taught me
as a schoolteacher teaches a pupil. (St. Ignatius)
I remind myself that there are things God has to teach me yet,
and ask for the grace to hear them and let them change me.

Consciousness
In the presence of my loving Creator,
I look honestly at my feelings over the last day,
the highs, the lows, and the level ground.
Can I see where the Lord has been present?

The Word
I take my time to read the Word of God, slowly, a few times, allowing myself to dwell on anything that strikes me. (Please turn to your scripture on the following pages. Inspiration points are there should you need them. When you are ready, return here to continue.)

Conversation
What feelings are rising in me
as I pray and reflect on God's Word?
I imagine Jesus himself sitting or standing beside me,
and open my heart to him.

Conclusion
Glory be to the Father, and to the Son, and to the Holy Spirit,
As it was in the beginning, is now, and ever shall be,
World without end. Amen

Sunday 16th October,
Twenty-ninth Sunday in Ordinary Time Matthew 22:15–21

Then the Pharisees went and plotted to entrap him in what he said. So they sent their disciples to him, along with the Herodians, saying, "Teacher, we know that you are sincere, and teach the way of God in accordance with truth, and show deference to no one; for you do not regard people with partiality. Tell us, then, what you think. Is it lawful to pay taxes to the emperor, or not?" But Jesus, aware of their malice, said, "Why are you putting me to the test, you hypocrites? Show me the coin used for the tax." And they brought him a denarius. Then he said to them, "Whose head is this, and whose title?" They answered, "The emperor's." Then he said to them, "Give therefore to the emperor the things that are the emperor's, and to God the things that are God's."

- This was an exquisite, malicious trap laid for Jesus: if he went one way he lost followers; if he went the other, he would be seen as a threat to public order.
- Jesus embraces the confrontation he did not seek, and turns it on its head. God is always the highest authority.
- When my beliefs are threatened, do I tend to embrace the quiet life and avoid confrontation, or do I stand up for what I believe?

Monday 17th October Luke 12:13–21

Someone in the crowd said to Jesus, "Teacher, tell my brother to divide the family inheritance with me." But he said to him, "Friend, who set me to be a judge or arbitrator over you?" And he said to them, "Take care! Be on your guard against all kinds of greed; for one's life does not consist in the abundance of possessions." Then he told them a parable: "The land of a rich man produced abundantly. And he thought to himself, 'What should I do, for I have no place to store my crops?' Then he said, 'I will do this: I will pull down my barns and build larger ones, and there I will store all my grain and my goods. And I will say to my soul, 'Soul, you have ample goods laid up for many years; relax, eat, drink, be merry.' But God said to him, 'You fool! This very night your life is being demanded of you. And the things you have prepared, whose will they be?' So it is with those who store up treasures for themselves but are not rich toward God."

- Possessions and wealth can bring us near to God, or away from God when we focus our goals on them.
- They can become the centre of self-absorption rather than a means of helping and coming closer to others. We come from God and go to God empty of possessions but full of God's love and the love we have tried to share.

Tuesday 18th October,
St. Luke, Evangelist **Luke 10:1–7**

After this the Lord appointed seventy others and sent them on ahead of him in pairs to every town and place where he himself intended to go. He said to them, "The harvest is plentiful, but the laborers are few; therefore ask the Lord of the harvest to send out laborers into his harvest. Go on your way. See, I am sending you out like lambs into the midst of wolves. Carry no purse, no bag, no sandals; and greet no one on the road. Whatever house you enter, first say, 'Peace to this house!' And if anyone is there who shares in peace, your peace will rest on that person; but if not, it will return to you. Remain in the same house, eating and drinking whatever they provide, for the laborer deserves to be paid."

- Jesus' instructions for these missionaries are similar to those given to the twelve: travel light; be prepared; bring healing and peace; spread word of the kingdom; accept hospitality.
- Let me make this my checklist for today. How do I measure up?

Wednesday 19th October **Luke 12:39–44**

Jesus said, "But know this: if the owner of the house had known at what hour the thief was coming, he would not have let his house be broken into. You also must be ready, for the Son of Man is coming at an unexpected hour." Peter said, "Lord, are you telling this parable for us or for everyone?" And the Lord said, "Who then is the faithful and prudent manager whom his master will put in charge of his slaves, to give them their allowance of food at the proper time? Blessed is that slave whom his master will find at work when he arrives. Truly I tell you, he will put that one in charge of all his possessions."

- The Lord can touch our lives with a mood of peace, a challenge, or a word of the scripture at any time if we are alert and open.
- Openness to God is the fruit of prayer in worship or personal time; it requires little human skill. Prayer is God's gift to us and God's work within us.

Thursday 20th October **Luke 12:49–53**

I came to bring fire to the earth, and how I wish it were already kindled! I have a baptism with which to be baptized, and what stress I am under until it is completed! Do you think that I have come to bring peace to the earth? No, I tell you, but rather division! From now on five in one household will be divided, three against two and two against three; they will be divided: father against son and son against father, mother against daughter and daughter against mother, mother-in-law against her daughter-in-law and daughter-in-law against mother-in-law.

- Jesus can bring division among people—those either with him or against him. He can bring division also inside each of us.
- Let me take time to sit with Jesus, to sift through the different desires and actions of my life. In prayer we ask for the grace to "know him more, love him more, and serve him."

Friday 21st October **Luke 12:54–56**

Jesus also said to the crowds, "When you see a cloud rising in the west, you immediately say, 'It is going to rain'; and so it happens. And when you see the south wind blowing, you say, 'There will be scorching heat'; and it happens. You hypocrites! You know how to interpret the appearance of earth and sky, but why do you not know how to interpret the present time?"

- We need to put aside time to notice God in our lives. We can look back over a day or a week and notice where we found love given and love received, where we found the moments of depth in our lives, the call to help or to serve.
- Let me think of some of the different ways I see the presence and activity of God, in my life and in my day.

Saturday 22nd October **Luke 13:1–5**

There were some present who told Jesus about the Galileans whose blood Pilate had mingled with their sacrifices. He asked them, "Do you think that because these Galileans suffered in this way they were worse sinners than all other Galileans? No, I tell you; but unless you repent, you will all perish as they did. Or those eighteen who were killed when the tower of Siloam fell on them—do you think that they were worse offenders than all the others living in Jerusalem? No, I tell you; but unless you repent, you will all perish just as they did."

- In the different desires and activities of life we can be with God or not with him. We can love him fully or find ourselves tempted.
- Jesus calls us all the time to turn back, to change so that we live out of the best side of ourselves to become more like him.

october 23–29

Something to think and pray about each day this week:

Reading the Good News

One scene I would love to have witnessed is described by Luke when Jesus reads the book of Isaiah in the Nazareth synagogue (Luke 4:14–22). Incidental details tell us much about the ordinary life of Jesus. It was his custom to go to the synagogue on the sabbath. Though he took issue with details of the Law proclaimed there, he chose to join with his community in the worship of God. Though he wrote nothing (as far as we know), he read, and was chosen to read to the assembly. He read standing, handed back the scroll to the attendant, then he sat down—the posture for serious teaching. The eyes of all in the assembly were fixed on him. It is a moment of grace and promise, as he brings the good news to his own people.

For those few minutes, history is holding its breath. The anointed one, the Messiah, has arrived and declared himself. I watch the scene unfolding, the tension in Jesus as he makes his claim, the anticipation among those present, then the mixture of excitement and rejection.

Jesus is in his hometown, a handsome young man who has already been talked about for his teaching and cures. I listen, Lord, as you start to proclaim the good news. But this is different. It is not just that you proclaim the good news. You are the good news in your person.

Presence of God
What is present to me is what has a hold on my becoming.
I reflect on the presence of God always there in love,
amidst the many things that have a hold on me.
I pause and pray that I may let God
affect my becoming in this precise moment.

Freedom
If God were trying to tell me something, would I know?
If God were reassuring me or challenging me, would I notice?
I ask for the grace to be free of my own preoccupations
and open to what God may be saying to me.

Consciousness
Knowing that God loves me unconditionally,
I look honestly over the last day, its events and my feelings.
Do I have something to be grateful for? Then I give thanks.
Is there something I am sorry for? Then I ask forgiveness.

The Word
God speaks to each one of us individually. I need to listen to what he is saying to me. (Please turn to your scripture on the following pages. Inspiration points are there should you need them. When you are ready, return here to continue.)

Conversation
What is stirring in me as I pray?
Am I consoled, troubled, left cold?
I imagine Jesus himself standing or sitting at my side,
and share my feelings with him.

Conclusion
Glory be to the Father, and to the Son, and to the Holy Spirit,
As it was in the beginning, is now, and ever shall be,
World without end. Amen

Sunday 23rd October,
Thirtieth Sunday in Ordinary Time **Matthew 22:34–40**

When the Pharisees heard that he had silenced the Sadducees, they gathered together, and one of them, a lawyer, asked him a question to test him. "Teacher, which commandment in the law is the greatest?" He said to him, "'You shall love the Lord your God with all your heart, and with all your soul, and with all your mind.' This is the greatest and first commandment. And a second is like it: 'You shall love your neighbor as yourself.' On these two commandments hang all the law and the prophets."

- The gospel today centres the message of Jesus on love; on two loves united in each of us. Love God, love the neighbour—this is the only commandment of Jesus. Without this, all we say we do for him is really done for ourselves.
- No detail of religious observance is above this law of love. Jesus said this and lived it in his life. He never allowed the laws of religion to overtake the need for love.

Monday 24th October **Luke 13:10–17**

Now Jesus was teaching in one of the synagogues on the sabbath. And just then there appeared a woman with a spirit that had crippled her for eighteen years. She was bent over and was quite unable to stand up straight. When Jesus saw her, he called her over and said, "Woman, you are set free from your ailment." When he laid his hands on her, immediately she stood up straight and began praising God. But the leader of the synagogue, indignant because Jesus had cured on the sabbath, kept saying to the crowd, "There are six days on which work ought to be done; come on those days and be cured, and not on the sabbath day." But the Lord answered him and said, "You hypocrites! Does not each of you on the sabbath untie his ox or his donkey from the manger, and lead it away to give it water? And ought not this woman, a daughter of Abraham whom Satan bound for eighteen long years, be set free from this bondage on the sabbath day?" When he said this, all his opponents were put to shame; and the entire crowd was rejoicing at all the wonderful things that he was doing.

- Religion in Jesus' time forbade even helping someone on the sabbath. Jesus holds out against that. We can be kept in religious bondage, and he was comparing the woman's physical bondage to the way the others were stuck in legalisms which had no heart.
- Through prayer, through time with the Lord, we can go deeper than ritual, deeper than laws, to sharing the saving love of Jesus.

Tuesday 25th October **Luke 13:18–19**

He said therefore, "What is the kingdom of God like? And to what should I compare it? It is like a mustard seed that someone took and sowed in the garden; it grew and became a tree, and the birds of the air made nests in its branches."

- *The God of Small Things* is the title of a popular novel. God is the God of the mustard seeds. Not alone do we grow from small beginnings of faith. We grow in faith and love through the small and ordinary experiences of life with one another.
- God, creator of heavens and earth, is interested in the things of our lives which loom large for us but may seem trivial to others—our hurt and grief, our aches and pains, our work, and all that goes to make up our lives.

Wednesday 26th October **Romans 8:26–27**

The Spirit helps us in our weakness; for we do not know how to pray as we ought, but that very Spirit intercedes with sighs too deep for words. And God, who searches the heart, knows what is the mind of the Spirit, because the Spirit intercedes for the saints according to the will of God.

- Paul teaches us that the Holy Spirit is central to our prayer. Whatever our human limitations, they are no barrier to the Spirit working through and in us.
- We always need the Spirit to help us carry through the work of sharing the good news.

Thursday 27th October **Luke 13:31–35**

At that very hour some Pharisees came and said to him, "Get away from here, for Herod wants to kill you." He said to them, "Go and tell that fox for me, 'Listen, I am casting out demons and performing cures today and tomorrow, and on the third day I finish my work. Yet today, tomorrow, and the next day I must be on my way, because it is impossible for a prophet to be killed outside of Jerusalem.' Jerusalem, Jerusalem, the city that kills the prophets and stones those who are sent to it! How often have I desired to gather your children together as a hen gathers her brood under her wings, and you were not willing! See, your house is left to you. And I tell you, you will not see me until the time comes when you say, 'Blessed is the one who comes in the name of the Lord.'"

- Jesus' heart goes out to the people of his beloved city, Jerusalem. His heart goes out today in every city, for he lives among us everywhere.
- We pray that our hearts become like his and that we will look on the needs of people and hear their cries as he does.

Friday 28th October,
Sts. Simon and Jude, Apostles **Luke 6:12–16**

Now during those days he went out to the mountain to pray; and he spent the night in prayer to God. And when day came, he called his disciples and chose twelve of them, whom he also named apostles: Simon, whom he named Peter, and his brother Andrew, and James, and John, and Philip, and Bartholomew, and

Matthew, and Thomas, and James son of Alphaeus, and Simon, who was called the Zealot, and Judas son of James, and Judas Iscariot, who became a traitor.

- After prayer, Jesus chose his first community. The beginnings of the Church are here. These are the ones who would gather with others at Pentecost and move out into the whole world to proclaim the good news.
- As the gospel goes on, we will get to know some of them well. They are just like each of us—and we are just like each of them.

Saturday 29th October **Luke 14:1, 7–11**

On one occasion when Jesus was going to the house of a leader of the Pharisees to eat a meal on the sabbath, they were watching him closely. When he noticed how the guests chose the places of honor, he told them a parable. "When you are invited by someone to a wedding banquet, do not sit down at the place of honor, in case someone more distinguished than you has been invited by your host; and the host who invited both of you may come and say to you, 'Give this person your place,' and then in disgrace you would start to take the lowest place. But when you are invited, go and sit down at the lowest place, so that when your host comes, he may say to you, 'Friend, move up higher'; then you will be honored in the presence of all who sit at the table with you. For all who exalt themselves will be humbled, and those who humble themselves will be exalted."

- We are often drawn to humble people. In Jesus, we see the humility of the one who knew who he was—loved by the Father—and knew his mission—to serve others.
- He is among us as one who serves, the one who sees the needs of his people and does his best to meet them. In word and action he served us in love—even on to death.

october 30–november 5

Something to think and pray about each day this week:

How God Loves

Working as a therapist, I have to be a methodological atheist. I do not take it for granted that anybody believes in God. God gave us our heart. If you can get back to the healthy centre of it, you can trust it. Religious friends sometimes protest if I write something that does not stress the God factor. I trust the God factor in an experience with people if I can help them to their inner health and freedom. Freud offered an elegant definition of mental health: the ability to love and to work. If I can help people to love again (and to work again if they are of such an age), if I can help the love to flow again in a family, the Lord is there. You do not need a label or picture of the Sacred Heart. God is there.

One scriptural phrase that stays with me is that the love of God is poured out in our hearts through the Holy Spirit who is given to us. I see that in a tangible way when confronted by people with serious problems, people often weeping on the phone, in enormous emotional tension. Under their distress, they are still driven by love.

The Presence of God

God is with me, but more, God is within me.
Let me dwell for a moment on God's life-giving presence
in my body, in my mind, in my heart,
as I sit here, right now.

Freedom

I need to close out the noise, to rise above the noise;
The noise that interrupts, that separates,
The noise that isolates.
I need to listen to God again.

Consciousness

I remind myself that I am in the presence of the Lord.
I will take refuge in his loving heart.
He is my strength in times of weakness.
He is my comforter in times of sorrow.

The Word

I read the Word of God slowly, a few times over, and I listen to what God is saying to me. (Please turn to your scripture on the following pages. Inspiration points are there should you need them. When you are ready, return here to continue.)

Conversation

Do I notice myself reacting as I pray with the Word of God?
Do I feel challenged, comforted, angry?
Imagining Jesus sitting or standing by me,
I speak out my feelings, as one trusted friend to another.

Conclusion

Glory be to the Father, and to the Son, and to the Holy Spirit,
As it was in the beginning, is now, and ever shall be,
World without end. Amen

Sunday 30th October,
Thirty-first Sunday in Ordinary Time 1 Thessalonians 2:7–9, 13

We were gentle among you, like a nurse tenderly caring for her own children. So deeply do we care for you that we are determined to share with you not only the gospel of God but also our own selves, because you have become very dear to us. You remember our labor and toil, brothers and sisters; we worked night and day, so that we might not burden any of you while we proclaimed to you the gospel of God. We also constantly give thanks to God for this, that when you received the word of God that you heard from us, you accepted it not as a human word but as what it really is, God's word, which is also at work in you believers.

- Paul shares with us these images of God's love and his own—the devoted parent, the hard worker, the brotherly protector, the leader who passes on the gospel.
- Lord, give us church leaders with the zeal, the care, and the devotion of Paul. Encourage me with your parental love.

Monday 31st October Luke 14:12–14

Jesus said also to the one who had invited him, "When you give a luncheon or a dinner, do not invite your friends or your brothers or your relatives or rich neighbors, in case they may invite you in return, and you would be repaid. But when you give a banquet, invite the poor, the crippled, the lame, and the blind. And you will be blessed, because they cannot repay you, for you will be repaid at the resurrection of the righteous."

- Jesus is saying something here about not expecting thanks. He is hinting that we do what we do out of love, out of care, because we follow him. We invite to share in what we have people who have no way to return the favour.

- In our time with the Lord, we can offer what we do for God to God, knowing that this is reward enough.

Tuesday 1st November,
Feast of All Saints **Matthew 5:2–12**

He began to speak, and taught them, saying: "Blessed are the poor in spirit, for theirs is the kingdom of heaven. Blessed are those who mourn, for they will be comforted. Blessed are the meek, for they will inherit the earth. Blessed are those who hunger and thirst for righteousness, for they will be filled. Blessed are the merciful, for they will receive mercy. Blessed are the pure in heart, for they will see God. Blessed are the peacemakers, for they will be called children of God. Blessed are those who are persecuted for righteousness' sake, for theirs is the kingdom of heaven. Blessed are you when people revile you and persecute you and utter all kinds of evil against you falsely on my account. Rejoice and be glad, for your reward is great in heaven, for in the same way they persecuted the prophets who were before you."

- It is easy to recite these "blesseds" as a sort of mantra. They are the vision statement of Jesus. He lived what he said—that all of life is blessed, even the experiences we might never ask for.
- All who live according to his way of life are—and will be—richly blessed.

Wednesday 2nd November,
Feast of All Souls **Matthew 25:31–40**

When the Son of Man comes in his glory, and all the angels with him, then he will sit on the throne of his glory. All the nations will be gathered before him, and he will separate people one from another as a shepherd separates the sheep from the goats, and he will put the sheep at his right hand and the goats at the left. Then the king will say to those at his right hand, "Come, you that are blessed by my Father, inherit the kingdom prepared for you from the foundation of the world; for I was hungry and you gave me food, I was thirsty and you gave me something to drink, I was a stranger and you welcomed me, I was naked and you gave me clothing, I was sick and you took care of me, I was in prison and you visited me." Then the righteous will answer him, "Lord, when was it that we saw you hungry and gave you food, or thirsty and gave you something to drink? And when was it that we saw you a stranger and welcomed you, or naked and gave you clothing? And when was it that we saw you sick or in prison and visited you?" And the king will answer them, "Truly I tell you, just as you did it to one of the least of these who are members of my family, you did it to me."

- The death of Jesus reminds us that, as we will die, he has died. He has breathed his last as all will do. The Resurrection reminds us that as he has risen, we too will rise.
- The one who was the son of God on earth, and son of Mary, is in eternity the Son of God. As he is, we shall be.

Thursday 3rd November **Luke 15:1–10**

Now all the tax-collectors and sinners were coming near to listen to him. And the Pharisees and the scribes were grumbling and saying, "This fellow welcomes sinners and eats with them." So he told them this parable: "Which one of you, having a hundred sheep and losing one of them, does not leave the ninety-nine in the wilderness and go after the one that is lost until he finds it? When he has found it, he lays it on his shoulders and rejoices. And when he comes home, he calls together his friends and neighbours, saying to them, 'Rejoice with me, for I have found my sheep that was lost.' Just so, I tell you, there will be more joy in heaven over one sinner who repents than over ninety-nine righteous people who need no repentance. Or what woman having ten silver coins, if she loses one of them, does not light a lamp, sweep the house, and search carefully until she finds it? When she has found it, she calls together her friends and neighbours, saying, 'Rejoice with me, for I have found the coin that I had lost.' Just so, I tell you, there is joy in the presence of the angels of God over one sinner who repents."

- A painting of this scene shows a woman bent over looking intently for what she has lost. The coin was precious to her, a tenth of all her wealth. Jesus compares his care for us to this; he really wants us near him, faults and all.
- Our prayer time is that—the whole self is the self I bring to prayer, searching for the God who loves all of creation.

Friday 4th November **Luke 16:1–8**

Then Jesus said to the disciples, "There was a rich man who had a manager, and charges were brought to him that this man was squandering his property. So he summoned him and said to him, 'What is this that I hear about you? Give me an accounting of your management, because you cannot be my manager any longer.' Then the manager said to himself, 'What will I do, now that my master is taking the position away from me? I am not strong enough to dig, and I am ashamed to beg. I have decided what to do so that, when I am dismissed as manager, people may welcome me into their homes.' So, summoning his master's debtors one by one, he asked the first, 'How much do you owe my master?' He answered, 'A hundred jugs of olive oil.' He said to him, 'Take your bill, sit down quickly, and make it fifty.' Then he asked another, 'And how much do you owe?' He replied, 'A hundred containers of wheat.' He said to him, 'Take your bill and make it eighty.' And his master commended the dishonest manager because he had acted shrewdly; for the children of this age are more shrewd in dealing with their own generation than are the children of light."

- The quiet time we spend with the Lord can be a time of growing in wisdom and discernment; to put a question or decision before the Lord can put it into the wide perspective of love, mission, and gratitude.
- Can I use my *Sacred Space* time like that today?

Saturday 5th November **Luke 16:9–13**

Jesus said to the disciples, "And I tell you, make friends for yourselves by means of dishonest wealth so that when it is gone, they may welcome you into the eternal homes. Whoever is faithful in a very little is faithful also in much; and whoever is dishonest in a very little is dishonest also in much. If then you have not been faithful with the dishonest wealth, who will entrust to you the true riches? And if you have not been faithful with what belongs to another, who will give you what is your own? No slave can serve two masters; for a slave will either hate the one and love the other, or be devoted to the one and despise the other. You cannot serve God and wealth."

- This is a series of words, "sound bites," and varied instructions of Jesus. We mull over each of them and see which might touch us most. The scripture always has something new to say. Rather than read the word of scripture as you might read a newspaper, you might allow the gospel words to read you.
- The words of Jesus are like the words of a friend or a loved one. They brighten up our day.

november 6–12

Something to think and pray about each day this week:

Testing Signs and Wonders

Jesus was wary of those who wanted signs and wonders. He discouraged his disciples from speculating about when the end of the world would be. This has not deterred later would-be prophets from foretelling doomsday or offering private revelations. The Church has always said, "Be skeptical. Believing in private revelations is not part of our faith, but an optional extra, to be treated with caution." Look to the quality of the prophet's life, the absence of ego, greed, or self-seeking. Don't just listen to the words; test the spirits.

The Presence of God

As I sit here, the beating of my heart,
the ebb and flow of my breathing, the movements of my mind
are all signs of God's ongoing creation of me.
I pause for a moment, and become aware
of this presence of God within me.

Freedom

Lord, grant me the grace to be free from the excesses of this life.
Let me not get caught up with the desire for wealth.
Keep my heart and mind free to love and serve you.

Consciousness

In God's loving presence I unwind the past day,
starting from now and looking back, moment by moment.
I gather in all the goodness and light, in gratitude.
I attend to the shadows and what they say to me, seeking healing, courage, forgiveness.

The Word

I take my time to read the Word of God, slowly, a few times, allowing myself to dwell on anything that strikes me. (Please turn to your scripture on the following pages. Inspiration points are there should you need them. When you are ready, return here to continue.)

Conversation

Remembering that I am still in God's presence,
I imagine Jesus himself standing or sitting beside me,
and say whatever is on my mind, whatever is in my heart,
speaking as one friend to another.

Conclusion

Glory be to the Father, and to the Son, and to the Holy Spirit,
As it was in the beginning, is now, and ever shall be,
World without end. Amen

Sunday 6th November,
Thirty-second Sunday in Ordinary Time Matthew 25:1–13

Then the kingdom of heaven will be like this. Ten bridesmaids took their lamps and went to meet the bridegroom. Five of them were foolish, and five were wise. When the foolish took their lamps, they took no oil with them; but the wise took flasks of oil with their lamps. As the bridegroom was delayed, all of them became drowsy and slept. But at midnight there was a shout, "Look! Here is the bridegroom! Come out to meet him." Then all those bridesmaids got up and trimmed their lamps. The foolish said to the wise, "Give us some of your oil, for our lamps are going out." But the wise replied, "No! there will not be enough for you and for us; you had better go to the dealers and buy some for yourselves." And while they went to buy it, the bridegroom came, and those who were ready went with him into the wedding banquet; and the door was shut. Later the other bridesmaids came also, saying, "Lord, lord, open to us." But he replied, "Truly I tell you, I do not know you." Keep awake therefore, for you know neither the day nor the hour.

- Jesus, you were in Jerusalem, close to the showdown with your people. Many of them would be like the foolish virgins, caught unawares. The wise virgins would be those who recognized and followed you.
- Today this speaks to me of moments of grace and opportunity, as when a great love comes into my life, or a chance to reconcile, or an unexpected blow. It comes unexpectedly, as a shock.
- Lord, give me the grace today to find you in every encounter. Make me ready to recognize you.

Monday 7th November **Luke 17:1–6**

Jesus said to his disciples, "Occasions for stumbling are bound to come, but woe to anyone by whom they come! It would be better for you if a millstone were hung around your neck and you were thrown into the sea than for you to cause one of these little ones to stumble. Be on your guard! If another disciple sins, you must rebuke the offender, and if there is repentance, you must forgive. And if the same person sins against you seven times a day, and turns back to you seven times and says, 'I repent,' you must forgive." The apostles said to the Lord, "Increase our faith!" The Lord replied, "If you had faith the size of a mustard seed, you could say to this mulberry tree, 'Be uprooted and planted in the sea,' and it would obey you."

- This is a harsh message from Jesus about scandal and leading others astray. Alongside that, Jesus places the necessity of forgiveness and reconciliation to meet genuine repentance. The disciples recognize just how hard it is to forgive sinners.
- Lord, increase my faith; clothe me in the power of God.

Tuesday 8th November **Luke 17:7–10**

Jesus said to his disciples, "Who among you would say to your slave who has just come in from plowing or tending sheep in the field, 'Come here at once and take your place at the table'? Would you not rather say to him, 'Prepare supper for me, put on your apron and serve me while I eat and drink; later you may eat and drink'? Do you thank the slave for doing what was commanded? So you also, when you have done all that you were ordered to do, say, 'We are worthless slaves; we have done only what we ought to have done!'"

- We are slaves—not a title we like. But we remember that slaves in Jesus' culture were very often welcomed and accepted members of the family circle. Even though they were without rights and not fully included in the family, they knew that they were not worthless. They were valued members of a household as we are.
- We can always ask a further question about what Jesus means, not concluding that we can easily know what he meant.

Wednesday 9th November,
Dedication of the Lateran Basilica **John 2:13–22**

The Passover of the Jews was near, and Jesus went up to Jerusalem. In the temple he found people selling cattle, sheep, and doves, and the money changers seated at their tables. Making a whip of cords, he drove all of them out of the temple, both the sheep and the cattle. He also poured out the coins of the money changers and overturned their tables. He told those who were selling the doves, "Take these things out of here! Stop making my Father's house a marketplace!" His disciples remembered that it was written, "Zeal for your house will consume me." The Jews then said to him, "What sign can you show us for doing this?" Jesus answered them, "Destroy this temple, and in three days I will raise it up." The Jews then said, "This temple has been under construction for forty-six years, and will you raise it up in three days?" But he was speaking of the temple of his body. After he was raised from the dead, his disciples remembered that he had said this; and they believed the scripture and the word that Jesus had spoken.

- The people of Jesus' time took pride in the Temple as a place. Jesus saw that it had a more important value: it pointed to the presence of God in our midst.

- Some people in Jesus' time valued the Temple as a commercial centre, allowing their greed to exploit the poor. I pray for the poor who are exploited and hungry today.

Thursday 10th November **Luke 17:20–25**

Once Jesus was asked by the Pharisees when the kingdom of God was coming, and he answered, "The kingdom of God is not coming with things that can be observed; nor will they say, 'Look, here it is!' or 'There it is!' For, in fact, the kingdom of God is among you." Then he said to the disciples, "The days are coming when you will long to see one of the days of the Son of Man, and you will not see it. They will say to you, 'Look there!' or 'Look here!' Do not go, do not set off in pursuit. For as the lightning flashes and lights up the sky from one side to the other, so will the Son of Man be in his day. But first he must endure much suffering and be rejected by this generation."

- We have to look hard sometimes to see the kingdom of God and its qualities. We may not notice the things of Jesus' kingdom immediately among the neighbourhood, community, or family.
- Wherever we find the qualities of the beatitudes, or the qualities of sincere love, there we find the kingdom of God.

Friday 11th November **Luke 17:26–37**

Just as it was in the days of Noah, so too it will be in the days of the Son of Man. They were eating and drinking, and marrying and being given in marriage, until the day Noah entered the ark, and the flood came and destroyed all of them. Likewise, just as it was in the days of Lot: they were eating and drinking, buying and selling, planting and building, but on the day that Lot left Sodom, it rained fire and sulfur from heaven and destroyed all of them—it will be like that on the day that the Son of Man is revealed. On that day, anyone on the housetop who has belongings in the house must not come down to take them away; and likewise anyone in the field must not turn back. Remember Lot's wife. Those who try to make their life secure will lose it, but those who lose their life will keep it. I tell you, on that night there will be two in one bed; one will be taken and the other left. There will be two women grinding meal together; one will be taken and the other left.

- The "end" gospels call on us to trust. Losing and saving our lives is in the hands of God, as is all else. Trust is the big call of every relevant relationship.
- Prayer is a gateway to growth in trust in God.

Saturday 12th November **Luke 18:1–8**

Then Jesus told them a parable about their need to pray always and not to lose heart. He said, "In a certain city there was a judge who neither feared God nor had respect for people. In that city there was a widow who kept coming to him and saying, 'Grant me justice against my opponent.' For a while he refused; but later he said to himself, 'Though I have no fear of God and no respect for anyone, yet because this widow keeps bothering me, I will grant her justice, so that she may not wear me out by continually coming.'" And the Lord said, "Listen to what the unjust judge says. And will not God grant justice to his chosen ones who cry to him day and night? Will he delay long in helping them? I tell you, he will quickly grant justice to them. And yet, when the Son of Man comes, will he find faith on earth?"

- The widow had the right to pester the judge for what she wanted. The judge was meant to be the defender in this culture of the widow and the orphan.

- Jesus says that God is on our side at least as much as the judge is on the side of the widow. Can we bring ourselves in humility and poverty to God, knowing we have then found something of our true identity?

november 13–19

Something to think and pray about each day this week:

Facing up to Ourselves

Confession, or the sacrament of Reconciliation, has a long history among Christians, but it is often misunderstood. "Putting words on it"— that's what makes confession at once so painful and so healing. All of us build defenses against accepting guilt, against facing what is mean or cowardly or cruel in us. In Confession we are not looking for counseling or psychotherapy, or for a warm blanket of forgetfulness to be cast over our past. In our own minds we tend to be vague about what we have done, and easily excuse it. In Confession we try to see our meanness as others might see it, putting it in words to an anonymous priest. "That is what I did, it was bad, and I am sorry." In all our religious life, there is no act as personal as this. The other sacraments can easily turn into empty rituals. Confession, taken seriously, makes the most intense personal demands on us; and it brings a comfort we can feel.

The Presence of God
As I sit here, the beating of my heart,
the ebb and flow of my breathing, the movements of my mind
are all signs of God's ongoing creation of me.
I pause for a moment, and become aware
of this presence of God within me.

Freedom
I will ask God's help,
to be free from my own preoccupations,
to be open to God in this time of prayer,
to come to love and serve him more.

Consciousness
Help me, Lord, to be more conscious of your presence.
Teach me to recognize your presence in others.
Fill my heart with gratitude for the times your love
has been shown to me through the care of others.

The Word
I take my time to read the Word of God, slowly, a few times, allowing myself to dwell on anything that strikes me. (Please turn to your scripture on the following pages. Inspiration points are there should you need them. When you are ready, return here to continue.)

Conversation
Remembering that I am still in God's presence,
I imagine Jesus himself standing or sitting beside me,
and say whatever is on my mind, whatever is in my heart,
speaking as one friend to another.

Conclusion
Glory be to the Father, and to the Son, and to the Holy Spirit,
As it was in the beginning, is now, and ever shall be,
World without end. Amen

Sunday 13th November,
Thirty-third Sunday
in Ordinary Time **Matthew 25:14–15, 19–21**

Jesus told his disciples this parable, "For it is as if a man, going on a journey, summoned his slaves and entrusted his property to them; to one he gave five talents, to another two, to another one, to each according to his ability. Then he went away. After a long time the master of those slaves came and settled accounts with them. Then the one who had received the five talents came forward, bringing five more talents, saying, 'Master, you handed over to me five talents; see, I have made five more talents.' His master said to him, 'Well done, good and trustworthy slave; you have been trustworthy in a few things, I will put you in charge of many things; enter into the joy of your master.'"

- Wealth can lead to happiness and to generosity, if we remain masters of money rather than letting money—or its equivalents like property, or job, or reputation—master us. Money can also engender anxiety and will never, of itself, make us happy.
- Jesus was one who founded his happiness on his relationship with God and on the fulfillment of his mission in life. We can find a true happiness when our lives are guided towards God and live in the values of the gospel of Jesus Christ.

Monday 14th November **Luke 18:35–43**

As he approached Jericho, a blind man was sitting by the roadside begging. When he heard a crowd going by, he asked what was happening. They told him, "Jesus of Nazareth is passing by." Then he shouted, "Jesus, Son of David, have mercy on me!" Those who were in front sternly ordered him to be quiet; but he shouted even more loudly, "Son of David, have mercy on me!" Jesus stood still and ordered the man to be brought to him; and when he came near, he asked him, "What do you want me to do for you?" He said, "Lord, let me see again." Jesus said to him, "Receive your sight; your faith has saved you." Immediately he regained his sight and followed him, glorifying God; and all the people, when they saw it, praised God.

- What did this man see when he was cured? Whatever he saw encouraged him to follow Jesus with praise and glory. Whatever the people saw in the blind man's cure, they too praised the Lord.
- Can we look over a day or a week and recall what would lead us to praise God? Let that be part of my conversation with the Lord.

Tuesday 15th November **Luke 19:1–10**

Jesus entered Jericho and was passing through it. A man was there named Zacchaeus; he was a chief tax-collector and was rich. He was trying to see who Jesus was, but on account of the crowd he could not, because he was short in stature. So he ran ahead and climbed a sycamore tree to see him, because he was going to pass that way. When Jesus came to the place, he looked up and said to him, "Zacchaeus, hurry and come down; for I must stay at your house today." So he hurried down and was happy to welcome him. All who saw it began to grumble and said, "He has gone to be the guest of one who is a sinner." Zacchaeus stood there and said to the Lord, "Look, half of my possessions, Lord, I will give to the poor; and if I have defrauded anyone of anything, I will pay back four times as much." Then Jesus said to him, "Today salvation has come to this house, because he too is a son of Abraham. For the Son of Man came to seek out and to save the lost."

- Short in stature and big in greed is one description of Zacchaeus. He was hated and rejected socially; the acceptance and welcome of Jesus somehow changed him. His moment with the Lord, his moment of prayer, changed him.

- Ask today for what change you might like in your life which Jesus could give. Zacchaeus, small in body-size, grew tall "on the inside" on meeting Jesus.

Wednesday 16th November **Luke 19:11–28**

As they were listening to this, he went on to tell a parable, because he was near Jerusalem, and because they supposed that the kingdom of God was to appear immediately. So he said, "A nobleman went to a distant country to get royal power for himself and then return. He summoned ten of his slaves, and gave them ten pounds, and said to them, 'Do business with these until I come back.' But the citizens of his country hated him and sent a delegation after him, saying, 'We do not want this man to rule over us.' When he returned, having received royal power, he ordered these slaves, to whom he had given the money, to be summoned so that he might find out what they had gained by trading. The first came forward and said, 'Lord, your pound has made ten more pounds.' He said to him, 'Well done, good slave! Because you have been trustworthy in a very small thing, take charge of ten cities.' Then the second came, saying, 'Lord, your pound has made five pounds.' He said to him, 'And you, rule over five cities.' Then the other came, saying, 'Lord, here is your pound. I wrapped it up in a piece of cloth, for I was afraid of you, because you are a harsh man; you take what you did not deposit, and reap what you did not sow.' He said to him, 'I will judge you by your own words, you wicked slave! You knew, did you, that I was a harsh man, taking what I did not deposit and reaping what I did not sow? Why then did you not put my money into the bank? Then when I returned, I could have collected it with interest.' He said to the bystanders, 'Take the pound from him and give it to the one who has ten pounds.' (And they said to him, 'Lord, he has ten pounds!') 'I tell you, to all those who have, more will be given; but from those who have nothing, even what they have will be taken away. But as for these enemies of mine who did not want me to be king over them—bring them here and slaughter them in my presence.'" After he had said this, he went on ahead, going up to Jerusalem.

- As we live in the spirit of the gospel, our souls grow. More is given to those who have a lot. It's not meanness on the part of God—God wants the best for all.
- When we give what we are and what we have in the service of the Lord, we receive more than we give. Nothing given is wasted in the hands of God.

Thursday 17th November **Luke 19:41–44**

As he came near and saw the city, he wept over it, saying, "If you, even you, had only recognized on this day the things that make for peace! But now they are hidden from your eyes. Indeed, the days will come upon you, when your enemies will set up ramparts around you and surround you, and hem you in on every side. They will crush you to the ground, you and your children within you, and they will not leave within you one stone upon another; because you did not recognize the time of your visitation from God."

- Lost chances—that's what he was weeping over. Not that Jerusalem had done something awful, but the city had not realized what was best and had ignored the message of peace and hope it could have heard.
- Don't we regret more the fullness of life we could have had than the faults and failings which led us astray for a short while?
- Let our quiet time today be a moment of fullness—the heart open to the fullness of God.

Friday 18th November **Luke 19:45–48**

Then Jesus entered the temple and began to drive out those who were selling things there; and he said, "It is written, 'My house shall be a house of prayer'; but you have made it a den of robbers." Every day he was teaching in the temple. The chief priests, the scribes, and the leaders of the people kept looking for a way to kill him; but they did not find anything they could do, for all the people were spellbound by what they heard.

- What Jesus said offended the powerful but kept the ordinary ones spellbound.
- Only when I am poor and needy and open to life, love, and the challenge of goodness can I hear the Lord. Only the humble find themselves at home in the house of God.

Saturday 19th November **Luke 20:27–40**

Some Sadducees, those who say there is no resurrection, came to him and asked him a question, "Teacher, Moses wrote for us that if a man's brother dies, leaving a wife but no children, the man shall marry the widow and raise up children for his brother. Now there were seven brothers; the first married, and died childless; then the second and the third married her, and so in the same way all seven died childless. Finally the woman also died. In the resurrection, therefore, whose wife will the woman be? For the seven had married her." Jesus said to them, "Those who belong to this age marry and are given in marriage; but those who are considered worthy of a place in that age and in the resurrection from the dead neither marry nor are given in marriage. Indeed they cannot die any more, because they are like angels and are children of God, being children of the resurrection. And the fact that the dead are raised Moses himself showed, in the story about the bush, where he speaks of the Lord as the God of Abraham, the God of Isaac, and the God of Jacob. Now he is God not of the dead, but of the living; for to him all of them are alive." Then some of the scribes answered, "Teacher, you have spoken well." For they no longer dared to ask him another question.

- Jesus avoids the problems of the situation described here by summing up that God is the God of the living, and we can leave the questions of details after death in the hands of the living God.
- Wherever there is real life, the sharing of physical life as in parenthood and the sharing of the life of love and justice, God is present. God is alive where people are alive to each other and to each other's needs and joys. God is the one who sent Jesus that we too might have life to the full.

november 20–26

Something to think and pray about each day this week:

Time at the Table

Perhaps a test of family health is: can they eat together? Family meals are at risk. The table can be a place where the preparation of food reflects a mother or father's care, and where parents and children can sit, enjoy, argue, joke, listen, have their voice heard, attack and be attacked, but not walk out. Young couples prize a chance to enjoy a meal with their children. As work or other pressures increase, fast food and television can take over, and you find families who never eat together. In some parts of the world the children grab something from the fridge and "graze," a can in one hand, fast food in the other, their eyes fixed on a TV screen. It is no accident that at the centre of the Christian family Jesus placed a meal, the Eucharist. It is round a common table that a family really lives together. Try to find a time, at least once a week, for slow food, not fast.

The Presence of God
I pause for a moment
and reflect on God's life-giving presence
in every part of my body, in everything around me,
in the whole of my life.

Freedom
God is not foreign to my freedom.
Instead the Spirit breathes life into my most intimate desires,
gently nudging me towards all that is good.
I ask for the grace to let myself be enfolded by the Spirit.

Consciousness
I exist in a web of relationships—links to nature, people, God.
I trace out these links, giving thanks for the life that flows through them.
Some links are twisted or broken: I may feel regret, anger, disappointment.
I pray for the gift of acceptance and forgiveness.

The Word
God speaks to each one of us individually. I need to listen to what he is saying to me. (Please turn to your scripture on the following pages. Inspiration points are there should you need them. When you are ready, return here to continue.)

Conversation
How has God's Word moved me? Has it left me cold?
Has it consoled me or moved me to act in a new way?
I imagine Jesus standing or sitting beside me,
I turn and share my feelings with him.

Conclusion
Glory be to the Father, and to the Son, and to the Holy Spirit,
As it was in the beginning, is now, and ever shall be,
World without end. Amen

Sunday 20th November,
Feast of Christ the King **Matthew 25:31–46**

When the Son of Man comes in his glory, and all the angels with him, then he will sit on the throne of his glory. All the nations will be gathered before him, and he will separate people one from another as a shepherd separates the sheep from the goats, and he will put the sheep at his right hand and the goats at the left. Then the king will say to those at his right hand, "Come, you that are blessed by my Father, inherit the kingdom prepared for you from the foundation of the world; for I was hungry and you gave me food, I was thirsty and you gave me something to drink, I was a stranger and you welcomed me, I was naked and you gave me clothing, I was sick and you took care of me, I was in prison and you visited me." Then the righteous will answer him, "Lord, when was it that we saw you hungry and gave you food, or thirsty and gave you something to drink? And when was it that we saw you a stranger and welcomed you, or naked and gave you clothing? And when was it that we saw you sick or in prison and visited you?" And the king will answer them, "Truly I tell you, just as you did it to one of the least of these who are members of my family, you did it to me." Then he will say to those at his left hand, "You that are accursed, depart from me into the eternal fire prepared for the devil and his angels; for I was hungry and you gave me no food, I was thirsty and you gave me nothing to drink, I was a stranger and you did not welcome me, naked and you did not give me clothing, sick and in prison and you did not visit me." Then they also will answer, "Lord, when was it that we saw you hungry or thirsty or a stranger or naked or sick or in prison, and did not take care of you?" Then he will answer them, "Truly I tell you, just as you did not do it to one of the least of these, you did not do it to me." And these will go away into eternal punishment, but the righteous into eternal life.

- In Jesus, we are all brothers and sisters in the image of God. God is so big that we are all like God.
- But what does that mean? This is the big act of faith that we will soak ourselves in during Advent, that God became one like us, one of us, born, lived, suffered, and died like the rest of us. The real God is found in real people.

Monday 21st November **Luke 21:1–4**

Jesus looked up and saw rich people putting their gifts into the treasury; he also saw a poor widow put in two small copper coins. He said, "Truly I tell you, this poor widow has put in more than all of them; for all of them have contributed out of their abundance, but she out of her poverty has put in all she had to live on."

- Take, Lord, receive—all I have and possess. You have given all to me, I now return it.
- Give me only your love and your grace; that's enough for me.

Tuesday 22nd November **Luke 21:5–11**

When some were speaking about the temple, how it was adorned with beautiful stones and gifts dedicated to God, Jesus said, "As for these things that you see, the days will come when not one stone will be left upon another; all will be thrown down." They asked him, "Teacher, when will this be, and what will be the sign that this is about to take place?" And he said, "Beware that you are not led astray; for many will come in my name and say, 'I am he!' and, 'The time is near!' Do not go after them. When you hear of wars and insurrections, do not be terrified; for these things must take place first, but the end will not follow immediately." Then he said to them, "Nation will rise against nation, and kingdom against kingdom; there will be great earthquakes, and in various places famines and plagues; and there will be dreadful portents and great signs from heaven."

- The temple, beautiful as it is, and so essential to the life of the people, will not last. In other places in scripture Jesus says of himself that he is the temple.
- He is asking the people to listen to his words, the new temple speaking of the old. As we spend more time with Jesus, the old passes away and new life, new beauty, and new commitment is found.

Wednesday 23rd November **Luke 21:12–19**

Jesus said to his disciples, "But before all this occurs, they will arrest you and persecute you; they will hand you over to synagogues and prisons, and you will be brought before kings and governors because of my name. This will give you an opportunity to testify. So make up your minds not to prepare your defense in advance; for I will give you words and a wisdom that none of your opponents will be able to withstand or contradict. You will be betrayed even by parents and brothers, by relatives and friends; and they will put some of you to death. You will be hated by all because of my name. But not a hair of your head will perish. By your endurance you will gain your souls."

- The word of the Lord is a "two-edged sword," dividing even families. Truth is seen in different ways by different people.
- Prayer helps us keep strong, courageous, and faithful. Our endurance with God's love wins out in many of life's struggles.

Thursday 24th November **Luke 21:20–28**

Jesus said to the disciples, "When you see Jerusalem surrounded by armies, then know that its desolation has come near. Then those in Judea must flee to the mountains, and those inside the city must leave it, and those out in the country must not enter it; for these are days of vengeance, as a fulfillment of all that is written. Woe to those who are pregnant and to those who are nursing infants in those days! For there will be great distress on the earth and wrath against this people; they will fall by the edge of the sword and be taken away as captives among all nations; and Jerusalem will be trampled on by the Gentiles, until the times of the Gentiles are fulfilled. There will be signs in the sun, the moon, and the stars, and on the earth distress among nations confused by the roaring of the sea and the waves. People will faint from fear and foreboding of what is coming upon the world, for the powers of the heavens will be shaken. Then they will see 'the Son of Man coming in a cloud' with power and great glory. Now when these things begin to take place, stand up and raise your heads, because your redemption is drawing near."

- In the midst of all sorts of destruction, redemption, new life, and joy can be just around the corner. No matter how life may frighten us, the care and the protection of God is near. Jesus uses creation signs to indicate this.

Friday 25th November **Luke 21:29–33**

Then Jesus told them a parable: "Look at the fig tree and all the trees; as soon as they sprout leaves you can see for yourselves and know that summer is already near. So also, when you see these things taking place, you know that the kingdom of God is near. Truly I tell you, this generation will not pass away until all things have taken place. Heaven and earth will pass away, but my words will not pass away."

- In the middle of all sorts of natural, economic, and other types of disasters, the Word of God offers truth and a strong place. It is a rock on which we stand, and on which we withstand forces of evil in the culture and in our own lives.
- There is something about Jesus which never passes away. We find that in prayer.

Saturday 26th November **Luke 21:34–36**

Jesus said to his disciples, "Be on guard so that your hearts are not weighed down with dissipation and drunkenness and the worries of this life, and that day catch you unexpectedly, like a trap. For it will come upon all who live on the face of the whole earth. Be alert at all times, praying that you may have the strength to escape all these things that will take place, and to stand before the Son of Man."

- Prayer roots us in the strong desires of our lives, calms worries, and gives a fulfillment that the excesses of neither alcohol nor work can bring. We can stand before the Son of Man in prayer filled with the Spirit of God.
- This is what we can ask for in prayer. Amen.

Founded in 1865, Ave Maria Press, a ministry of the Congregation of Holy Cross, is a Catholic publishing company that serves the spiritual and formative needs of the Church and its schools, institutions, and ministers; Christian individuals and families; and others seeking spiritual nourishment.

For a complete listing of titles from

Ave Maria Press

Sorin Books

Forest of Peace

Christian Classics

visit www.avemariapress.com

ave maria press® / Notre Dame, IN 46556
A Ministry of the Indiana Province of Holy Cross